Jonathan Goldberg

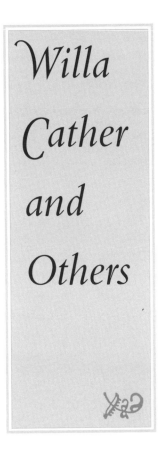

Willa Cather and Others

Duke University Press

Durham & London 2001

© 2001 Duke University Press

All rights reserved

Printed in the United States of America

on acid-free paper ⊗

Designed by C. H. Westmoreland

Typeset in Bembo by Tseng Information Systems, Inc.

Library of Congress Cataloging-in-Publication

Data appear on the last printed page of

this book.

Willa Cather and Others

Edited by Michèle Aina Barale, Jonathan Goldberg,

Michael Moon, and Eve Kosofsky Sedgwick

for Sharon Cameron

Contents

Preface

I first read Willa Cather when I was in high school. I can no longer remember which novel we were assigned—it must have been *O Pioneers!* or *My Ántonia*—but I can still recall what it felt like to be reading Cather then. Once I had read the assigned novel I went on to others—among them, I am certain, *The Professor's House,* the novel that prompted the first essays I wrote on the way to this book. Back then, I didn't know Cather's well-known pronouncement in "The Novel Démeublé" about "the thing not named," but it was just that quality in Cather's writing that spoke to me:

> Whatever is felt upon the page without being specifically named there—that, one might say, is created. It is the inexplicable presence of the thing not named, of the overtone divined by the ear but not heard by it, the verbal mood, the emotional aura of the fact or thing or the deed, that gives high quality to the novel or the drama, as well as to poetry itself.[1]

I found the writing intense, atmospheric, heavy with something that was not said which I nonetheless recognized. I couldn't tell what it was, aslant the calm surface of narration, that I heard. But whatever it was sounded along the wavelengths of a silence that I found irresistible. It was as if, somehow, the novels were written in a language which I could not myself articulate and yet in which I found myself articulated. Not, I should add, that I knew what they said, or what part of me they found; or, rather, I knew somehow that my own incipient, incoherent sexuality was being addressed, but couldn't tell how the novels I was reading spoke so uncannily, couldn't see what it was in the novels that made the connection. My experience then was like the one I have now, writing these sentences only to discover that they come from *The Song of the Lark,* the scene when its heroine, Thea Kronborg, is being told about "something in the inside from the beginning" which "she did not altogether understand . . . and yet, in a way she knew. She knew, of course, that there was something in her that was different."[2]

I find myself now as then similarly rapt by "something"; indeed, I can recall a dizzying identification with Niel Herbert's voyeurism in *A Lost Lady* I experienced then, without quite knowing whose eyes it was that I was seeing through, or what it was that held my gaze; I remember the fevered sense that overcame me when I first read "Tom Outland's Story"; at that time I knew nothing about the Anasazi ruins at Mesa Verde, and read the story as if it were some kind of science fiction. The place was unimaginable, I could not imagine it as being real. It was the place of reading. It was where I was. It is still—amazingly—where I often find myself reading Cather.

Now, in hindsight, I know several names for that place, even as I continue to find it not exactly nameable. While it remains the case for me that Cather speaks uncannily for my own sexuality, the very obliquity in which that occurs is, for me, even more interesting than any self-discovery her work occasions. Or, rather, what it allows, I think, is the recognition that categories of identity are far more complicated than might be suggested by the autobiographical framing with which I have begun. Understandably, much of the work of gay and lesbian studies in the post-Stonewall era has been concerned with questions of identity, with historical inquiry that seeks to validate queer existence by finding where "we" came from. Richly productive as such work has been, it is also the case that much of it has been guided by a legislative appeal, a narrowing of the question of identity. Having been defamed so long, it seemed necessary to write the history of that defamation and oppression, to claim value in what was so long and so variously despised. But to do so meant locating martyrs for a cause or delineating the terms under which people fearfully lived in hiding. While much work in the wake of Foucault has necessarily complicated this tidy picture, it does not invalidate the agenda of preserving imperiled lives— even as it seems crucial not to make such appeals in strictly identitarian terms. Any number of current events could be adduced to show this. From the current U.S. military policy of "don't ask, don't tell," which has proved even worse than previous policies (here Janet Halley is the guide to follow), to the agendas of gay normalization that effectively stigmatize whole segments of the gay and lesbian population (here Michael Warner's the voice to be heard), a notion that there is such a thing—something singular—that constitutes gay identity is supposed.[3] While the closet that the military imposes testifies to an anxiety about the porousness of identities, which it wishes to deny, the furthering of gay assimilation is fixated on a vision of straight normalcy that is a phantasm. Both agendas cannot tolerate difference.

Yet it must precisely be the difference *in identity* that allows me (for example) to find myself solicited by Cather's texts, uncannily found by them, uncannily finding myself elsewhere thanks to them. Such identifications and transformations are not matters of identities that are to be imagined as utterly self-identical. It's for that reason that even as I open this preface with a bit of the history of my own relationship to Cather's work, I would not want to argue for that as anything but an example. There are not only many routes by which her texts solicit readers, there are also many routes to her writing. It is to the latter task of attending to these possibilities that this book is devoted. To feel what is not specifically named, as Cather invites, requires a heightened sense of attentiveness, a willingness to suspend determinate categories in order to allow resonances to sound. It requires more than a personal vantage point.

Luckily for me, I do not have to invent these possibilities. When I began working on Cather, two essays helped me most to find some language to name what cannot be named. From Eve Kosofsky Sedgwick's "Across Gender, Across Sexuality: Willa Cather and Others" I have borrowed the title for this book, and—I hope—profited from the wisdom contained in her unpresumptive insights into the always unpredictable ways in which gender and sexuality are inhabited, the ever ramifying and utterly contingent ways in which they cross in anyone's experience and in the relationships of identification that they make possible.[4] Her exemplary ability to name and find "unrecognized pockets of value and vitality that can hit out in unpredictable directions" (70) has posed for me the continual challenge and exhilaration of reading Cather and writing about her. Against the assumption that underlies much work that has been written about Cather's relationship to her sexuality—that she was closeted, or repressed, or self-hating—Sedgwick makes possible a nonprescriptive approach to Cather, one that assumes that questions of knowing are not answered by throwing off the veil of occlusion to reveal a singular truth. Sedgwick suggests kinds of identifications that seem taboo to a criticism bent on straightening and straitening identity and identification into determinate paths, ones in which gender and sexuality, for example, are assumed to be—desired to be—so aligned.

Here I approach the subject named in the other essay that galvanized my thinking about Cather, Judith Butler's "'Dangerous Crossing': Willa Cather's Masculine Names." In the first chapter of this book, I engage directly with this essay, aiming there to extend Butler's arguments about the complex crossings through which identity and identification occur.[5] Some of the passion of Butler's essay comes from her sense that Cather is not to be judged as errant in her masculinity, that one should not assume that to be properly feminine is a prerequisite for lesbian identity, or that masculinity is properly male. Butler works to exonerate Cather from charges of some failure of identity—as if identity could somehow ever be anything but failed; she works too to suggest the limits of historical contextualization when they are posed as some law imposed upon desire, some repressive hypothesis, even as she develops a strong sense of these rigorous exactions. What emerges, I think, from her work, as from Sedgwick's, are new possibilities of generosity and sympathy, recognitions that a politics of reading need not also be a matter of policing.

Shortly after I had published an essay on *The Professor's House,* Julie Abraham's *Are Girls Necessary?* appeared, supporting many conclusions to which I also had come; further along in my writing of this book, I encountered an essay by Christopher Nealon that was especially inspiring to me in writing about *One of Ours* in the third chapter, "War Requiems"; from these I gathered confidence that the project I had undertaken was worth pursuing and might find some sympathetic readers.[6] Abraham shows skillfully how impoverishing a certain form of lesbian writing must be, especially when it is assumed to be the only possible way to plot lesbian desire, and how Cather's project of cross-identification (moving not merely across genders, but across history) opens necessary vistas. Nealon writes movingly about a crucial form of such historical sympathy, the possibility of what he terms an "affect-genealogy" that allows connections to "our" past that are not tied to identitarian narratives. It suggests, rather, that "we" are precisely not singular, that therefore "our" history is carried along wavelengths that are not heard in the same way by each of us, and that telling the story of those strange coincidences is the task to pursue rather than the more determinative and judgmental agendas that have so often guided gay and lesbian criticism (and which, I would add, now seem to be the sole gesture available to cultural critique). *Willa Cather and Others* is committed to the task that Nealon enunciates. This means, on the one hand, validating Cather's project for the ways in which it allows us to think beyond paradigms of (self-identical) identity; it means, on the other hand, recognizing that the occlusions and limits in Cather would not simply have been resolved had she lived in a later, supposedly more liberal or enlightened era. Cather is offered here not as an exemplary model to follow or as a cautionary tale. Attempting to think these occlusions and facilitations together, I read Cather's texts as sites of dense transfer points that cannot easily be reduced to the singular terms through which identity often is posed.

Hence, "others" in the title of this book signals, at the highest level of generality, an alterity that I take to accompany all and any identity. More locally, the "others" in this study are, first of all, other women, for the most part Cather's contemporaries whose artistic projects allow for points of comparison with Cather's. While I begin with this seemingly determinate framework of shared gender and historical proximity, the very inhabitation of time or place or body is itself too various to be exactly caught within these guiding rubrics. For these proximate comparisons are most interesting insofar as they are entangled with other aspects of identity, sexuality and race, for example, categories mobilized in the pages that follow to pursue the affordances—as well as the damages—that such identity categories make possible. I aim, above all, to allow what remains unsettled to remain unsettling. Cather's relationship to her sexuality, her gender, her race and class are all fraught terrains, and how these impinge on her writing practices are consequential. When framed as a set of judgmental questions—was Cather a proper lesbian? does Cather identify with women? does Cather appropriate racialized bodies?—all criticism can do is to pass judgment, as if "we" were at some point in time in which we correctly inhabited all these frameworks, knew the truth, and embodied it. I know that in the pages that follow I have not always been able to suspend judgment (either of Cather or of her critics); nonetheless, the very possibility of doing any kind of historical work must involve something more than simply blaming the past for not being the present or nostalgically idealizing it. It's in this context that I would wish the "personal" appeal with which I opened this preface to be heard. Historical justice is not all that far from doing justice to the complexities, discontinuities, and disjunctions that structure identities over time.

The first chapter of this book serves as an introduction to the project. Taking Cather's numinous phrase "the thing not named" as its leitmotif, it works through several critical paths, assembles a range of critical takes on Cather, and traverses her career—a career of self-naming otherwise—from her first novels, *Alexander's Bridge* and *O Pioneers!,* through *My Ántonia* and her final novel, *Sapphira and the Slave Girl.* The Cather that I engage in this chapter is someone who divides and displaces herself, and a variety of identificatory stances are explored, including the troubled relationships between gender, race, and sexuality which are brought to a crisis point in her last novel. From this opening, I narrow my focus in the second chapter, "Cather Diva," to consider the most literal relationship between Cather and another that I take up in this book, charting the Wagnerian diva Olive Fremstad's inspiring role in *The Song of the Lark.* The leitmotif here could be summarized in another numinous phrase of Cather's, "the overtone divined by the ear but not heard by it." To suggest what Cather divined in the diva requires the resonance of some further frameworks, among them Fremstad's life as recorded by her faithful companion Mary Watkins Cushing and as fictionalized in Marcia Davenport's *Of Lena Geyer.* If these invite points of comparison with Cather, they also begin to suggestively place how divided an identification could be even when it might seem as straightforward as one woman's admiration and love for another. An ambivalence within sameness is lined with aggressivity, a topic further examined and extended in the chapter that follows.

"War Requiems," chapter 3, is built around *One of Ours* and counterposes Cather's World War I novel with an admittedly far-fetched comparison to the World War I novels that Pat Barker wrote in the 1990s. This historical swerve, however, is not unconnected to the resonance between two women novelists working out questions of sexuality often through homosexual figures, their extension of issues that might seem only psychological to encompass broader social implications. A set of strange and estranging affiliations sustains the possibility of juxtaposing Cather and the poets of her time who are central to Barker's novels, Siegfried Sassoon and Wilfred Owen. That Cather, in fact, befriended Sassoon's sometime lover Stephen Tennant and that he—an outrageously effeminate man—somehow, after Cather's death, took the place of Cather for Edith Lewis, Cather's lifetime companion, anchors a historical connection that further highlights complications around questions of cross-identification across time and space; these, in turn, figure in the project of *One of Ours* to imagine the (im)possibility of living as or in one of these "misfits." Owen's "Strange Meeting," with its stunning line, "I am the enemy you killed, my friend," underpins the trajectory of the chapter.

Finally, chapter 4, "Strange Brothers," weaves around *The Professor's House* the writing projects of Blair Niles and the photographs of Laura Gilpin. Unlike Fremstad, these contemporaries of Cather's, so far as I can tell, never met her, no personal relationship binds them. Yet the lack of literal connection seems to me merely that, and without reducing the three figures (Cather, Niles, Gilpin) to some set of identities, this chapter pursues the cross-cutting that locates them as women of a certain time, interested in racialized others, or in transporting lesbian, male homosexual, and heterosexual difference to other registers of representation. All of this has pertinence to the depiction of the family in *The Professor's House,* to the aching of male-male desire and its locus in the ruins of Anasazi civilization. Rather than a reductive contextualization, the aim in the final chapter, as throughout the book, is to allow for the resonance of alterities in the place of reading that Cather invites. A place, as I suggest at the end of this book, transcendentalized and rendered sublime in the ultimate union of the two brothers in *Death Comes for the Archbishop.* Yet even there, a language that ideological critique, for example, must render necessarily suspect, also metaphorizes the sympathetic vibrations Cather sets loose in "the inexplicable presence of the thing not named, . . . the overtone divined by the ear but not heard by it. . . ."

Acknowledgments

Willa Cather and Others would never have been written had Eve Kosofsky Sedgwick not invited me to contribute an essay to an issue of *Studies in the Novel*, "Queerer than Fiction," that she was editing. Portions of the final chapter of this book on *The Professor's House* and Blair Niles appeared as "Strange Brothers" in *Studies in the Novel* 28, no. 3 (fall 1996): 322–38, which was reprinted in a slightly revised version in *Novel Gazing: Queer Readings in Fiction* (Durham: Duke University Press, 1997), the volume that developed from that collection. So, once again, thanks Eve, for making this book possible, and not just by issuing that invitation. Other materials from the final chapter of this book were welcomed into *American Literature* 70, no. 1 (March 1998): 63–95, as "Photographic Relations: Laura Gilpin, Willa Cather," thanks to Cathy N. Davidson, whose response to the essay was everything an author could desire. Lauren Berlant's incisive and supportive comments on an earlier draft of those materials also were deeply appreciated, as are Tyler Curtain's for its published incarnation. I would never have known to write about Pat Barker had her novels not been recommended to me by colleagues at Duke: Jan Radway, Laurie Shannon, and Irene Silverblatt. To Laurie, additional thanks for comments on "War Requiems," as well as to Marcie Frank, Chris Nealon, and Michael Warner; your advice, too, was invaluable, and your support for this project deeply appreciated. My colleagues at Johns Hopkins —especially Toby Ditz, Frances Ferguson, Allen Grossman, Neil Hertz, Walter Benn Michaels, Ronald Paulson, John Plotz, Rochelle Tobias, Judith Walkowitz—also are to be thanked for their comments on "Cather Diva," which I presented at a General Seminar of the Program for Studies of Women, Gender, and Sexuality. For their warm endorsement of this project, I thank the two readers who recommended the book for publication, Chris Nealon and Lee Edelman, and Ken Wissoker for finding such sympathetic readers. Thanks to everyone at Duke University Press who saw this book into publication, particularly to Katie Courtland and to Lynn Walterick.

It is one of the pleasures of my friendship with Jonathan Brody Kramnick that he has come, in the years I have been working on Cather, to share my enthusiasm, and to reflect it back in ways that have renewed my confidence in this project. Michael Moon has read draft after draft of this book, and has always made me feel that it was worth writing. I wouldn't know what to do without you, Mike. Sharon Cameron read the book through and offered generous and incisive comments that guided me in the final stages of revision. It's not just for that, but in celebration of our long and dear friendship, that this book is dedicated to her.

Other Names

The basso ostinato that sounds throughout this chapter is the principle Cather enunciated in "The Novel Démeublé" as "the thing not named." In a groundbreaking essay, Sharon O'Brien affiliated Cather's artistic principle with her sexuality, and one translation of "the thing not named" is, undoubtedly, the love that dare not speak its name.[1] Whether that love is unspeakable because it is prohibited, or whether what it is *in itself* is unnameable *as such* is one complicating question that I bring in these pages to this primary translation. If a logic of identity cannot be mobilized to unfold what only can be said otherwise, the possibility of reading Cather's texts in terms of questions of sexuality cannot work from the assumption that sexuality and gender are aligned. Hence, in the pages that follow, Judith Butler's arguments about the lack of symmetry between identity and identification have been crucial. If, as I argue, "the thing not named" ramifies in a number of directions around an unnameable numinosity, further ranges of meaning can be posed, and not least important among these are the ways in which lesbianism and male homosexuality may be entangled and represented even through ostensible heterosexual figurations. These displacements along the axes of gender and sexuality do not exhaust the paths I wish to open here, the ramifications of Cather's phrase, for the crossings involved both facilitate and frustrate, and they can be charged with ambivalence, aggression, denial. These paths of sex and gender are involved in other crossings, most notably across the terrain of race, raising further complications and discomforts. None of these paths, none of these complications, can be separated from the kind of artistic project Cather pursues and the difficulty her work represents for a criticism that wishes or attempts to name what cannot be named, to respond in some way, however inadequate, to the stunning resonances of her laconic texts. In the pages that follow, I try out some initial mappings of the career of Cather's thing not named. The lack of specificity in Cather's phrasing provokes multiple possibilities that cannot be reduced to each other; each section of this chapter depends upon a signature-effect to lend precision in specifying these differences, but even the last of these, Cather's proper name, does not offer a singular translation of "the thing not named."

A. B.

Willa Cather repudiated her first novel twice, first in a preface she wrote when *Alexander's Bridge* (1912) was republished in 1922, the second time in 1931 in *The Colophon,* where she once again compared *Alexander's Bridge* invidiously with *O Pioneers!* (1913). Whereas the first novel everywhere betrayed the act of "inventing" (her scare quotes), in *O Pioneers!,* she claimed in the *Colophon* essay, "everything was spontaneous and took its own place, right or wrong." It was, she continued, like riding through "familiar" country, its subject matter "a kind of country I loved," its interest further heightened, she went on, "because it was about old neighbors, once very dear, whom I had almost forgotten in the hurry and excitement of growing up and finding out what the world was like and trying to get on in it."[2] *Alexander's Bridge,* on the other hand, was superficial, based on recent impressions, a working up of material chosen because it seemed artistic.

Cather's judgment is, in many respects, unexceptionable; the machinery of *Alexander's Bridge* is readily apparent, the archness of its language often shy-making, its tone frequently pseudo-Jamesian, its adultery plot the sort of thing that Edith Wharton did again and again. Nonetheless, it is worth noting that Cather's piece in *The Colophon* carries a rather ambivalent title, "My First Novels (There Were Two)." Ostensibly elevating *O Pioneers!* to an originary position, the essay also promotes what was probably by then — after the triumphs of novels that built upon the success of *O Pioneers!* — a forgotten first effort. Even as Cather ejects *Alexander's Bridge* from serious consideration, she includes it — there were two first novels. Indeed, by the end of the piece, the first first novel has its own germinative force; *The Song of the Lark* is seen as in its "road" and is compared (invidiously) to *My Ántonia,* the latter claimed as another spontaneous piece of writing — "it took no direction from me" — which nonetheless (unspontaneously?) followed "the road of *O Pioneers!* not the road of *The Song of the Lark*" (100). Cather's essay thus affirms herself as a writer with two origins, two paths. The repudiation of *The Song of the Lark* here is consistent with her ongoing discomfort with the novel (as I detail further in the second chapter, "Cather Diva"), a book that she nonetheless sometimes affirmed as a favorite. Even renunciation provides *The Song of the Lark* with a place, a genealogy in *Alexander's Bridge*. Cather does not merely begin twice; she continues along a double route. Denial is not quite to be taken at face value. Claims of spontaneity versus invention cross divided paths.

I am not the first person to think that connections can be found between Cather's double starts. "In her second novel," Sharon O'Brien writes, "Cather revises *Alexander's Bridge* when she turns Alexander into Alexandra"; "the similarity of the names," she continues, "shows what close relatives these two characters are."[3] Bartley Alexander, Alexandra Bergson: the orthographic play is insistent. *Alexander's Bridge,* moreover, reverses the initials of its hero in its title; Alexandra Bergson, the central figure in *O Pioneers!,* has initials that match the alphabetic order of the first novel: A. B. When, in 1931, Cather said she had written two first novels, she was only saying, in other words, what the play of alphabetic beginnings in her two first novels had intimated. Charting her forward movement along two "roads," she was perhaps saying something implicit in the alphabetic play of A. B. In choosing these originary letters (of the alphabet) to mark her beginning, she marked it twice from the start. A. B. are her initial initials. "Hers"—or do they belong to the alphabet, an order and origin in which she "spontaneously" found herself?

O'Brien connects Alexander and Alexandra only, in a Cather-like way, to deny the connection. For her, Alexander is Cather's "failed masculine hero," Alexandra the opposite; where he is riven by his "'double nature',," she integrates the two sides (392–93). For O'Brien, "double nature" is to be translated into male and female, and resolution will always be coded in the feminine. The difference between A. B. and B. A. is the difference that gender makes. Only when Cather can represent her artistic ambition through a heroine, O'Brien argues, wholeness, integrity, a proper mastery (no different from submission to a story that simply tells itself) will follow, lined up in neat symmetry. A=A. Identity is achieved.

Gender does make a difference, I would agree, but not necessarily this one. For I would notice first of all that the desire of the hero of *Alexander's Bridge* matches Cather's as enunciated in her 1931 piece. Alexander's adulterous affair begins when he encounters Hilda Burgoyne some dozen years years after having ended an affair with her that preceded his marriage: "He had not thought of Hilda Burgoyne for years; indeed, he had almost forgotten her" (21). This is exactly what Cather says in *The Colophon* about the material that came to her for *O Pioneers!,* a past almost forgotten, a love lost and necessarily so in order to learn the ways of the world. That, too, has been Bartley Alexander's experience; as soon as he met the marriageable Winifred, he married her, dropping Hilda to pursue a professional life that brought him middle-class comfort, indeed that has made him a poster boy for success: "There were other bridge-builders in the world certainly, but it was always Alexander's picture that the Sunday Supplement men wanted, because he looked as a tamer of rivers ought to look," all "rugged, blond good looks" (8). When he sees Hilda again, Alexander realizes that it has not been worth it. Indeed, even before he has resumed the affair, even before speaking to her, he knows that "none of the things he had gained in the least compensated" for what he had lost (26). Not success as an engineer, not his marriage, not his money and position, not what he summarizes as his "popularity," his having become a public person, having found out, as Cather says too about herself, what the world was like and what it took to have a place in it.

In these ways, then—as someone catalyzed by something almost forgotten in the course of meeting strenuous demands to conform to the ways of the world—Bartley Alexander is Cather's surrogate. The crisis of the novel (abandoning convention for passion, breaking the bridge) enacts Cather's own alphabetic move, her revisitation of Alexander as Alexandra. The "failure" of the first novel is the desire realized in the second. Or, to put this more exactly, it is the desire of the first—Bartley's for Hilda—that is embodied in Alexandra. Cather intimates this in another way when she ends her *Colophon* piece by recalling that William Heinemann, who had published *Alexander's Bridge* in England, rejected *The Song of the Lark;* "he thought in that book I had taken the wrong road," Cather paraphrases his letter to her—in the very terms she will appropriate a moment later, or has foisted upon him, to describe her various paths shuttling between her two beginnings, "and that the full-blooded method, which told everything about everybody, was not natural to me" (99). Cather faults *Alexander's Bridge* and *The Song of the Lark* essentially for being conventional realistic novels in which a narrator fairly cuddles up with the reader in offering a view of life as we know it (the procedures that, as D. A. Miller tellingly claims, mark the affinity between the novel and the police). Yet, as Cather says here (or has Heinemann say in her paraphrase), the conventional is, for her, "not natural"; it is the wrong road. Which is also to say that it is far more revealing than the unconventional novels upon which Cather's fame rightly rests, novels which, contra O'Brien, I would suggest do not offer the perfect symmetry of an identitarian achievement; rather it is the fact that they do not tell everything about everybody that makes them so powerful. Cather calls books like *O Pioneers!* and *My Ántonia* spontaneous, but they are the product of exaction. *Alexander's Bridge* fails, insofar as it does, because it is a tell-all book.

To say this invites the supposition that the secret in *Alexander's Bridge*—its open secret, indeed—is Cather's sexuality. Moreover, this suggests that the difference between one first novel and the next has everything to do with how Cather's sexuality is implicated in her writing. Since these are the guiding suppositions in the chapters that follow, it seems worth indicating what such a claim does not mean. I agree with Hermione Lee, for example, that "it is important not to collapse Cather's imaginative life into a simple matter of repression, nor to condescend to her for her lack of 'openness'."[4] For Lee, these are the only ways to take Cather's sexuality into account, and since they seem misguided, Lee ignores Cather's sexuality insofar as possible in the analysis of her life and work, attending only to the so-called larger issues of artistic meaning that transcend sex or gender, rather than enlisting Cather for a cause, whether feminist or lesbian.[5] There is, however, a clear alternative to this procedure once one grants that Cather's sexuality can be treated beyond the parameters that Lee provides, which are based on the assumption that sexuality is merely a narrow question of personal identity.

The procedures that Lee decries do continue in Cather criticism, although as Marilee Lindemann notes in the closing pages of *Willa Cather: Queering America,* the decade since the publication of Sharon O'Brien's 1987 *Willa Cather: The Emerging Voice* (the first book to make a connection between Cather's sexuality and her writing) has not exactly teemed with readings of gender and sexuality in Cather—in part, no doubt, because critiques like Lee's have denigrated such work as unimportant and misguided.[6] Cather would not have wanted to have been outed. Indeed, Lindemann's book continues in the familiar vein of the lesbian feminism that Lee deplores.[7] Approaching the secret similarity of *Alexander's Bridge* and *O Pioneers!*, for example, Lindemann finds that both novels exhibit "an ambivalent fascination with the chaotic force of illicit sexuality, a fascination that ultimately leads to the elimination of threat and the restoration of a conservative social order" (49). For Lindemann, there is no chance that Cather could be out; since she couldn't be, that must mean that she internalized society's homophobia; therefore her novels must echo social condemnation. That narrative, however, doesn't tally very well with the Cather of *The Colophon* essay, decrying convention, or even with the hero of *Alexander's Bridge,* repudiating the sacrifice of passion for the sake of passing as a model married man.

That even as late as 1931 Alexander might still serve as a surrogate for Cather would seem to be ruled out when Lindemann asserts that "Bartley Alexander is by no means 'queer'" (49). "Queer" thereby functions as an identity category, and there is no chance that Cather could possibly identify with her hero. Lindemann spends pages of her book—as well as the introduction to the edition of *Alexander's Bridge* that she edited for Oxford University Press—condemning his desire as infantile, regressive, sick, self-absorbed, narcissistic. Homophobia unleashed in the name of queer study; misandry in the name of feminism (Lindemann comes by the latter honestly enough; for O'Brien there is similarly no hope for Alexander simply because he is male; building bridges is always something one should not do since it is a form of masculine domination). Lindemann offers an instance of what Eve Kosofsky Sedgwick terms "punitive/pedagogical reading" that answers the question, How could this novel have been prevented?[8] The point is not that Cather simply endorses Alexander; the novel ends in his death, after all, but this does not exactly mean that she condemns him, although it does indicate the impossibility of his having his desire. The bridge that collapses marks the end of Alexander's "road," his path as a public person, his supposed maturity. But there is very little to suggest that Cather disagreed with the thought she assigns him, about how little these things mattered. These are, after all, the very terms in which she marks her first novel as failed—for attempting to accommodate herself to the ways of the world.

Cather's 1931 *Colophon* essay basically repeats what she had written in the preface that she provided for the 1922 republication of *Alexander's Bridge*. There, she repudiates the novel for a "subject-matter" in which she no longer finds herself at home; *O Pioneers!*, contrastively, invidiously—and in a stunning metaphor—is said to arise from material that the author can simply depend upon, a "something else" than the false consciousness of her first novel: "the thing by which our feet find the road home on a dark night, accounting of themselves for roots and stones which we had never noticed by day."[9] *Alexander's Bridge* once again—or, rather, at first—is said not to be in touch with what lies "at the bottom of consciousness" where the true materials are located, those that stimulate an author "whether he is aware of it or no" (94).

Cather's use of the masculine pronoun in this sentence and insistently throughout her preface is somewhat startling since the masculine author she is writing about is herself; it suggests the limits of the gender identification that O'Brien argues—and also may suggest some lingering identification with Alexander. More to the point, however, her assertion—that when a writer truly writes whether she/he knows it or not (s)he must write from a "bottom" that Cather locates in consciousness, and thereby dislocates—provides the very categorical ground for suspending the difference she claims between her first two novels. Cather develops in this preface the image of the road also to be found in the piece in *The Colophon*. Here she emphasizes the moment of coincidence, when the path of an author's life—his "life line"—realizes itself in writing, when the bottom becomes the surface of the text. The novel writes itself from this unconscious locale. Cather represents this meeting of lines as virtually uncrossable—and then crosses it. Once the lines meet, she says, the writer "will not often turn back to the building of external stories again." Not often, but not never, since "the young writer must have his affair with the external material he covets" (95). Only when the affair is over can "inner feeling" and its "deeper excitement" take over. Even as Cather frames this, these two supposed opposites, inner and outer, feed each other. Moreover, in distinguishing successful writing from failure, Cather seems to be enunciating her artistic principles through the novel she ostensibly repudiates. The image of the affair with externality, which might look like a way of describing Alexander's affair with Hilda (she is an actress, after all), fits even more exactly his relationship to his wife and through her the entire public world that claims him as its reflection. In that case, Hilda represents the call of the inner life, the demanding bottom. "He learns," Cather writes of the novelist—herself—"that it is not the adventure he sought, but the adventure that sought him, which has made the enduring mark upon him" (95), a summary that also applies to Alexander. To the end of the preface, Cather stresses that the true calling may go unheard, that "this guide is not always with him. . . . But when it is with him it corresponds to what Mr Bergson calls the wisdom of intuition as opposed to that of intellect" (96). Cather alludes here to the philosopher Henri Bergson, not the father of her heroine Alexandra Bergson, who may nonetheless get her Scandinavian name through this French connection.[10] Those intermittent "flashes that are as unreasoning, often as unreasonable, as life itself" (96) cannot be circumscribed. The very point of Bergsonian intuition is that it overrides the false divisions that intellect places upon experience, the ways in which it divides the world into mind and matter.[11]

If this is Cather's position, it is no stretch to call it queer in its refusal of boundaries. The very distinctions in her 1922 preface to *Alexander's Bridge*—between inner and outer, between her own materials and those that she misappropriates, between masculine and feminine, between forward and backward motion—all erected in an attempt to sink *Alexander's Bridge,* point, instead, to what supports it, its "double life." That phrase, subtitling Lee's book and invoked by O'Brien to distinguish the failure of *Alexander's Bridge* (divided, broken) from the integrity of *O Pioneers!,* comes, in fact, from an essay of Cather's on another writer, Katherine Mansfield.[12] Cather singles out for praise in Mansfield precisely what she avows as her own domain, and in a way that further torpedoes the line between external and internal, superficial and unconscious that supposedly divides her first two novels. Mansfield is a master of the "double life," Cather writes, showing in her most accomplished stories that what lies "underneath" and is "secret and passionate and intense . . . stamps the faces and gives character." No surface without depths. Life, as Cather characterizes it in this paradigm, represents a double tug, away from social relationships and their claims toward this secret self and yet toward others as where and how the secret life is lived to the extent that it can—for it cannot be fully: "human relationships are the tragic necessity of human life; . . . they can never be wholly satisfactory, . . . every ego is half the time greedily seeking them, and half the time pulling away from them" (136). Human psychology is necessarily ambivalent, founded in "secret accords and antipathies which lie hidden under our everyday behaviour," at its most extreme a battle of love and hate. Cather fights it over and again, as we have been seeing, in her accounts of *Alexander's Bridge,* and it is to these struggles, played out in a number of keys, that subsequent chapters will continue to attend. If Cather makes it difficult for the reader to exactly name the thing not named, it is in part because such struggles underlie her work. The thing not named does not simply translate something that can be said, and this is in part because of the deep ambivalences of the tug of war that Cather describes in her essay on Mansfield. As she argues, the successful writer—like Mansfield, like Cather—communicates "vastly more than she actually writes" in an "overtone, which is too fine for the printing press" (137). Crucially, in suggesting where the thing not said is yet to be found (in an overtone), Cather also suggests its necessary relationship to where it supposedly is not (on the page). The terms of Cather's analysis build the bridge from the novel that tells all to the reticent text.

Bartley Alexander therefore must have a "double nature"; indeed, Elizabeth Shepley Sergeant in her 1953 memoir claims that Cather used precisely that phrase to describe him.[13] In the novel, it is marked most visibly as he shuttles back and forth between his wife and mistress. Hilda, however, awakens a passion that is primordial, the one attached to his secret self. In her only positive recorded remarks about *Alexander's Bridge* (in an interview that she gave the New York *Sun* on 25 May 1912), Cather distinguishes her book from the industrial novel; it's not about building bridges, she says, but about "ever-kindling energy" in relationship to a hero who "began life a pagan, a crude force."[14] In other words, here too Cather discounts the externals and focuses on the internals, only this time *Alexander's Bridge* is not faulted on that account. Cather's remarks point to important moments in her novel; there is, for instance, the scene on the train as Alexander hurtles toward the bridge that will not hold. He sees himself in precisely those terms, about to crack under the strain of a "new force" that he cannot resist: "This new force was not he, it was but a part of him" (76). His terms for this experience—the irresistible passion kindled by Hilda—match Cather's own account of being overtaken by the spontaneous force that supposedly writes her best books. Bartley is represented as having—as being had by—that unsupportable experience. Hilda does not even begin to name what it is.

The passion for the actress is only partially "Alexander's masquerade," the title under which the novel first appeared serially in *McClure's,* presumably the name of the work as submitted by an author who had signed herself Fanny Cadawaller. Cather's pseudonym suggests that she was writing from her bottom, and Bartley's desire for Hilda is not just a passing fancy, but also the way in which lesbian desire is represented in the novel. As O'Brien suggests, the masquerade is Cather's way of presenting her desire for a woman under the guise of Bartley's desire for Hilda (385). O'Brien registers her discomfort with this, expressing distaste for Cather's masquerade; Lindemann, on the other hand, takes the affair straight.[15] Either way, however, heterosexuality is a masquerade, for Bartley Alexander's desire for his wife metonymizes the superficiality of worldly success and esteem. Bartley has had two loves, one represents conformity dressed up as romance, the other transgressive desire. Two loves, of comfort and despair.

The experience of desiring Hilda is even further a masquerade because it drives Alexander back upon himself, back in time to the primordial "pagan" condition that Cather names in the interview. In the novel, the form of the pagan is "boy." As Bartley rides the train of his thought, he sees the corollary outside the window, a scene of boys camping: "Alexander looked back wistfully at the boys, camped on the edge of the little marsh" (77). That backward glance is toward a point of origin that Cather shares with her hero, "the eternal boy in us," as she put it in an 1895 review.[16] Thus, Cather might well have understood the force of Gertrude Stein's question, "What is the use of being a boy if you are going to grow up to be a man?" Stein's query—used in the service of answering yet another question, "What are master-pieces and why are there so few of them?"—suggests that there is no necessary path, no conventional path, that produces masterpieces. They don't grow as men do from boys.[17] Stein decouples the usual trajectory from boys to men to allow for alternative possibilities, to account for the unaccountable process that produces masterpieces. So, too, Cather ostensibly attempting to carve out the road of her genius, a path connecting past to future, finds it crossed, not merely by a supposedly false road, but by an unsaid, unconscious, and overwhelming spontaneous force that underlies the two paths that Cather wishes to regard not merely as separate, but as representing a decisive, conscious choice.

If Bartley Alexander is queer insofar as his position is Cather's, so too is she insofar as she marks her origin as he marked his, in the masculine, in the boy that does not grow up to be a man. For Bartley resists being a man, if by "man" one means the socialized self, married, public. Boy resists that trajectory. The moment Alexander sees Hilda again, he feels "the boy he had been," a boy in full self-possession of himself:

> That consciousness was Life itself. Whatever took its place, action, reflection, the power of concentrated thought, were only functions of a mechanism useful to society; things that could be bought in the market. There was only one thing that had an absolute value for each individual, and it was just that original impulse, that internal heat, that feeling of one's self in one's own breast. (28)

A page later, he is described as having regained "a shadowy companion—not little Hilda Burgoyne, by any means, but some one vastly dearer . . . —his own young self, the youth who had waited for him upon the steps of the British Museum that night" (29). Alexander's desire has been faulted by O'Brien—how like a man to love only himself, the criticism goes—but the situation is less comfortably decided if Bartley's desire, and desiring position, also is Cather's. Moreover, his desire looks pederastic, as if the desire for the boy he was is a desire for a boy tout court, a reading suggested by phrasing the memory of meeting Hilda at the British Museum as a pickup scene. This passage, and others like it in the novel, anticipate *The Professor's House,* St. Peter's ultimate recovery of himself in similar reveries.[18] This suggests, at the very least, how central this fantasy was for Cather, simply by the fact that it recurs throughout her career. Readers who have noted this thematic have not seen that the professor's desire for the irrecoverable boy he was also doubles

his desire for the irrecoverably dead Tom Outland. I pursue this point in chapter 4, "Strange Brothers." Here I would merely reiterate the argument developed there, that Cather represents her own desire through a cross-gendered same-sex scenario. Doubly displaced, Alexander's desire for Hilda, which is his desire for a boy, is Cather's too. Even when she tells all, she tells it slant. A plot that looks heterosexual houses lesbian desire that is also figured as male-male desire. Male-male desire, indeed, figures the primordiality of desire through the "pagan" "boy" life-force of a secret self. Because of the enormous importance of these displacements—of this route to "the thing not named"—these configurations will be explored in each of the chapters to come. I turn now to the male-male erotics of *Alexander's Bridge*.[19]

This subject is perhaps most evident thanks to another shuttling figure in the novel, a premonition of professors to come. Lucius Wilson, Alexander's old teacher, ends the novel bridging Hilda and Winifred. He is the only character in the novel who knew Bartley as a boy, and he has been waiting to see him crack ever since. He knows, the old bachelor, that "predicting, in the case of boys, is not so easy as you might imagine" (7). He's spent his life observing boys, this "observer of women" (4). All he can think about, and the novel with him, almost from its first page to its last, is Alexander as a boy. He introduces those reveries as the novel opens; the protagonist himself comes to have them. When the boy-loving professor is not on the scene, Alexander is in the hands of another male mentor in London, Maurice Mainhall, a flamboyant, decadent theater person with Oscar Wilde tastes and associates. He takes Alexander around, much taken with his butchness—"Mainhall liked Alexander because he was an engineer" (16), a perfect cover. Mainhall can be presumed to have been drawn, like the narrator, to Bartley's rugged blond good looks (the first of Cather's hunks, anticipating Claude Wheeler in *One of Ours,* or the young Dr. Archie in *The Song of the Lark*). In this context, Bartley's worries about what would become of him if he left his wife (as he intends to do, although the letter declaring his intentions is rendered invisible when he drowns with it in his pocket) conjure up the fate of Oscar Wilde: "There would be nothing for him afterward. He seemed to see himself dragging out a restless existence on the Continent—Cannes, Hyères, Algiers, Cairo—among smartly dressed, disabled men of every nationality"

(76). Alexander's "unnatural excitement" (48) comes to its inevitable end: "The mind that society had come to regard as a powerful and reliable machine, dedicated to its service, may for a long time have been sick within itself and bent upon its own destruction" (88). A chilling conclusion. Cather seems to ventriloquize the judgmental voice of society; yet the vision of society turning the mind into a machine is at least as chilling; to be "sick" of that may not be a sign of disease. The sentence equivocates endlessly, but knows one thing, what Cather described in the Mansfield essay as "the tragic necessity of human life," that destruction is inevitable, relationships are impossible.[20] Between the impossibility of marriage and the impossibility of the affair with Hilda—or beneath these—is the secret Cather all but revealed in talking about (herself by considering) Katherine Mansfield.

This secret is not one thing. As we have seen, it implicates the specificity of Cather's sexuality in the existence of a secret self at war with itself and with the forms of social relationship in which it can at best only imperfectly be realized. It implicates itself in Cather's writing practices and their continual mobilization of an unsaid that may be unsayable because it is unconscious or because no set of words can quite capture something that resists conventional formalization. At the level of representation, the secret radiates, so that lesbian desire masquerades as heterosexuality, heterosexuality as homosexuality, and, even more to the point, heterosexuality as social convention necessarily fails to satisfy the deepest nature of the self. The domains of the speakable and nameable— the ordinary terms of social life—are no more divorced from the unspeakable than are Cather's double paths, the supposedly separate path of the repudiated first novel and secret pathway of the second first novel, which is said to have written itself. The "double life" of *Alexander's Bridge* ties it to *O Pioneers!*, for, as Julie Abraham has observed, "When the heterosexual couple made up of Emil and Marie is destroyed, so is a 'homosexual' couple—also Emil and Marie— who cannot speak their love" (42). Abraham assumes, commonsensically enough, to be sure, that Emil and Marie qualify as a heterosexual couple because he is male and she is female; it is their secret, unavowable passion that places them in a " 'homosexual' position" (42). Is gender, however, the stable ground that Abraham seems to assume? Is it only homosexuality that requires scare quotes? The very possibility that heterosexuality might figure homosexuality suggests that the notion of "coding" (heterosexual for homosexual) needs to be supplemented with "crossing." In *O Pioneers!,* crossing is marked almost from the first page, and precisely in terms of the instability of gender identity.

When Emil first appears, just a few pages into the novel, a five-year-old boy weeping because his kitten has climbed up into a tree, we see him wearing a dress (5).[21] A page later, his sister appears clothed in "a man's long ulster" and looking like a soldier (6). Enter Carl Linstrum, who climbs the pole to rescue the cat, but before we credit this as an exemplary act of gender-appropriate behavior, we must note that he is in town shopping, buying "chromo 'studies' which the druggist sold to the Hanover women who did china-painting" (9; Carl's artwork is similarly derivative). Carl may climb the tree, but his effeminacy is further conveyed by his bodily demeanor—he is "slight and narrow-chested" (9), in a word, "too sensitive" (10). To complete the scene, add Marie, clothed in a "fur tippet" that Emil "fingered admiringly" (12). Ultra femme Marie replaces the kitten; she is the one non-Swede in this cast of characters, the "dark child" seen as a "brunette doll" (11) in comparison to these very white blonds. Gender, in a word, is crossed from the start; desire even between those of different genders may be following a path that the term "heterosexual" seems too limited to describe.

The bodies, dress, deportment of these figures is scarcely simply aligned to their genitals. Marie's hyperfemininity, for example, seems almost to make her another species, certainly another "race." The next time we see Emil and Marie together, he's "a splendid figure of a boy" (77) splendidly singing the coloratura soprano aria from *Faust*—Marguerite on the verge of her transgressive path; Marie, however, is a "contralto" (79). In his next significant return, Emil will be wearing a Mexican costume that Alexandra insists he keep on at the church supper: " 'All the girls . . . are going to wear fancy costumes,' she argued, 'and some of the boys' " (212), which is somehow persuasive.

Marie and Emil are not the only couple to cross hetero- and homosexual desire; Alexandra and Carl do too, and in ways that complicate Julie Abraham's paradigm. For if Marie and Emil embody a destructive, transgressive, unutterable desire, Alexandra and

Carl are linked by a bond of "sympathy" (10) that requires no language. At the start of the novel, as at its end when they agree to marry, this couple is named "the two friends" (10, 15, 306). "The two friends stood for a moment on the windy street corner, not speaking a word, as two travelers, who have lost their way, sometimes stand and admit their perplexity in silence" (10–11). He looks back, she looks forward. They are, as it were, the two paths that meet and cross, and their sympathetic communication, as they go in opposite directions and yet toward each other, refigures the roads through which Cather figured her double journey. Carl has been "engraving other men's pictures" (116)—he is the kind of derivative superficial artist who wrote *Alexander's Bridge*—while Alexandra has "made her own" picture (116) directly on the land, like the author of *O Pioneers!* The couple they form is Cather twice over. If Emil and Marie mark the fatality of proscribed desire, Alexandra and Carl mark its productive possibility. " 'We've someway always felt alike about things.' 'Yes, that's it: we've liked the same things and we've liked them together, without anybody else knowing' " (52). Two forms of the thing not named are offered by the novel's two couples.

The union of Alexandra and Carl thus cannot quite support the conclusion that Lindemann reaches, in which Alexandra "stands at the pinnacle of the novel's bodily and ideological hierarchy . . . the " 'gleaming white body' of the un-queer entrepreneur" (44), "the transcendent, disembodied subjectivity of liberal individualism" (45), Alexandra the pedagogic police(wo)man, the embodiment of masculine values that Lindemann thinks feminism should repudiate and that Cather only embraced because she could not affirm her lesbianism. The point, rather, is that the "masculinity" of Alexandra can be taken to displace rather than simply to affirm suspect values. Alexandra occupies a position in the text not entirely delimited by gender difference. Her "Amazonian fierceness" (8), marked as such in her defiance against men, also allows for her alliance with a man who can say to her that it has been her fate "to be always surrounded by little men" (181), a category from which Carl himself is not excluded. Earlier, Carl's self-pitying extends to a description of the urban population to which he belongs (a backward path that further connects him to *Alexander's Bridge*), and which Alexandra has, in his view, mistaken for freedom. "We have no house, no place, no people of our own. We live in the

streets, in the parks, in the theatres. We sit in restaurants and concert halls and look about at the hundreds of our own kind and
shudder" (123).

The "shudder" that accompanies the recognition of "our own
kind" is the decisive indication of the "kind" in which Carl includes
himself. It's a teeming population. Having delivered this speech,
in the silence that ensues, "he knew that she understood what he
meant" (123), knows, that is, that Alexandra is one of "our own
kind" too. Lindemann marks Alexandra in the masculine in terms
of the ways she embodies what Carl says he lacks—possession, property, people. "He felt that men were too weak to make any mark
here" (15). Other readers, O'Brien, for example, have been more impressed with the "feminine" dispossession of Alexandra, the version
of things in which her entrepreneurial success is a function of the
desire of the land as it "yields itself" (76) to her, not of her putting
her mark upon it. In fact, Cather's text offers support for both views,
and, indeed, prevaricates possession as dispossession by calling it, in
one of the most famous passages of the novel, "love and yearning":

> For the first time, perhaps, since that land emerged from the waters
> of geologic ages, a human face was set toward it with love and yearn-
> ing. It seemed beautiful to her, rich and strong and glorious. Her
> eyes drank in the breadth of it, until her tears blinded her. Then
> the Genius of the Divide, the great, free spirit which breathes across
> it, must have bent lower than it ever bent to a human will before.
> The history of every country begins in the heart of a man or a
> woman. (65)

The ideological trick of writing possession as dispossession, of this
mutualized desire, doubles Cather's own insistence that she wrote
novels that wrote themselves. In making such a point, Cather is
not simply voicing her privilege as a disembodied liberal subject
(a subject that ideological critique will unmask as white and male
by definition). Arguably, Cather's gender interrupts this, but even
more so does the figuration of desire in this passage. For it natural-
izes queer desire, the "kind" to which Carl and Alexandra belong.
If the Genius of the Divide, who elsewhere Alexandra fantasizes as
a huge male figure carrying her off, here bends to her, she bends
to a land in which she feels her heart stirring (76), a land that, in
the final phrases of the book, will be both her burial place and the

seedbed of the eternal youth that Alexandra embodies as the figure of futurity. These figurations refuse the hetero/homo divide even as they increasingly weight an identification between heroine and land that is a same-sex desire: "There were certain days in her life, outwardly uneventful, which Alexandra remembered as peculiarly happy days; days when she was close to the flat, fallow world about her, and felt, as it were, in her own body the joyous germination in the soil" (203–04).

> And now the old story has begun to write itself over there. . . . Isn't it queer: there are only two or three human stories, and they go on repeating themselves as fiercely as if they had never happened before; like the larks in this country, that have been singing the same five notes over for thousands of years. (119)

The queer story that writes itself, one that refuses the division of internal and external, of activity and passivity, of gendered difference, is plotted in Alexandra's final response to Carl's vision of himself as a failure living the life of urban anonymity and dispossession, for she goes further than acquiescing in silent understanding of what he says. "And yet," she adds, "I would rather have Emil grow up like that than like his two brothers" (123).

Alexandra has two projects in the novel. One involves settling the land, the other is her brother whom, as this and similar pasages indicate, she treats as if he were her son, and for whom she wishes what Carl has, distance from the land, "a personality apart from the soil" (213). "She had always believed in him, as she had believed in the land" (239). The connection here is as queer as the one Alexandra's father notes when he sees in her, but not in his eldest sons, a reflection of his father; John Bergson attempts a biological explanation for lines of affiliation that refuse the proprieties of gendered difference, a sameness posited upon difference as in a first that was double from the start.

Emil also is a substitute for Carl; if Alexandra projects his future as Carl's, when Carl departs earlier in the novel, she says to him, "Now I shall have nobody but Emil" (54). Brother and sister are capable of the same silent communication, the same sharing of memory, the "likeness" that Alexandra and Carl share, "that warm, friendly silence, full of perfect understanding, in which Emil and Alexandra had spent many of their happiest half-hours" (238). "I've had a pretty lonely life, Emil," Alexandra tells her brother, explaining her desire for Carl, who has only received scorn for his weakness from the rest of the family (the older brothers whom Alexandra has displaced). Carl mistakes Alexandra's position—as landowner, as a kind of patriarch—in much the same way Lindemann does. "Besides Marie, Carl is the only friend I have ever had" (177), she tells Emil, who only has ears for Marie's name. In this moment of failed sympathy for the untowardness of Alexandra's desire for Carl ("He was a little ashamed for his sister" [179]), Emil nonetheless pursues his own comparable desire. Hence, in exile from Marie, the letters he writes to Alexandra from Mexico are as much to Marie, as she sees: "Marie knew perfectly well that Emil's letters were written more for her than for Alexandra. They were not the sort of letters that a young man writes to his sister" (199). Marie voices a conventional sense of propriety here that may be mistaken (the intense and incestuous desires of Emil and Alexandra have a place in the economy of forbidden desire), but she is acute about the double destination of the letter, for it is also how Cather's text is written. As the rather convoluted discussion in this paragraph has aimed to suggest, the paths of the plotlines of O Pioneers! continually cross each other.

Emil's desire for Marie is so intense that he is unable to show interest in other women; at college he is therefore thought "queer" (180). Even Amadee, Emil's best friend, with whom he characteristically goes arm-in-arm (163), wonders if Emil would rather be a priest than married, as Amadee has just become. As Abraham points out, another reason for reading cross-gendered couples as same-sex ones is the fact that the dissolution of the same-gender coupling of Amadee and Emil—first by marriage, then by Amadee becoming a father, finally by Amadee's death—coincides with the explosion that precipitates the tragic denouement of the novel. It is in his inconsolable mourning for Amadee that Emil, thinking he is going to say goodbye to Marie forever instead has sex with her, which turns out to be the same thing. There is a parallel here for Alexandra as well; Marie is, as she says in the passage cited above, her only friend besides Carl. In fact, she says it to him, explaining that Marie now lives in the very house he abandoned, at the other end of the field that divided/joined their properties: "It has been so nice for me to feel that there was a friend at the other end of it again" (130).

Marie is for her something like the kitten was for Emil, "a little brown rabbit" (130), and Marie reciprocates enough to be able to tell Emil that "his sister was a handsome woman" (235). Yet Marie's desire for Emil drives a wedge in her friendship with Alexandra—it is the one thing that cannot be said, just as it is what Emil cannot tell Amadee. And although it is right in front of Alexandra's face if she could only see it, she does not see that Emil and Marie are desperately in love with each other. Alexandra is blind to them because she is blind to herself: "Her personal life, her own realization of herself, was almost a subconscious existence" (203). The novel depends upon these opacities which it marks as the sign of the *shared* difference of its central figures, two couples who cross each other and in whom same- and other-sexed desires also cross.

It is perhaps this that explains the difficult ending of *O Pioneers!*, Alexandra's move to identify with Frank Shabata, the jealous husband who kills Emil and Marie, as well as her insistence on blaming Marie. Lindemann reads this as evidence that Alexandra distances herself from the queerness of the transgressive couple, following in this respect Abraham, who writes: "If in *O Pioneers!* shotgun blasts are directed at the heterosexual couple to obliterate the heterosexual plot, they are also blasts this lesbian writer is turning on herself" (42). As I've suggested, the final union of Carl and Alexandra in part disputes this reading. Alexandra identifies with Frank because she feels that she too has been victimized; Frank is a stranger who had ruined himself by making a mistake, marrying Marie not because he loved her but because she wanted him, having mistaken him for something he was not; his dandified exterior covered sadistic brutality. Emil is who Frank appeared to be. "They were the best you had here," Carl says to Alexandra (305), and he is the substitute for Marie and Emil. Alexandra's rage can be understood as the other side of her loss, the other side of her desire and guilt, for "she had omitted no opportunity of throwing Marie and Emil together" (284): the rage at herself for not knowing, for not allowing herself to know, for not being allowed to know. Carl says it for her. You should have told me, she says, and he replies:

"My dear, it was something one felt in the air, as you feel the spring coming, or a storm in summer. I didn't *see* anything. Simply, when I was with those two young things, I felt my blood go quicker, I felt—how shall I say it?—an acceleration of life. After I got away, it was all too delicate, too intangible, to write about." (305)

The line between transgressive and permissible desire all but disappears. Bordering/dividing "the thing not named" is the destructive passion that Alexandra unleashes in the final section of *O Pioneers!* It's intimated in the poem that Cather wrote to stand before the novel, "Prairie Spring," in which a land that always is "silent" is met by another silence—of "Youth,/Flaming," singing, flashing, fierce and sharp in its desire, "Singing and singing,/Out of the lips of silence."

Wick Cutter

Another way to understand Alexandra's identification with Frank Shabata—her identification, that is, with the man who kills the two whom she loved best—would be to recall Judith Butler's observations about mourning as constitutive of the imperfect formation of sexual identity. This argument in *Gender Trouble* is implicit in her complex and important essay about Cather, " 'Dangerous Crossing': Willa Cather's Masculine Names." [22] There, working toward an understanding of Cather's cross-positioning, Butler urges that one think, contra O'Brien, that identification is not "a sign of loyalty and affiliation" but rather of "unresolved aggression or, minimally, ambivalence" (143–44). Butler's account of identification presumably applies whether one identifies with someone who is nominally the same or nominally different, although her aim is to explain why Cather as a woman and a lesbian necessarily writes in the masculine (why, that is, referring to Cather as a woman or a lesbian is not to make some sort of simple and transparent statement about her gender and sexuality). Cather inhabits positions of gender equivocation that do not easily subscribe to the univocity of a singular nomination. Her texts have "as one of their persistent features," Butler announces as she opens her essay, "the destabilization of gender and sexuality through the name" (143). This "name," unspecified here, presumably names the thing not to be named, or so Butler glosses it further into the discussion: "Of course, it was in the prosecution of Oscar Wilde that homosexuality became associated with the unspoken and unspeakable name" (152; indeed, the crime not to be named among Christians is far more ancient than Wilde).[23] Butler's argument glosses this unspeakable name, and, in seeking to ally it to Cather's writing practice furthers the consideration of Cather's "thing not named."

To follow Butler, one would understand Alexandra's identification with Frank as a surfacing of the murderousness that is involved in the very desire that she instantiates, a desire that cannot name itself except as otherwise, through the radiating displacements of the kind we have noted in *O Pioneers!,* and which Butler would read as signs of the ambivalence of identification, which must always involve translation, substitution, displacement, "a taking on of a position that is at once a taking over, a dispossession, and a sacrifice" (148). The bloodbath that ends the lovemaking of Emil and Marie is a horrific figure for this sacrifice, while the second-best union of Alexandra and Carl could stand in for the coupling that the text continually refigures but never realizes as such, "figuration that enables precisely the sexuality it thematically forecloses" (161), to borrow Butler's parsing of another of Cather's texts. It is Butler's point that there only are these murderous refractions. At the end, then, Alexandra's identification with Frank could be read as her—or as Cather's—acknowledgement of the cost involved in the desire that cannot affirm itself, a cost that a heterosexuality that claims for itself normative gender and sexuality occludes, and that is more apparent, although necessarily not therefore more sayable, for those who have seen though and suffered the masquerades of the norm. The dynamic of (dis)possession that Butler traces also relates to Cather's problematic figuration of Alexandra's relationship to the land.

Although Butler emphasizes that "the name . . . functions as a kind of prohibition, but also as an enabling occasion" (152), her phrasing of the (im)possibility of "direct and transparent visibility" (144) of lesbian representation lodges any enablement within a prohibition that Butler attributes over and again to an agency she names "the law." This monolithic generalization plausibly attaches to its instantiations as mandatory heterosexuality and the proscription of homosexuality, and in terms of male dominance. While Butler wishes to maintain the case of the law that is not one, the displacements, multiplications, crossings, and refractions that are the inevitable routes by which prohibited desire comes to be articulated can seem like sad substitutes for a real when they are said to involve a "practice of dissimulation" (145) or a "false transfer" (148). Sexuality exists under the sign of its erasure and always must be experienced as an act of mourning. In this rigorous light, it is difficult to know what the "enabling" side of the prohibition amounts to, so narrow is the distance between its possibility and its impossibility. The kind of world-building that might be imagined through Carl and Alexandra, networks of possible alliance that "heterosexuality" barely describes (and does not at all in its compulsory normative form), is blasted with Frank's shotgun. In this respect, Butler's argument is close to Julie Abraham's claims about the foreclosure of same-sex desire in the routing of heterosexual coupling. Butler's mournful embrace of "a prohibition in desire that necessitates the sacrifice of desire" (156) sounds stronger than any enablements the argument seeks to offer. Nonetheless, what Butler does show is that if Cather could not represent lesbian desire directly, the indirect modes she chose—or, rather, that were the necessary conditions of her practice—do the job.

Butler's arguments have been crucial in my thinking about Cather (the consideration of disidentification in "Cather Diva," for example, of a murderousness that accompanies lesbian desire, would have been impossible without her work). In the pages that follow I want to build upon her reading of *My Ántonia,* a novel that Cather claimed had written itself, for further consideration of its dangerous crossings in the direction of the masculine.[24] Butler focuses on two moments in the novel: on the "Introduction" to the text, as it installs Jim Burden as authorial surrogate, a round-robin, as Butler acutely reads it, of authorial agency and dispossession. The other involves an episode early in the novel, when Jim kills a monstrous rattlesnake. The snake lies in coils that make a *W,* and Butler reads this, entirely persuasively, as a truncated signature, the *W* of "Willa," where the scene of a threatening phallic assault, and a threatening castration, is answered by a self-castration of the letter and the name which nonetheless points to Cather's phantasmatic appropriation of the phallus, the snake, against her masculine double, Jim Burden, whose last name names his burden of supporting her.

"In 1918, Cather began her novel *My Ántonia* with a prologue," Butler begins (145); however, the "Introduction" she reads is the one

Cather provided in 1926, a revision of the original 1918 "Introduction." I would briefly compare them, not to deny the acuity of Butler's reading, but to see again how a supposedly self-written text underwent a revision fully congruent with Cather's repudiation and affirmation of the doubled paths of her first two novels.[25]

In the 1918 "Introduction" to *My Ántonia* there is no ambiguity about the gender of its author; she needs Jim to tell the tale because she had been "a little girl" who lacked Jim's "opportunities" to know Ántonia (xiii). Cather's explanation—in terms of gendered debility—while undoubtedly true to the paradigm that Butler endorses (of the exchange of women who can never affirm the name since it is always the name of the father) rings false here precisely in its affirmation of a transparency between the author and the "I" who speaks in the "Introduction." Insofar as that "I" once was a girl, she is all the more likely now to be Willa Cather. And insofar as that is true, it must be patently untrue that the book one is reading is the manuscript represented as inscribed by Jim as *My Ántonia*. Moreover, Jim explicitly asks the narrating "I" why she has "never written anything about Ántonia," and the two enter into a contest to produce her story: "I would set down on paper all that I remembered of Ántonia if he would do the same" (xii–xiii). The struggle for (dis)possession that Butler reads in the later preface is thus explicit in the first one, but here too the literalization of Cather as author—in this case as failed author since she never does produce the text she promises Jim—only further fabricates, making Jim-as-author an insupportable fiction. The original "Introduction" seeking to explain literally how it came to have a male narrator explains instead how it came to be a false text of the kind that Cather would repudiate for superficiality and conventionality. Making Jim more real by making herself more real—giving them definitive gendered histories in the original tell-all preface—makes it all less real.

Cather's original "Introduction" offers much more than the remark in the later edition about finding Jim's wife insufferable: "I do not like his wife" (1). Here we get a full page on the woman Jim married; she has a name—Genevieve Whitney; a genealogy—"the only daughter of a distinguished man"; a character—headstrong; a story—she married Jim on the rebound. Her instability and willfulness are marked by the causes she takes up, women's suffrage and strikers, for instance, as well as the supposedly advanced artistic set she patronizes, the sign that Cather let stand in 1926 to show how "unimpressionable" Jim's wife is (x–xi). Cather's account is a paroxysm of misogyny, male identification with Jim, saddled with a woman who is irritated by "her husband's quiet tastes" (xi). If he is properly femininely demure, this woman isn't. The page-long portrait brings to the surface an antagonism that is unambiguously that of one woman against another. The plot sketched comes straight from *Alexander's Bridge,* and Jim's wife is first cousin to Alexander's. In this initial "Introduction," Cather aggressively and in her own name adopts a point of view that could be called male; yet the misogyny is directed not at all women, but at one who seems to violate the proprieties of marriage. If this is Cather calling out the law, it rings utterly false since she was herself no one's wife, even if her insubordination did not take the form of advocating the vote for women or the rights of workers.

(Dis)identification with Jim's wife extends beyond her refusal of subordination; as someone who married a westerner "out of bravado" (x), Genevieve Whitney's marriage could be taken to figure Cather's writing project; in fact, she is a writer with a self-produced play to her credit (or shame). Faulted for the insincerity of her views, she takes up causes because her marriage is a lost cause. What Cather values in the marriage is a man who keeps quiet, hardly a conventional view of marriage or of gendered relations. Undoubtedly Cather dropped all this because of its literality. The two introductions, nonetheless, remain in the usual double relationship, and the suppressions of the later one are not just the result of forces bearing down upon Cather from some domain of "the law." They are exactions that allow her to ambiguate positions that, in either instance, do not seem bent on observing the law. For the original "Introduction" represents compulsory heterosexuality as failed, while the author's male identification does not seem necessitated by an attempt to evade a singular prohibitive law.

Butler's reading of the truncated *W* follows upon her reading of the 1926 "Introduction." Beside its abbreviation, I would put another nomination in the masculine, Wick Cutter, a name that rhymes aslant with the author's even as it too conjures up phallic dispossession. What might be made of this (dis)identification?

Wick Cutter first appears in *My Ántonia* at a moment when the text momentarily and awkwardly falters: "Wick Cutter, the merciless Black Hawk money-lender, a man of evil name throughout the country, of whom I shall have more to say later" (34–35). There is no other character in the novel whose future appearance is so awkwardly forecast, while the emphasis on his "evil name" and his monstrous appropriation of others' resources clearly situates Wick Cutter within the problematic that Butler identifies: whatever Wick Cutter lends, he takes more than he gives. Cather intrudes this naming of herself in the masculine with the kind of self-consciousness she regularly excoriated in her affirmations of texts that write themselves. The narrating "I" splits into this alterity.

Wick Cutter looms over the ruin of "our friends the Russians" (34), Peter and Pavel, the first of several male couples in the novel (including Jake and Otto, the hands who bring up Jim and who depart together never to be heard of again). They are "our friends" because they are Mr. Shimerda's, a couple joined from the moment they threw a newly wed bride and groom to wolves pursuing the sled they were driving (a rear attack like Jim's with the snake). Mr. Shimerda also is depleted by the demands of marriage, and he pines for a trombone-playing friend with whom he made music back in Bohemia: "He love very much the man who play the long horn," Ántonia tells Jim (59). Wick Cutter is the double for Krajiek, a fellow Bohemian who also extorts money from the Shimerdas, and who acts guilty when Ántonia's father commits suicide. The path to his suicide begins when Pavel dies and Peter leaves, his property turned over to Cutter. The moneylender is the embodied antipathy to their gentleness. Similarly, Mr. Shimerda's fault is that he would give everything away, and finally does by taking his own life.

An explanation of sorts for Cutter's behavior is offered when he appears again in the text, this time for his story to be told. In "perpetual warfare with his wife" (135), he is mainly concerned to make sure that neither she nor her family inherit any of his money or property after he dies. His exaggerated possessiveness therefore contrasts with even as it shares the point of origin that coupled the Russians or led Ántonia's father to the grave: antipathy to marriage. From this central point (one established from page one in the dismissal of Jim's wife) radiate a number of points of disavowed identification. Cutter is emphatically described as "fussy" and "fastidious and prim" (Ántonia's father engages in a similarly fussily neat suicide), and is reduced physically to little more than a "pink, bald head" and "yellow whiskers, aways soft and glistening . . . brushed every night, as a woman does her hair" (134–35), features Jim "detests." The monstrosity of masculine appetitiveness—including being "notoriously dissolute with women" (135)—couples with excessive femininity, and Wick Cutter's gender cannot be stabilized: "It was a peculiar combination of old-maidishness and licentiousness that made Cutter seem so despicable" (135). The sentence functions apotropaically, as Cutter edges near to the divided state of the author.

Cutter's story is introduced as Ántonia leaves the employ of the Harlings to go and work for him. She makes this move when she refuses to stop attending dances as Mr. Harling has demanded as a condition of her employment. At this moment an entire nexus of connections between Bohemian girls and sexuality is cemented. This section of the novel is called "The Hired Girls" and prevaricates between one kind of labor and another, as when Wick Cutter takes one of the Swedish girls he had employed to Omaha in order to establish her "in the business for which he had fitted her" (135; other girls he has gotten pregnant return to domestic service after bearing his illegitimate children or aborting them). The hired girls are assumed to be promiscuous because they are foreign; the world divides into nice Black Hawk girls and these girls: "The daughters of Black Hawk merchants had a confident, unenquiring belief that they were 'refined,' and that the country girls, who 'worked out,' were not" (128). Ántonia will seem to fulfill these expectations when she has an illegitimate child. Cutter's mix of primness and promiscuity combines the divided traits of femininity in the novel. In him—and in Ántonia—these also are marked as male and female. Ántonia works in the field "like a man" (95) and is "saved" from this by being turned into a hired girl.

"The Hired Girls" ends when Wick Cutter attempts to rape Ántonia. He fails because Ántonia is not in her own bed; she has asked Jim to sleep there. Cutter's failure thus has two failed objects; "Jim has literally taken Ántonia's place and experienced the rape intended for her," as Judith Fetterley notes (157): "A hand closed softly on my shoulder, and at the same moment I felt something hairy and cologne-scented brush my face" (158). Butler has noted that Ántonia touches Jim on the shoulder (19), indicating that he is the one who carries the burden of the text. A moment later,

Mr. Shimerda touches him there as well (20); here Wick Cutter does. The touching becomes insistently sexual at this moment. Jim dives out the window, Cutter panting behind. Stripped a page later, his bruised body is exposed. Like Alexandra with Marie, he blames Ántonia for this: she put him in the position to be raped. "She had let me in for all this disgustingness" (159). In the relay in which Jim substitutes for Ántonia, she, in his recoil, substitutes for Cutter. The evil name of Cutter so multiplies. Humiliated, Jim can "well imagine what the old men down at the drugstore would do with such a theme" (159).

The desires of the author, enacted, repudiated, displaced through all these circuits, crystallize in the name Wick Cutter. He appears finally in the last pages of the novel, having succeeded in depriving his wife of his fortune by first murdering her and then committing suicide (231–33). His suicide answers Mr. Shimerda's, joined through marital antipathy. The murdering of wives hyperbolizes Cather's antipathy to marriage in this "text whose hostility to marriage would be hard to exceed," to borrow Judith Fetterley's words (150). The hired girls Tiny and Lena, thought to be promiscuous, in fact never marry, and Lena announces over and again that she never would (Fetterley takes her refusal and her ongoing relation with Tiny to mark her as a feminine-identified lesbian). Of course the grand exception to this is Ántonia, teeming mother at the end of the novel, a figure virtually declared to have always already been "a natural-born mother" (204). Jim's famous declaration to her encompasses that possibility too: "I'd have liked to have you for a sweetheart, or a wife, or my mother or my sister—anything that a woman can be to a man" (206). At the end she speaks of Jim, only a few years younger than she is, as if he were one of the Harling children she brought up: "I declare, Jim, I loved you children almost as much as I love my own" (215). Placed in this "maternal" position, Ántonia's maternity seems somewhat separated from its actuality as a biological function: she is so "naturally" a mother that she mothers virtually anyone. By the end of the novel she assumes the kind of originary position that "mother" might metaphorize. "She was a rich mine of life, like the founders of early races" (227).

Ántonia produces what the final section names, "Cuzak's Boys," and although she has daughters, they don't figure. Her boys are for Jim—"I would like to sleep in the haymow, with the boys," he tells her as soon as she invites him to spend the night (221), and immediately he feels "like a boy in their company" (222). His future is the boys: "trips I meant to take with the Cuzak boys. . . . There were enough Cuzaks to play with for a long while yet. Even after the boys grew up, there would be Cuzak himself" (237). Gentle Anton might finally replace Gaston Cleric, the man with whom Jim went east, and who died of a fever contracted in Italy. (Does one need to decipher that story? As Lindemann notes, this narrative would seem to testify to "Jim's unfinished mourning for his lost male companion" [68].) The displacements are stunning; even as Ántonia "lent herself to immemorial human attitudes" (226), it is in the time-out-of mind possibility of these teeming male couples that her maternity is realized. Wick Cutter's murder/suicide, recounted by Ántonia's children in the final pages of the novel (" 'Hurrah! The murder!' the children murmured" [231]), is the counterimage to her hyperfecundity. Indeed, his story is to be associated with the other omphalos of the novel, that little spot of unploughed land at the crossroads covered in undulating red grass where Mr. Shimerda, the genius loci that ties Ántonia to Jim, lies buried. The dead father there, dead WC at the end, are the poles of (dis)possession that permit the teeming possibilities of life, of desires that do not subscribe to the law of compulsory heterosexuality. The abjection of Wick Cutter is the dissimulation of the desire of the text, the crossing performed and disavowed by the author who takes this bad name almost as her own.

Willa Cather

"Is it not obvious why Jim can't marry Ántonia?" Judith Fetterley queries (158). The answer to her rhetorical question echoes Butler's argument—he can't because he really isn't male. One problem with this answer, however, is that, at least in the "Introduction," Jim has a wife. However much the novel codes the impossibility of coupling Jim and Ántonia as the interdiction of same-sex union, that translation overlooks the explanation that the novel does provide. Jim and Ántonia are divided by class, and his refusal of the Black Hawk views about the difference between nice white girls and promiscuous immigrants is one that he only is able to make retrospectively. Ántonia is not for him to marry, while his failed marriage to a woman of the right class allows Cather here, as in *Alexander's Bridge,* to underline how conventional choices are devastating to those who could and should have chosen otherwise.

Although class is the impediment to marriage, this literal answer to the question is no more satisfactory than the coded one if only because class is figured in racial terms, the hired girls as "almost a race apart" (127).[26] Hence the novel's insistence on describing Ántonia as "brown," from Jim's first sight of her brown eyes, brown hair—"her skin was brown, too, and in her cheeks she had a glow of a rich, dark colour" (17)—to his final vision of her as a broken woman of forty-plus, "brown and hardened" but still emitting "the fire of life" (217). Ántonia is as brown as Marie in *O Pioneers!* and for the same reason: to register sexual allure. Marie is compared to animals, Ántonia is the mother of primitive races. A Bergsonian life force is embodied in racialized forms that here unmistakably evoke the Native Americans who are remarkably absent from Cather's plains, only mentioned, not otherwise represented in *My Ántonia.*

Jim's luxuriance in erasure, in being "blotted out" (8) and "dissolved into something complete and great" (14), or the intensity of feeling generated in the novel for the "unbroken" land covered in red grass, has to be read in the light of the history that Mike Fischer has insisted stands behind Cather's novels, the violent removal of Native Americans that produced Nebraska as empty virgin territory.[27] As Fischer details, this history was still in the making when the Cathers arrived in Nebraska, and the town in which they settled—Red Cloud—was named for a chief forced to sign away land to the United States. Cather's renaming of the town as Black Hawk in *My Ántonia* pushes this history back to the earlier moment of Indian removal under Andrew Jackson, although, as Fischer points out, the Black Hawk Wars of 1831–32 had been given romantic sheen in an autobiography attributed to Black Hawk. Cather, he argues, was doing little more than reproducing a widespread cultural nostalgia for the Indian that had developed once Native Americans had been eliminated and space had been created for the immigrants, a fitting conclusion for the career of "the little girl who had been photographed as Hiawatha" (35). Convincing as this is, one has to ask whether Ántonia's brownness or the redness of the grass really suppresses the materials that ideological critique unmasks. Fischer's claims about a textual unconscious seem difficult to sustain next to a description like this one of the red grass that ends with this comparison: "as if the shaggy grass were a sort of loose hide, and underneath it herds of wild buffalo were galloping, galloping . . ." (13). The novel continually evokes such scenes of breaking and ploughing (the author is a cutter), and with them a continued invitation to the thing not named, which, in this case, lodges a history of relations between whites and natives that cannot be entirely unconscious.

When Jim opines that the snake he killed "must have been there when white men first came, left on from buffalo and Indian times" (32)—all of twenty-four years before, as Fischer notes—the prevaricating primordiality is drawn into the orbit of conflicted gendered and sexed identity played out in this scene. Butler's analysis of sacrifice and appropriation seems apt in both cases. The snake is said by Jim to be "like the ancient, eldest Evil. Certainly his kind have left horrible unconscious memories in all warm-blooded life" (32–33). The disavowal here ("the ancient, eldest Evil") simultaneously relegates to the unconscious a motivating force comparable to the energy associated with Ántonia. Is only an invidious sentimental appropriation of the native involved when Cather assumes the part of an Indian boy?

Tabooed desire figured as tabooed racial crossing: Cather could be said to attempt to rewrite and reappropriate the native by making Ántonia brown, ur-mother of primitive races—erasing the real Indian in this masquerade. In figuration, if not directly, the text registers the Indian removal that it performs. White ascendency is rendered ambivalently. Consider the oft-cited image of the plough set against the blazing sun: first it is "heroic in size, a picture writing on the sun"; a moment later, it is gone, absorbed in darkness, returned to "its own littleness": "the forgotten plough had sunk back to its own littleness somewhere on the prairie" (156). As picture writing, it is a hieroglyph, pioneer achievement scripted in ancient form, and as fleeting as the fate of ancient empires. The elegiac tone of the novel builds on an expanding repertoire of loss, the "picture writing on the sun" retracing a primordial circle of the kind still visible after Indian removal. While Jake and Otto believe a circle still to be seen on the land marks a site where Indians tortured white men, Jim's grandfather believes it was where they raced horses. Jim sees the circle beneath the snow, and says it looked "like strokes of Chinese white on canvas" (42). Is this effacement? or remembrance, reorigination, reinscription?

It is difficult to answer these questions, but not to see that they are allied to the problematic of dispossession and disidentification, of not saying and yet saying aslant, that is explicitly connected to Cather's writing. The strokes of Chinese white on white match Jim's estimation of the "perfect utterance" in Virgil's *Georgics,* "where the pen was fitted to the matter as the plough is to the furrow" (170), a description that names Cather's ambition—and suggests its cost, for *My Ántonia* begins with an epigraph from the *Georgics,* "Optima dies . . . prima fugit,*" the best days are the first to flee, and Ántonia is in that "prima" position. Her teeming loins perform the work that Virgil's lines urge even as fecundity is placed in a losing struggle. Mortality is not all that is involved, although we recall that Jim read Virgil with Gaston Cleric, and mourns his death. The allusion draws Ántonia's body and Cather's writing project into the orbit of male-male erotics. The racialization of difference (which, of course, remains a questionable if entirely commonplace fantasy) and the literal removal of native Americans from the novel are involved in mourning the impossibility of fulfilled or realized desire, here displaced and articulated in Jim's relationship to his former tutor. Just as Cather scorned any reader who might think that *Alexander's Bridge* really was about engineering, so too the rescripting and refusal of the literal histories of Native Americans in *My Ántonia* is woven into Cather's forays into things unnamed.

This is not to deny the point that a number of critics have made about Cather's participation in a range of racist ideologies. Alexandra's claims to the land—as if no one before her had ever turned toward it with love and desire—certainly supports the claim that Cather could be oblivious to the fate of Native Americans, to their history and their relationships to the land taken from them. Nonetheless, there is more to say about Cather'smobilization of racial alterity in the service of questions of gender and sexuality. For, like Randolph Bourne, who admired *My Ántonia,* Cather could think about race most productively in her estimation of immigrant culture, the plains as a site of a new cosmopolitanism.[28] Cather was vocal in her opposition to Americanization insofar as that meant homogenization, blandness, vapidity, a kind of common measure that for her was the inevitably cheapening effect of mass culture, the very opposite of her white on white. Only from preserved differences could a complex whole be made. And this is thought in terms of new relations: Jim's marriage to someone who is the same as he is, in terms of race and class, is opposed to the kind of union he might have had—and, in a displaced fashion, does with Ántonia. Across time and distance, they are coupled (but not married to each other). The pair derives its figural force, its pathos and promise, from the ways in which it variously minoritized difference—male homosexual, lesbian, immigrant, Native American—to glimpse a future that does not efface difference.

This is a project limited, of course, by Cather's own limits; as Guy Reynolds notes, in the fullest treatment of Cather's progressive vision in *My Ántonia,* "Cather's heterogeneous, pluralist immigrant culture is, nonetheless, essentially white and of North European descent."[29] Such a judgment is easy to make; it nonetheless ignores the evidence that Matthew Frye Jacobson offers in *Whiteness of a Different Color,* which shows how the white "essentialism" that Reynolds supposes is the endpoint of a historical process barely completed at the time of Cather's writing. Nor do Cather's sympathies for immigrants simply echo the agendas of a Woodrow Wilson, as Mike Fischer claims they do (Wilson only supported Czechs because they were also anti-German). As I point out in "War Requiems," Cather's pro-war novel, *One of Ours,* also is pro-German. Fischer further underlines the hollowness of Wilson's position by pointing to his imperialist designs in the Southern Hemisphere; these attitudes do not translate in Cather's case. In *The Song of the Lark,* Thea Kronborg argues with her parents—and confronts their "race prejudices"—when they object to how much time she spends with Mexicans.[30]

Reynolds treats questions of race apart from questions of gender and sexuality (topics, in fact, to which he gives only a passing glance). Yet it is worth considering whether the "not naming" around race is connected to other things not said, and not merely in the identitarian vein offered by Katrina Irving, who argues that immigrants stand for the necessarily repudiated sexual part of Cather, while Jim is her normative Anglo half.[31] In this account, Cather's text veils a singular, forbidden sexuality, while her characters enact as all-too-familiar drama of a divided self structured by repression.

Cather's Jim, rather, vehiculates desire. Cather explained her choice of a male narrator in a 1921 interview:

> One of the people who interested me most as a child was the Bohemian hired girl of one of our neighbors, who was so good to me. . . . Annie fascinated me, and I always had it in mind to write a story about her.
>
> But from what point of view should I write it up? I might give her a lover and write from his standpoint. However, I thought my Ántonia deserved something better than the *Saturday Evening Post* sort of stuff in her book. Finally I concluded that I would write from the point of view of a detached observer, because that was what I had always been.
>
> Then, I noticed that much of what I knew about Annie came from the talks I had with young men. She had a fascination for them, and they used to be with her whenever they could. They had to manage it on the sly, because she was only a hired girl. But they respected and admired her, and she meant a good deal to some of them. So I decided to make my observer a young man.[32]

Cather's fascination becomes the young man's fascination; a marriage plot is eschewed, detachment becomes attachment "on the sly." Access to the Bohemian woman who is off-limits is displaced onto the young men who, in this telling, shuttle between Cather and Annie Sadilek.

The vicarious positioning of writing and desiring, and its imbrication with race, is perhaps nowhere more acute than in Cather's final novel, *Sapphira and the Slave Girl*. Its final two words—"Willa Cather"—are uncharacteristically proprietary, a signature—in the text—and seemingly undisguised.[33] It would seem that here displacements end. So, too, when an "I" intrudes into the second—and last—section of the concluding portion of the novel, "Nancy's Return." This "I" comes from nowhere, a five-year-old child, sick in bed, as immobilized as the title figure of the book, Sapphira, and similarly luxuriating in her incapacity as a scene is staged for her (as for Sapphira in the earlier portions of the novel) of compliant black female bodies placed at her disposal. Nancy, the slave girl of the title, returns after the flight, twenty-five years earlier, that virtually concludes the main story of the novel; she returns to be reunited with her mother Till: "The actual scene of the meeting had been arranged for my benefit. When I cried because I was not allowed to go downstairs and see Nancy enter the house, Aunt Till had said: 'Never mind, honey. You stay right here, and I'll stay right here. Nancy'll come up, and you'll see her as soon as I do'" (282). This presumably autobiographical moment, unlike the deployment of such material throughout Cather's career, is remarkably straightforward even if the "I" remains unnamed and ungendered. It is moments like these that Toni Morrison has subjected to exacting scrutiny in *Playing in the Dark*.[34]

For Morrison, *Sapphira and the Slave Girl* reveals "the sycophancy of white identity" (19); it is as evident in the scene of Nancy's return as in the main part of the novel, depicting how Nancy's life becomes fully intolerable when Sapphira, her mistress, turns on her and maneuvers her nephew Martin Colbert into position to rape her. The child, the author, her central character, all, Morrison charges, shore up their identities at the expense of black women. Even Nancy's escape from these plots is less her doing than engineered by a white woman—Sapphira's daughter Rachel Blake. In every respect, then, the novel entertains the fantasy of "one woman's absolute power over the body of another woman" (23), "the reckless, unabated power of a white woman gathering identity unto herself from the wholly available and serviceable lives of Africanist others" (25).

In a footnote to her essay on Cather in *Bodies That Matter*, Judith Butler endorses Morrison's thesis. Summarizing Morrison's point, that "the credibility of Cather's narrative is undermined by a recurring and aggrandizing racism," and offering the final scene of Nancy's reunion with Till as prime evidence, Butler then draws Morrison's critique into her own project: "Such a displacement resonates with the displacements of Cather's cross-gendered narrations as well, raising the question of the extent to which fictional displacement can be read as a strategy of repudiation" (274 n. 21). Butler's comment seems to brush against the grain of her thesis, since it suggests that Cather's racism damages her cross-gendered project, that in both instances what is needed is a text without displacement. With Elizabeth Ammons, if not so overtly, Butler would seem to be saying: "Willa Cather shared and acted upon standard white racist attitudes of her day, and that fact must be stated and faced."[35] Facing racism would seem to make it impossible to think productively about sexuality in the charged situation represented by *Sapphira and the Slave Girl.* Butler's critique—or Ammons's, for that matter—assumes that once Cather's appropriation of black bodies has been condemned, there can be little more to say.

Cather's final novel, set for the most part in the antebellum South, undoubtedly perpetuates racist attitudes that persist to this day. "Aunt Till" in the final pages may not be a slave anymore, but she remains a household servant (Nancy's position too after her escape from slavery). The text uses the words "darky" and "nigger" repeatedly, and not merely in a distanced way, as the language of a bygone time (there is, moreover, as critics have noted, a nostalgia for those days). A moment before Nancy is subject to Martin Colbert's most direct assault on her, for example, Cather represents her sitting in the branches of a cherry tree: "Someway no troubles followed a body up there; nothing but the foolish, dreamy, nigger side of her nature climbed the tree with her. She knew she had left half her work undone, but here nobody would find her out to scold her" (178). Cather is capable of registering that the supposed deformations of character here summarized as "the nigger side of her nature"—the slave as shiftless, lazy, mindless—is not a question of nature at all but a possible effect of slavery. Sapphira's husband, Henry Colbert, for example, ponders "the dark lethargy of the cared-for and irresponsible" (228), a phrase that seems to attempt a description of the symbiosis of slaveholder and slave, an already suspect equation tipped a moment later even further in the direction of justifying the very institution that he—and Cather—deplore when Colbert thinks that his wife's "darkies were better cared for" than "poor whites" (229) and yet understandably desired freedom, however painful. So, too, the passage describing Nancy's "nigger side" seems to move from inhabiting her consciousness to introducing the very judgment for failing to do her "work" that Nancy thought to have evaded. In this instance, the work she shirks is making up Martin Colbert's room, a task Sapphira has assigned her precisely because it affords him repeated occasions to make attempts on her.

Why does Sapphira have these designs on Nancy? As Naomi Morgenstern has suggested, Morrison, believing that Sapphira's plan is aimed somehow at resecuring her marriage, faults its logic (how would "ruining" Nancy save her from her husband?) without seeing what she all but says, that this false belief hides what is at stake in these "fantasies of sexual ravish": "one woman's absolute power over the body of another woman"; "an uncontested assumption of the sexual availability of black females"; "the bottomless devotion of the person on whom Sapphira is totally dependent." These are Morrison's phrases and they add up to a point that Morrison herself evades, or, rather tallies otherwise.[36] For her, these "fictional demands . . . stretch to breaking all narrative coherence" (23), and make the novel and its characters incredible, unbelievable. Is it female-female desire, one wonders, that constitutes the unbelievable, incredible fiction? Does a refusal of the erotics of the novel lead to Morrison's charges of "sterility of the fiction-making imagination"; of "bizarre and disturbing deformations of reality" (23)? Sapphira's plan to have Nancy raped reveals her sexual desire for Nancy; her nephew is her surrogate, much as Wick Cutter transported Cather's desire. For all the seeming directness of Cather's signature-effect in *Sapphira and the Slave Girl,* this last novel is as divided as her earlier ones between the sayable and the unsayable. Whiteness is not one thing in this novel.

"The Colberts were termed 'immigrants,'—as were all settlers who did not come from the British Isles" (23). This racialized difference divides Colbert from his slaveholding Anglo-Saxon wife. He knows slavery is wrong; he also profits from the institution (upon his marriage to Sapphira Dodderidge, her slaves become his legal property). Rachel, the only child of the marriage actually represented in the novel, looks and acts like her father, and is more overtly antipathetic to her mother than her father is. Her marriage to Michael Blake had surprised her mother, who had not expected her to marry well—perhaps had not expected her to marry at all. "Well, Mrs. Colbert reflected, there was no accounting for tastes. Blake was Irish, and the Irish often leap before they look" (132). Sapphira's explanation here is fully in line with her racism, and illuminated by the now well-studied phenomenon of how long it took for the Irish to become white. Blake is a phoneme away from black; this is also the same surname Cather used for Tom Outland's companion Roddy. The difference between mother and daughter is, in this way, racialized, and perhaps cross-gendered as well.

All of which is to say that Cather's racial representations are complex; writing Cather off as a deplorable nativist modernist or as guilty of an aggrandizing and unchecked racism is to go even further than Morrison does.[37] She describes Cather's project as one that both "poses and represents" (18) its central problematic, something "the novel obscures even as it makes a valiant effort at honest engagement: the sycophancy of white identity" (19).

Cather's text luxuriates in a disavowed power emblematized, as Morrison suggests, by representing Sapphira as an invalid supposedly sympathetic for the strength with which she faces bodily debility. Confined to her wheelchair and dependent upon the ministrations of her black body servants, her entrapment is equated with slavery. Appropriation once again masquerades as disappropriation —intolerably. "The surrogate black bodies become her hands and feet," Morrison acutely observes, "her fantasies of sexual ravish and intimacy with her husband, and, not inconsiderably, her sole course of love" (26). If Morrison distrusts this love as much as she deplores Cather's racism, it would seem that for her "reality" equals "mother love" (23), parent-child, husband-wife relationships. Sapphira's desire does not run along these tracks. Her desire *for* Nancy, which is also her desire to be *rid* of Nancy (because Nancy does not return her desire—and therefore *resists* it), crystallizes in a desire to *ruin* Nancy, which satisfies both of these conflicting and conflicted aims. This is a situation of desire and disavowal at once, desire made all the more intense by its overlap with the institution of slavery, seemingly unchecked power checked and crossed by the necessity marked by the fiction of imagining that only a man can do what Sapphira wishes—rape another woman—and the reality that her slaves are legally her husband's property, not hers to do with as she would, and the fact that while Nancy is not having sex with Henry Colbert she is devoted to him in a way that she is not to her mistress. As in other Cather texts, as Morrison sees through the lens of mother-daughter relationships, female-female desires are intense, murderous, incoherent, and incapacitated. Sapphira's desire to have Nancy raped can stand beside Alexandra's identification with Frank Shabata, with the position named Wick Cutter, while "yellow" Nancy is where before there had been "brown" Marie or Ántonia.

Whereas Morrison faults *Sapphira and the Slave Girl* for denying agency to Nancy, who is throughout in something like a dream state (or the terrified state of a paralysis that amounts to the same thing), she nonetheless finds "wholly credible" (23) Martin's agency. Is this believable because it is heterosexual, because men can be assumed to have such power? Martin doesn't succeed, and in the final pages of the novel, when Nancy asks Rachel "with a smile . . . what had become of Martin Colbert" (290), Rachel reports Martin's death. What is Nancy's affect at this moment? It tallies with the dispatch of Martin, who disppears from the novel the moment that Nancy escapes, only to be heard of and dispatched again in this question in which the entire story of his attempted rape is relegated to silence. If he is the fantasized lesbian phallus, the novel also suggests that Rachel occupies that position when she foils her mother's plot, and that Nancy does too in this final moment when the memory of Martin Colbert provokes her derision.

Nancy, for Morrison, is nothing but a pawn in the struggle between white mother and daughter. She is, moreover, represented as abandoned by her own mother, who seems to have more regard for her mistress than for her child. For Morrison the clinching moment comes when Till turns to Rachel to belatedly voice her concern for the child that has fled. For Morrison, her question — "you ain't heard nothin', Miss Rachel?" (239) — signals Cather's false conscience, the necessary eruption of motherly feeling that Cather has systematically denied Till, and through her, all black women. It is odd that Morrison here forgets what she knows so well in *Tar Baby,* that it can be or can be perceived as a matter of survival for black servants or slaves to identify with their masters, even against their fellows. "I can't say no more," Till ends the brief exchange, "I don't want them niggers to see me cryin'" (249). Surely the novelist who in *Beloved* treated the extreme situation in which a slave mother shows her love by killing her child could understand better how Till's abandonment could still be motivated by love, and where the question represents a bursting out — a speaking of the unspeakable that one can assume creates the intolerable silence that precedes it. Till finds it impossible to ask Nancy anything or to tell her anything. Nancy, likewise, has never asked her mother who her father was, if "father" even is the right word to name the man who presumably raped Till. (The man who Till has for a husband was assigned to her by Sapphira precisely because he is sexually incapable; this is how Sapphira guarantees that Till is hers.) The grammar of such relationships, as Hortense Spillers has argued, is built on such estrangements, and mother love cannot be a simple matter when her child belongs to her master — or mistress.[38]

The solution to female-female betrayal staged in the embrace of Nancy and Till is the final displacement in a novel that continually displaces female same-sex relationships and yet that also represents them much more fully than in any other Cather novel. Mother-daughter pairs and cross-raced parallels are the displaced forms of such representations. Till's story of female relationships begins with a mother who burned before her eyes, a white servant woman, and then Sapphira who replaced her mother at the cost of further abandonment. Till apparently cannot rebel against her surrogate mother. Nancy cannot turn to her mother but goes instead to Sapphira's daughter. Rachel asks: "'Have you said anything to Till?' Nancy looked up at her with wondering, startled eyes. 'To Maw? How could I, mam?'" (218). It is unthinkable to tell Till what she already knows and can do nothing about. For Morrison, this signals "the complicity of a mother in the seduction and rape of her own daughter," and she assumes that Cather believes that is something "the reader does not object to" (21). That would be unbelievable, and perhaps Nancy's question to Rachel should be given more credit for understanding the situation. The reader need not treat Nancy as Rachel does, as a child (Rachel always addresses Nancy as "child," even in the final pages of the novel). Assuming this false maternal position, Rachel's estrangement from her mother is marked, as well as the fact that slavery has always stood between them, leading Rachel as a child to take a white abolitionist woman as her surrogate mother. These estrangements put Rachel in something like Till's position; but in taking control of Nancy, she also doubles her mother.

These duplicitous displacements could be related to something Naomi Morgenstern notes, that Sapphira's name could as easily be a version of a black woman's name (Sapphire) as a form of Sappho. They are counters in the novel's failed project to equate displacements, joining mistress and slave. This is a falsification writ large as the echo effect that Morgenstern examines in the opening pages of her essay, the looping road that the novel names the "double S," alliterating slave girl and Sapphira, naturalizing the relationship as had earlier novels in which (love of) the landscape had served as the displaced site of same-sex desire. Cather's novel is like Henry Colbert's Bible. He marks every passage on slavery with an S in the hope that he will finally find one that unequivocally condemns an institution that he knows to be wrong. He doesn't. "But nowhere did his Bible say that there should be no one in bonds, no one at all"; from this Henry comes to the ideological conclusion that omission fosters: "were we not all in bonds?" (110).

"Unspeakable Things Unspoken": Morrison's title for an earlier version of the arguments in *Playing in the Dark* might also be Cather's.[39] *Sapphira and the Slave Girl* is about the unspeakable that Morrison speaks as well as the one she does not. In Cather's novel, the slaves keep silence and know everything (and know they must not be known to know), while Sapphira is maddened at the thought that everyone knows about her husband and Nancy (the silence of the slaves covers what Sapphira cannot acknowledge, her own even more unspeakable desire). Everyone knows that Sapphira has turned on Nancy but no one knows why and no explanation ever is offered, while any answer to the question leads along the path of the linked displacements that structure the novel. This is signaled when the narrator remarks that every time Henry Colbert and Sapphira talk about one of their slaves—Bluebell—they really are talking about Nancy (52, 100). Bluebell is represented in the novel as a slave who cannot be made suitable for service the way Nancy can be (and who therefore has not been separated from her mother); she can be brought into the Colberts' conversation as the safe and displaced substitute for Nancy, the slave who has been taken into the house and the orbit of further ramifying unspeakable desires.

Exactions and deformations occur at every level and in every relationship in the novel, not only across race but across gender, starting with the "strange couple" (4) of Henry and Sapphira Colbert, a cross-classed union in which the mistress is the master (50), while his "long lashes would have been a charm in a woman" (5). These crossings cross Nancy. If Sapphira knows Henry's desire as her own, and foists it upon her nephew, Henry sees himself there as well in the Colbert "blood" (191) he and his nephew share. "He knew the family inheritance well enough. He had his share of it" (192). His solicitude for Nancy (represented as the supposed benevolence behind his refusal to sell her—or even more egregiously in the claim that the slaves he wished to sell didn't want to be sold) is the other side of the desire for her. Recognizing himself in his nephew's behavior, he recoils at her, much as Jim turns on Ántonia after Wick Cutter attempted rape. All he will do for Nancy is allow his daughter to steal money from him for her escape. He voids his agency and silently sides with Sapphira. The novel shows that the two sides are one side, his and his wife's. Martin Colbert stands in both places.

These "wrong" and crossed desires intersect in Nancy. The agency that has been taken from her is also what possesses her as a fantasy of powerlessness. Forced by Sapphira to sleep in the hallway, just beneath Martin's room, Nancy is convinced that Martin will get her if she closes her eyes: "If I was to sleep sound, he could slip in to me any time," she tells Rachel (217). Rachel is amazed when Nancy hands over to Martin a basket of mountain laurel that the two women have gathered when Rachel joins Nancy to safeguard her from Martin (174). The explanation is not that Nancy desires Martin, nor is it simply a matter of his power over her. It is rather that the central fantasy of the novel—of an abandonment without end, of displacements that never stop—is located at this site of absolute blockage and disconnection between conscious and unconscious desires; what one knows, what one can say, what one can do, never can line up. The state of slavery—literal (legal) dispossession—makes it impossible to know what would constitute one's own interest (tell, keep silence; succumb, resist). "He kin jist slip into my bed any night if I happens to fall asleep. I got nobody to call to. I cain't do nothin'!" (217).

At the locus of the unspeakable unspoken, Nancy is at the place of crossed desires. She is their product, a "mulatto," fathered perhaps by a Cuban painter, perhaps by a Colbert (Henry's brother? Martin's father? if so, Martin and Henry's desire would also be incestuous). In the racist taxonomies of the novel she is "yellow," miscegenated. In her double and doubtful and illegitimate paternity, the child of rape is either a painter's doing—an artist's representation—or, within the fiction, a Colbert, either way, doubly raced and yet not quite the product of black and white (the painter was Cuban; the Colberts are not Anglo-Saxon).

The product of such crossings, Nancy's "nature" is a question that the novel leaves unresolved, her figuration matched by a sentence that the child Cather is reported to have addressed to her genteel southern mother: "I'se a dang'ous nigger, I is."[40] Although she was presumably not dressed up for her Hiawatha recitation that day, it is still altogether likely that Cather looked more like a boy than not even as she declared herself to be black. Perhaps this is nothing but appropriation; perhaps a way of signaling differences between daughter and mother, for opening the possibility of identifying otherwise. And perhaps in her last novel Cather returned to the primal scene of those possibilities, in ways that are not comfortable in terms of their racial—or sexual—imaginaries, another instance of what Eve Sedgwick also finds in the "steely and unutopic plot" of *The Professor's House:* "plots of lesbian desire, nurturance, betrayal, exploitation, creativity" (69). Sedgwick's understated apposition of opposing nouns provides the grammar for the crossings of race and sex in Cather's final novel and the torsions of Cather's "thing not named."

Other Names

Cather Diva

Critics writing about *The Song of the Lark* have not failed to mention that Cather's heroine Thea Kronborg was inspired by Olive Fremstad, a Wagnerian soprano acclaimed for her Isolde and Kundry.[1] Certain obligatory citations appear, to "Three American Singers," for instance, an article Cather published in *McClure's* in 1913, at least to note the fact that Cather devotes half of its pages to Fremstad.[2] This is often all that is said, but even it serves as a simple indication that Cather esteemed Fremstad above Louise Homer and Geraldine Farrar, the other singers discussed; figure 1, showing Fremstad as Isolde, is the illustration that filled the first page of Cather's article. In it, Cather makes clear, moreover, that Homer's equanimity—and devotion to her children—did not inspire her, even if Homer's accomplishments as a singer were undeniable; nor did the charms of Farrar—not even her "frank" declaration that art and motherhood are incompatible—seem to Cather quite to make up for the easy popularity she had achieved.[3] In the solitary Fremstad, Cather saw an artist who "came out of a new crude country, fought her way against every kind of obstacle, and conquered by sheer power of will and character" (33).[4] Among those obstacles had been her voice, "reconquered," in Cather's account, from the contralto range "to invade soprano territory" (45).

Fremstad is taken to have provided a model for artistic achievement, hard won, singleminded and long in the making, through which Cather could figure her own career. Thea Kronborg's life story is rich in correspondence with Cather's, the friends of her childhood (to recall the title of the long first section, almost a third of *The Song of the Lark*), for instance, modeled on people important to Cather as she was growing up.[5] But equally, Thea's singing at revival meetings, her early training as a pianist, her studying with Lilli Lehmann and first singing opera professionally in Germany are among the many details culled from Fremstad's life. These facts are all duly reported as well in the article in *McClure's*, one of Cather's last contractual appearances there. *O Pioneers!* had been published six months earlier.

1. Olive Fremstad as Isolde. *(Courtesy Metropolitan Opera Archives.)*

I begin with these commonplaces not because it is my intention to dispute them—I too am convinced that Fremstad lies behind Kronborg, that Cather recast herself as much as she did Fremstad in her novel's protagonist—but because I wish to pursue these connections in the pages that follow. There is perhaps no better place to start than with Cather's first meeting with Fremstad, whom she had gone to interview for *McClure's.*

Usually cited is the account given by Cather's lifelong partner Edith Lewis in her 1953 reminiscence, *Willa Cather Living.*[6] Lewis describes the encounter of some forty years earlier as "a curious one" (91), although its curiosity is muted by her characteristic mode of narration, which barely allows the event to break its calm surface, a style comparable to Cather's ideal of writing as enunciated in "The Novel Démeublé." The chapter in which the episode is told is named for the Bank Street apartment that Lewis and Cather began sharing in 1913, the year Cather met Fremstad. Setting her story there and establishing their domestic arrangements as a frame, Lewis then recalls that she and Cather had been inveterate operagoers from 1905 on. Of all the singers they heard, she reports, "the most thrilling, to us, . . . was Olive Fremstad" (90). From this retrospective and shared perspective, Lewis narrows in to a night at the Metropolitan Opera; *The Tales of Hoffman* is about to begin, she and Isabelle McClung wait for Cather to arrive from the interview with Fremstad. Cather arrives, and tells them "to our great disappointment, that the interview had not come off" (91).

There are features in this narration worth interrupting its summary to notice, if only because they reappear in the critical literature describing Cather's autobiographical use of Fremstad. There is, for example, the sharing of expectations that allows Cather's diva worship also to be Lewis's ("the most thrilling, to us")—or McClung's, a *folie à trois* as uninflected as Lewis's flat declaration that McClung was in their company because "she was visiting us" (91). Lewis's "us" or "our" seems able, at once, to embrace herself and Cather as a couple equally involved with McClung—or Fremstad, or to include all three as identically disappointed when the interview with Fremstad failed to materialize. Lewis's prose effaces differences: McClung, with whom Cather had lived before meeting Lewis, and who is usually taken to have been the great passion of Cather's life, certainly had no such relationship with Lewis. Likewise, there was more to Cather's relationship to Fremstad than a fandom equally shared: only she transformed herself and Fremstad into Kronborg. That coupling needs to be decoupled from the kind of bland identification that can be found in Lewis's narration, where it can be questioned too.

To return to Lewis's story:

She had gone to Fremstad's apartment—waited—Fremstad was away on a motor ride, and there was some delay about getting back.

Finally she came in, very tired, and began at once to apologize; but she could scarcely speak—her voice was just a husky whisper. She was pale, drawn—"Why, she looked forty years old!" Willa Cather told us. She begged Fremstad not to try to talk—she said she would come back for the interview another time, and left. (91)

[Now, the first act of *The Tales of Hoffman* is over and the intermission drags, until the announcement is made that the Guilietta is ill and Fremstad has agreed to sing the part.]

Then the curtain went up—and there, before our astonished eyes, was Fremstad—whom Willa Cather had left only an hour before—now a vision of dazzling youth and beauty. She sang that night in a voice so opulent, so effortless, that it seemed as if she were dreaming the music, not singing it.

"But it's impossible," Willa Cather kept saying. "It's impossible." (92)

It's impossible: how does one become someone else? A worn-out woman a dazzling diva? An aspiring novelist a writer of distinction? And how might these impossible stories be joined? The answer, I suggest, does not lie in the critical commonplace that metaphorizes Cather's artistic identification with Fremstad, her self-representation as a diva, as an achievement of voice somehow comparable to Fremstad's soprano conquest of contralto territory.[7] The questions need to be asked again. They are pertinent, moreover, to Cather's assessment of Fremstad in *McClure's,* the first section of which is headlined "*Fremstad's Mysterious Personality,*" while the last (literally about her costumes) is titled "*Fremstad's Power of Transformation.*"

"It's impossible" is Cather's virtual refrain in *McClure's* as she tries—and fails—to explain how Fremstad achieved her effects. "After you have heard her sing Isolde, for instance, you are unable to say by what means she communicated to you the conception that is all too-present with you" (46). By conception Cather does not mean some gimmick of performance; rather, Fremstad conveys, she claims, "habits of mind and body which, by repeating themselves, define human nature." It is these that are somehow impressed upon a "scarcely conscious" viewer: "we get the feeling, but we do not know how we got it" (46). Moreover, the diva also is transformed: "It is difficult to believe that her voluptuous Venus and her girlish Brünhilde are made out of the same body" (47). The diva who looked forty—and was—also is voluptuous, beautiful, young.[8] "Her body she is able to manage and readjust very much as she does her fabrics. . . . How, for instance, when she sings Giulietta, in 'Tales of Hoffman,' does she remold her own strongly modeled countenance into the empty, sumptuous face of the Venetian beauty?—lifted, one might say, from a Veronese fresco" (47). Cather calls "human" what seems to be a fantasy, a dream somehow realized in the scarcely conscious mode by which performer and audience are joined. "You are driven back to the conclusion that whatever happened during the performance, happened in Mme. Fremstad; that the fateful drama actually went on behind her brow" (46).

The pages that follow drive toward that region, an interiority that the first edition of *The Song of the Lark* terms "unconscious memory" (1915, p. 449), but one that cannot be separated from its embodiment, much as the thing not named must have a relationship to words on the page.[9] Like previous critics I am taken with "Cather's fascination with the transformation processes which Fremstad revealed to her," to cite Hermione Lee: Cather desired "to turn herself into the singer, in order to find out how the singer could turn herself into, say, Isolde," she continues.[10] But whereas Lee figures this process of identification as a transcendent fusion that manifests the "impersonal power of the artist" (127), I want to validate the sexual terms she explicitly denies when she explains the process— for Cather, for Fremstad—as the story of "a heroic artist who fuses together 'gendered' characteristics—female nurturing, male strenuousness—so as to transcend them" (129). Theoretically put, this is a disagreement about the entanglements of identity and identification, the overlap of "being" and "having" that throws into havoc the terms that are supposed to secure the difference between ego ideal and object of desire.[11] It's for that reason that I paused over Edith Lewis's account of the meeting of Cather and Fremstad, and I return to Lewis now to further suggest torsions in identificatory transformation that hardly qualify as transcendent or as necessarily desexualized.

Lewis reports that after Fremstad read *The Song of the Lark* she "flung her arms about Willa Cather, exclaiming that she could not tell where *Thea* left off and she began" (93).[12] Just a few lines later, she adds: "perhaps the faults that she [Cather] found in this book came in part from working too directly from immediate emotions and impressions." A tinge of aggressivity (in Cather's name, in Lewis's deadpan identification) is launched at the novel for Cather's overinvestment in Fremstad. One reason for the hostility might be found by putting Lewis's account, which calmly equates Fremstad's embrace of Cather with her identification with Thea, beside the ventriloquizations of Cather offered by Elizabeth Sergeant, another intimate friend (although not Cather's partner): "Fremstad, Fremstad, wonderful Fremstad . . . Nothing, nothing, Willa murmured . . . could equal the bliss of entering the very skin of another human being. Did I not agree? And if this skin was Scandinavian— then what?" (121). A few pages later, as if it needed saying, Sergeant concludes: "Fremstad had somehow ignited Willa Cather's inner fires" (128).

The fire had long been burning. Lewis's simple statement—"we heard her nearly every time she sang" (90)—may be saying a great deal if taken literally; by the time that Cather met her on 12 March 1913, Fremstad had given close to two hundred performances in some eighteen roles at the Metropolitan Opera.[13] She had debuted as Sieglinde in *Die Walküre* some ten years earlier, on 25 November 1903, and ended her career at the Met (and effectively as an opera singer) with a performance as Elsa in *Lohengrin* on 23 April 1914, a little more than a year after Cather met her. Cather and Lewis were present at that final perfomance, which elicited unprecedented demonstrations from the audience.[14] In *McClure's* in December 1913, Cather hailed Fremstad as a singer climbing to the heights of her power; by the time she sent the final draft of *The Song of the Lark* to her publisher in April 1915, Fremstad's career was all but over. And, I would argue, the flame also had been consumed.

This supposition runs against the grain of the assumption that Cather and Fremstad had a long friendship, or that the transformation that produced Thea Kronborg was a matter of idealizing identification, a fusion without tension or residue. Evidence is easily found, however, in the preface that Cather provided to *The Song of the Lark* in 1932 (Lewis seems to have had it in mind in her remarks faulting the novel). There Cather declares the heroine's success the least interesting aspect of the novel, finding value only in the earlier sections depicting Kronborg's hard struggle:

The chief fault of the book is that it describes a descending curve; the life of a successful artist in the full tide of achievement is not so interesting as the life of a talented girl "fighting her way," as we say. Success is never so interesting as struggle. . . . The story set out to tell of an artist's awakening and struggle. . . . It should have been content to do that. I should have disregarded conventional design and stopped where my first conception stopped, telling the latter part of the story by suggestion merely. (xxxi–xxxii)

By the time she wrote her 1932 preface, Cather "had convinced herself that Fremstad had little to do with the characterization of Thea Kronborg," Cather's most recent biographer, James Woodress, comments, pointing to a letter of the same year to the publisher of *The Song of the Lark* in which Cather says just that.[15] By 1932 Cather sought to obscure Fremstad's inspiring role in *her* autobiographical novel.

And what did Fremstad think? Did she embrace the novel and its writer as Lewis claims? Not according to a source usually ignored by Cather's critics, *The Rainbow Bridge* by Mary Watkins Cushing, the only full-scale biography of Fremstad.[16] This 1954 book looks mainly at the years 1911 to 1918 when, as the young Mary Watkins, Cushing served as Fremstad's companion. Cushing echoes Lewis describing Fremstad's response to Cather's piece in *McClure's*: "Madame was delighted with the article, and told the author that her penetration and insight were uncanny; but," — here she diverges crucially — "she was less enthusiastic about *The Song of the Lark*. . . . 'My poor Willa,' she once said in my hearing, 'it wasn't really much like that. But after all, what can you know about me? Nothing!'" (243–44). This dismissal is confirmed by another account that appears also to have come directly from Fremstad, presumably years later, which reports that "characteristically the singer never found either leisure or opportunity to read the novel, until in her last year, when fatigue and illness made her return the book with regrets."[17] Fremstad's story of returning the book unread cannot entirely be trusted — by Fremstad's last year, Cather had been dead for several. But it does suggest a long-lasting antipathy to Cather's novel.

Perhaps in 1932 Cather was responding to Fremstad's dismissal ("My poor Willa . . ."), perhaps Fremstad dismissed the book when

Cather began to act as if she had not been its inspiration. I would suggest that these antipathies were written into Cather's project from the start. Disidentification inevitably accompanies identification. The fusion that produced Thea Kronborg may have been explosive. Fires burn.

The Song of the Lark ends with the diva's first spectacular performance at the Metropolitan Opera. The success that Cather wished she had cut is merely the beginning of a career, a performance of the part of Sieglinde in *Die Walküre* that marks Kronborg's arrival at the threshold of stardom. Kronborg assumes Fremstad's debut role, adding it to a repertoire that matches Fremstad's pre-Metropolitan repertoire of contralto parts (Venus in *Tannhäuser*, Fricka in *Rheingold*—even Thea's reference to a performance of *Trovatore* [384] may allude to Fremstad's debut role as Azucena in Cologne in 1895). However, in Cather's telling, Thea first gets the chance to sing the part only when the original singer falls indisposed and she is called in at short notice to finish the performance. This rewrites the circumstances of the *Hoffman* appearance, and while it heightens the drama of Kronborg's achievement, it also deflates it insofar as the end of Fremstad's career seems imminent in Thea's beginning.[18] This chronological manipulation is paralleled by the fact that Cather does represent Kronborg as having one soprano role in her repertoire before she sings Sieglinde, Elsa in *Lohengrin*. Giving Kronborg the role in which Fremstad made her final appearance, Cather even more emphatically makes Fremstad's demise Kronborg's prelude, not least because Elsa is explicitly not a role well suited to Kronborg's voice; "*Elsa* is not really in my voice," Thea says (371). Nor was it in Fremstad's. When Fremstad was told that her contract was not being renewed, she asked to sing Isolde, one of the roles in which she had triumphed, for her final performance; the management instead assigned her Elsa. Cather's chronological reversals—and the humiliations implicit in them—suggest that as she insinuated herself beneath the Scandinavian's skin—as she underwent the transformation from aspiring to accomplished writer—Fremstad needed to be sacrificed, a point underscored in the 1932 preface when Cather regrets the success, Fremstad's success, accorded her heroine.

These effects were furthered by cuts Cather made to *Song of the*

Lark in 1937, most of which were to the final part of the novel (the section called "Kronborg"). These include omission of the prediction made by Thea's sometime lover and eventual husband Fred Ottenburg that "you'll probably be singing *Brünnhilde* pretty soon now" (1915, p. 465), as well as one voiced by Andor Harsanyi, the teacher who first recognizes that Thea is a singer and not a pianist, that her Sieglinde will soon be topped by her performance as Isolde (1915, p. 477). These cuts truncate the trajectory of Thea's career; unlike Fremstad, she will not go on to conquer soprano territory.

Cather also excises a remark Fred utters as he makes his prediction, and presents Thea with a spear to confirm it: "it takes a great many people to make one—*Brünnhilde*" (1915, p. 465). That cut is even more symptomatic of what Cather did to her novel in 1937. Thea's aggressivity, her ferocity, are reduced. In the revised version of the novel she does not get to carry a spear. Nor does anyone now report that as a struggling singer in Germany she was called by her fellow singers "*die Wölfin*" (1915, p. 449); the "dog eats dog" aspect of Kronborg's career is played down as Ottenburg tells how Thea is assuming the parts of a soprano who is at the end of her career and "paying for it with the last rags of her voice" (1915, p. 439). Whose antagonisms are cut as Thea is "softened" in the 1937 version of the novel? Fremstad's? Cather's? Should we note that this soprano with her voice in ruins *also* could be Fremstad, who, some critics felt, had damaged her voice irreparably when she insisted on singing soprano parts?[19] Necker, the fictional soprano in question, may be a version of Lilli Lehmann or, more likely, of Lillian Nordica; like her fictional counterpart, Fremstad had performed Brangaene to both their Isoldes; but a detail only in the 1915 version, that "Madame Necker was forty, and her voice was failing just when her powers were at their height" (1915, p. 470), tilts the identification toward Fremstad.

Cather certainly knew these complaints; she quotes one in *McClure's,* W. J. Henderson in the New York *Sun,* writing on 17 December 1905, reviewing Fremstad's first Brünnhilde (13 December 1905): "About 11:15 p.m., Olive Fremstad awoke from the dream that she was a dramatic soprano. . . . The high notes which do not belong to her scale . . . refused to come. They were pitiful little head tones." Algernon St. John-Brenon, in the *Morning Telegraph,* similarly describes Fremstad in a slightly later concert performance of the same part, Brünnhilde's awakening in the last act of *Siegfried:* "Miss Fremstad . . . we have long given up in despair. She is lacerating her fine dramatic contralto voice, throwing the shreds at us and calling them Brünnhilde."[20] His "shreds" would appear to be the "rags" in Cather's description of the soprano whose early demise has made room for Kronborg's ascendency: "Every fresh young voice was an enemy, and this one was accomplished by gifts which she could not fail to recognize" (1915, p. 470). This diva struggle is also the dynamic of Cather and Fremstad.

In this context can be placed a change noted as well by Hermione Lee, the replacement of Fred's characterization of Thea's voice as "virile" with the adjective "warm" (365; 1915, p. 420), a softening of Thea that also feminizes her. In 1937 Cather revised the novel to make Thea less obviously a version of Fremstad and to diminish her. These are the last traces of the struggle that *The Song of the Lark* records, its desire to represent the "impossible": the impossible desire to be Fremstad, to have Fremstad, to replace Fremstad; to cross the boundaries of identity toward the totality of an identification that also entails the totality of repudiation, possession and dispossession at once.[21]

To highlight Cather's procedures one might compare *The Song of the Lark* to Marcia Davenport's *Of Lena Geyer,* a 1936 novel also inspired by Fremstad, who is fictionalized in the novel by enhancing her career with achievements of various other singers (among them Davenport's mother, Alma Gluck).[22] Fremstad is nonetheless the central model for the diva, in everything from her immigrant background (Geyer is Bohemian rather than Scandinavian, however, conflating Gluck and Fremstad) to her characteristic stride, whispered hoarseness after performance, habits of extravagance and parsimony (like Fremstad, Geyer always demands artist discounts), and the like. In its broad outline, Geyer's career matches Fremstad's: early years in New York (where she arrives on Christmas day, as had Fremstad), study with Lilli Lehmann in Germany and early success in European opera houses (although Geyer's triumph in Paris as Elisabeth in *Tannhäuser,* and her singing of other major parts in Berlin and Vienna, considerably embellishes on Fremstad's career); brilliant final years at the Met.

Whereas Cather truncates Fremstad's career, Davenport adds to it. Geyer is not merely a Wagnerian soprano, but also an accomplished singer of Verdi and Mozart. Like Fremstad, she has her first success in Germany in the part of Carmen (a role Fremstad performed to critical success a few times at the Met). She is, as much as Fremstad, a singer Gustav Mahler highly regarded (he was the conductor when Fremstad sang Brangaene to Lehmann's Isolde in Vienna on 22 May 1898, and he tried to lure her away from Munich to Vienna, where Fremstad was a guest artist for only that one season).[23] Fremstad sang her first Isolde at Mahler's Met debut on New Year's Day in 1908. Davenport makes Geyer's Met debut coincide with Mahler's; she appears as Donna Anna in *Don Giovanni,* a part Fremstad never sang at the Met but is said to have performed in Philadelphia under Mahler's direction, if so probably only once in her career.[24] Davenport chooses it as the debut role for the frisson of a great Wagnerian soprano displaying the agility required of Mozart singing. Soon, however, Mahler is replaced as Geyer's mentor by a conductor named Guido Vestri, a version of Toscanini, under whom Fremstad sang her first *Götterdämmerung* Brünnhilde. Fremstad went on to sing Isolde under his direction, as does Geyer, and Davenport gives lavish descriptions of her performances—that is, of Fremstad's performances, which Davenport witnessed as a very young child.[25] Toscanini chose Fremstad to open the 1910 season as Gluck's Armida, a momentous event in Davenport's novel as well (her mother also sang in this performance). In *The Rainbow Bridge,* Cushing describes a *Tristan* rehearsal with Toscanini of extraordinary intensity, beyond anything Fremstad had ever done. For Cushing this displays "the almost mystical Fremstad-Toscanini *rapprochement*" (132) whereas Davenport sexualizes the rapport with Vestri in order to further heighten the relationship. On the last page of the novel, Geyer dies listening to Vestri on the radio. Cushing reports that for her eightieth birthday (her last?), Toscanini sent Fremstad "a memento inscribed '*To my unforgettable Armida,*' which she kept beside her to the last hour of her life" (198).

Davenport often signals that she is describing Fremstad precisely by denying the comparison. For example, she comments on the difficulty of the role of Sieglinde: "There have been only a few memorable Sieglindes since Wagner composed the opera, though every capable dramatic soprano has sung it. Olive Fremstad was often called the greatest, but in her time Lena Geyer was the only Sieglinde. She used to move through the part building up an atmosphere of loneliness and terror and tragedy, against which the passion of her love for Siegmund was like fire" (212). Since Geyer is a fiction inspired by Fremstad, the denied comparison to Fremstad would seem to signal that Fremstad is the model for Geyer's accomplishment. Similarly, Geyer debuts as Donna Anna because "there were already in the company two splendid new Wagner singers, Olive Fremstad and Johanna Gadski" (252). The point—as in the ultimate novel about diva madness, James McCourt's *Mawrdew Czgowchwz*—is to indulge the fantasy of the diva who can sing everything.[26] This fantasy may correspond better to part of Fremstad's career that is not well documented, her years in Germany, when she sang at least sixty roles ranging from Amneris in *Aida* to Prince Orlofsky in *Fledermaus* and including, in some accounts, a blackface performance. The early Fremstad may have been a great deal less remote and mysterious than the Wagnerian soprano whom Cather presented in *McClure's*.[27]

Of Lena Geyer preserves the austerity along with a roughhouse quality as it charts Geyer's success. Geyer's voice encompasses so many parts and styles, such diverse ranges, that "critics . . . go wild looking for terms in which to describe it" (55), a fantasy of critical hysteria worth contrasting to Cather's account of naysaying critics in "Three American Singers." True, Cather cites W. J. Henderson describing Fremstad's initial *Siegfried* Brünnhilde so that she can quote a later review in which he praised Fremstad's "splendid vocal equipment" performing Isolde, and clearly takes pleasure in having Henderson eat his words. The question, however, is why she needs to represent Fremstad as maligned in the first place. For while the New York reviewers *did* worry that Fremstad was attempting parts that lay beyond her range, none did so more than Henderson. Even in his review of her Met debut (in the *Sun* on 26 November 1903), the role of Sieglinde is described as "a trifle high for her warm mezzo soprano voice." This was not, however, the view of the other major critics. Henry Krehbiel praised Fremstad's debut in the *New York Tribune* (25 November 1903): "Miss Fremstad has everything appertaining to voice and appearance in her favor"; while Richard Aldrich in the *New York Times* (26 November 1903) comes close to Davenport's ecstatic critics: "Her voice is of extraordinarily beautiful quality and large range, in the lower notes, particularly, of the richest contralto coloring, and its freedom and flexibility, the volume with which she poured it out, the nobility and broad sweep of her phrasing, showed in her the true artist." Aldrich reviewed Fremstad in such warm terms throughout her career even when he expressed concern about the suitability of some parts for her voice. In presenting her diva as triumphing over adversity—including adverse critical response—Cather seems to go out of her way to dampen the kind of enthusiasm that Davenport unleashes. Perhaps this is so, as Davenport says, because the critical excitement she imagines is difficult to separate from sexual excitement: "Her low voice was more thrilling than her fiery middle and high one, and in later days the critics used to go wild looking for terms in which to describe it. It was pure earth, female, sex if you want to call it that. You might say that where her high tones were enchanting to the imagination, her low ones warmed the body like an embrace" (55).

If Cather felt compelled to answer Henderson, she also seems to have had a need to echo him. These are the two sides of her complex identification with the diva. Emphasizing how few admirers were Fremstad's cuts in more than one direction. Cather shields herself from the kind of self-betraying enthusiasm that Davenport imagines and that is most evident, for example, in the writing of James Huneker, a critic of the arts with often advanced and sometimes outré views, who was an early admirer of Fremstad's in more than one sense of the word. Huneker goes overboard in the *Musical Courier* reviewing Fremstad's performance as various Rhinemaidens in the *Ring* at Bayreuth in 1896 (her sole appearances there). On August 5, as Flosshilde "our Olive deserved the crown," he writes; a week later, he singles out her performance in *Götterdämmerung* as "miles away from her companions in beauty of voice, plasticity of pose and artistic singing." At about the same time, Huneker published a story, "Venus or Valkyr," that thinly fictionalizes Fremstad and his attraction to her; letters exist that further suggest, at the very least, an early flirtation.[28] Although the affair—if it ever got started—went nowhere, Huneker remained an avid reviewer. One piece, "A New Isolde: Olive Fremstad," published after her first performance in that part, valuably suggests the extraordinary nature of her accomplishment, how Isolde had been transformed from exaggeration and overstatement to a subtlety conveyed by the "opalescent . . . hues of her powerful and plangent organ."[29]

Cather's praise could be equally extravagant, as we will see shortly, and I have mentioned Huneker here because he is fictionalized in *The Song of the Lark*. The resistances that seem evident in *McClure's* can be connected to the fact that, unlike Huneker, Cather could not claim either male or heterosexual privilege. Davenport manages to write so enthusiastically because she offers a version of Geyer's intoxicating "versatility" (the key term in the novel) as her own narrative strategy: *Of Lena Geyer* is structured as a multivoiced text, offering accounts of Geyer by narrators that include a young acolyte, Geyer's manager, a former lover, and her lifelong female companion. The question of where Davenport might be located is thus to some degree mooted. The remarks cited above about critical enthusiasm, for instance, are voiced by the male acolyte who convinces Geyer to allow her story to be told—by others; the fiction of the novel is thus that neither the soprano nor the female author are in the text except by proxies, male in every instance save one.[30] That figure, the lifelong female friend, was certainly suggested by Mary Watkins, and Davenport characteristically hyperbolizes the seven-year stint Watkins served. Here, too, there is a comparison to be drawn: *The Song of the Lark* includes male figures like those Davenport assembles, although not as explicitly as narrators, but has no female companion. In *The Diva's Mouth,* Susan Leonardi and Rebecca Pope take this to show Cather's "effeminophobia" as compared to Davenport's "almost candid exploration of [female] homoeroticism."[31] I will return to this point.

Let's start again, with the meeting of Cather and Fremstad, this time as Cushing tells it—in a possibly even more undramatic (i.e., threatened?) fashion than Lewis does. Here too a "we" is in evidence. "We had met Miss Cather," Cushing begins her narration (243), constituting herself and Fremstad as some kind of couple, much as Lewis gives the Bank Street address before allowing the intruder into her story. Like Lewis, too, Cushing situates her narrative retrospectively; before the meeting is narrated, Cather is first introduced as a mutual friend, indeed as an "ally" (242) in her attempt to get Fremstad to be just a bit less relentless in her working habits.[32] Cather then appears to occupy the companion's position vis-à-vis Fremstad even before the first meeting; it therefore follows, in Cushing's view at least, that Cather was only "somewhat thwarted" by Fremstad's nonappearance. What more could a worshipper expect than to be rebuffed? (That Fremstad rejected Cather's portrait of her as Thea is perfectly consistent with this.) Cushing continues:

> How deadly to be confronted by a humble young acolyte instead of the priestess herself! I was much embarrassed, and expected to see her [Cather] turn on a peevish heel and slam the door in my face. But this was not Willa Cather's way. She sat down quite happily with me and asked me all the questions which she thought it would be fair for me to answer. She laid the groundwork for her article, and had a fleeting glimpse of her heroine—rather tired and wind-blown—as a consolation at the end. (243)

Cushing expects Cather to slam the door on her—expects her to act like Madame, who has deliberately gone off for a ride, leaving Cushing in her official role as Fremstad's "buffer" to cope with the interviewer from *McClure's*. Instead, in Cushing's account, Cather is not mortified by the mortified buffer, rather, happy to be with someone in her own position, sharing the mistreatment which, in part, it is Cushing's role to impart.

One explanation for the difference between the wind-blown heroine of Cushing's story and Lewis's hoarse and ravaged diva may be that Lewis conflated Cather's initial meeting with Fremstad with one that took place a few days later after a performance of *Parsifal* in which Fremstad had sung Kundry (Fremstad usually spoke in a hoarse whisper after she sang). More significant is the possibility that Lewis depends upon a scene in *The Song of the Lark* that conflates the two meetings. By attending to it, I think we may come closer to the truth underlying both Cushing's and Lewis's accounts of the meeting—that is, the truth for Cather. In the novel, Cather's place is taken by Dr. Archie, the arch-friend who sees Thea through from childhood on (he pays for her to go to Germany to study with Lehmann). This is the first time Archie has heard Thea at the Met; after the performance of *Lohengrin*, waiting for her at her apartment, he sees a tall, veiled woman, whom he "confronts" at the elevator, and who returns the assault:

> She gave him a piercing, defiant glance through the white scarf that covered her face. Then she lifted her hand and brushed the scarf back

from her head. There was still black on her eyebrows and lashes. She was very pale and her face was drawn and deeply lined. She looked, the doctor told himself with a sinking heart, forty years old. (361)

Upstairs in her apartment Thea speaks to him "in a hoarse voice" (361) and urges him to come the next day—"I shall be more recognizable to-morrow" (362), she assures him; "This is not I" (363).

What makes this scene of failed meeting, blank (mis)recognition, loss of identity, voicelessness, and shocking transformation particularly powerful is the way in which it replays Archie's experience in hearing Kronborg sing. The impossibility of recognizing the off-stage Thea is matched by the impossibility of recognizing her on-stage.

As Elsa comes onstage, Archie is frightened: "It flashed across him that this was something like buck-fever, the paralyzing moment that comes upon a man when his first elk looks at him through the bushes, under its great antlers; the moment when a man's mind is so full of shooting that he forgets the gun in his hand until the buck is gone" (358; the 1915 text elaborates the comparison so that it is sustained throughout the passage including even the moment when he does see her). This extraordinary metaphor conveys the aggressivity in spectating as well as the confounding aggressivity of the performer who literally disarms and emasculates the spectator (a point all the more complicated in its reversals insofar as Archie stands in for Cather, while Elsa turned elk recalls even as it rewrites the fate of Actaeon for spying on Diana). When Archie thinks he has recovered from his "buck-fever" he realizes rather that even when he sees her he remains in that state:

> Yes, it was exactly like buck-fever. Her face was there, toward the house now, before his eyes, and he positively could not see it. She was singing, at last, and he positively could not hear her. He was conscious of nothing but an uncomfortable dread and a sense of crushing disappointment. He had, after all, missed her. Whatever was there, she was not there—for him. (359)

It is as a consequence of this absolute dissociation that her performance becomes available to him, for a moment later Archie is "not listening to, but dreaming upon, a river of silver sound. . . .

This woman he had never known; she had somehow devoured his little friend, as the wolf ate up Red Ridinghood" (359). Thea has become Kronborg; the Wölfin has been wolfed; the shooter shot. Archie dreams the dream that Lewis described, "a voice so opulent, so effortless, that it seemed as if she were dreaming the music, not singing it" (92). This is a state that Thea herself enters earlier in the novel, the first time she hears the music of Wagner: "She heard it as people hear things in their sleep" (181). Archie "hears" Thea singing Elsa's dream. (Figure 2 captures the all but unrecognizable Fremstad as Elsa.)

Cather's depiction of Archie's encounter with Thea's voice and person complexly entwines Lewis's account of Cather's disappointment/amazement ("it's impossible") with Cushing's picture of the impossible diva in an estrangement that knows no bounds, an estrangement that is the key to the position of the spectator as well as the singer. Dr. Archie sees the performer in her "wholly estranging beauty" (360) and feels "admiration and estrangement" (359). In this he is Cather's surrogate. Hence her painful citation of negative criticism in *McClure's*. Hence the tense dynamic of her relationship with Fremstad, a series of rebuffs and displays of friendship concluded (at least on Cather's part) with the writing of *The Song of the Lark*, a process continued in the preface added in 1932 and through the final revisions of 1937. Cather worked on *The Song of the Lark* from the beginning to almost the end of her career. No other novel of hers has this textual history.

It was not only Cather who struggled with Fremstad. Elizabeth Wood notes the "unacknowledged butch-femme implications in Cushing's blithe account of her relationship with Fremstad [that] seem obvious to a lesbian reader today." [33] Here is an example: Fremstad and Watkins vying over a motto, "dienen, dienen," the only words that Kundry sings in the final act of *Parsifal*. In a passage remarkable for its traversal of languages (the diva speaks no recognizable tongue), the two address each other in a private language. Watkins is Tinka, Fremstad's Scandinavian for Mary, as well as a play on the sound of her last name, which Fremstad found risible; Fremstad is Livan, a childhood diminutive of her proper name Anna Olivia:

2. Olive Fremstad as Elsa. *(Courtesy Metropolitan Opera Archives.)*

"Livan, I have decided," I ventured in a small, weak voice, to adopt '*Dienen, dienen!*' as my own motto in life!"

I had imagined this would please her, but she pounced at once.

"I'm sorry, child, but that belongs to me, you know . . . to me and to the Prince of Wales, of course."

"But I thought you had adopted '*Kunst heisst Können!*' You said that that was yours!"

"Mine and Lilli Lehmann's, yes!"

Cather Diva

"But why all this talk? Now listen to me once for all. I have already told you this and you will learn it for yourself someday. It is not exactly a motto, Tinka, just a truth, a very sad truth. A great man said it—'*Dort wo du nicht bist, dort ist das Glück!*'" (145)

Even Kundry does not own "dienen, dienen," words couched in the infinitive, not the first person, not the "I serve" which is the motto of the Prince of Wales. Fremstad insists on a kind of mistaken royal prerogative; she also usurps her teacher's motto, Lilli Lehmann's "Art means Knowledge." This serves as a reminder of the contested relationship hinted in the account of Kronborg's relationship to Necker in the 1915 *The Song of the Lark*. Fremstad may have had a picture of Lehmann among her effects, but Lehmann never refers to her in her autobiography and it is clear that the two divas were estranged after Fremstad's career took off. Some commentators claim that the rift was caused after Fremstad ran off with Lehmann's husband, but a much-repeated anecdote seems more to the point here, and consonant with accounts of other terror tactics Lehmann's pedagogy featured: performing Isolde, Lehmann commanded the neophyte Fremstad, who was singing Brangaene, Isolde's companion, to feel beneath her costume—ostensibly to see that she was not even sweating (Cushing 183–84).

Fremstad certainly knew about terrorizing seduction, as her first meeting with Cather suggests, at least in Cushing's version. More often she employed a seemingly opposing strategy, at least with Cushing. While the harried buffer likes to remember herself as abjectly tied to Fremstad, a pawn to her Kundry-like "witchery," "swallowed," enchanted," "enslaved" (120), this is not, even for Cushing, the entire story of how the young Mary Watkins and Olive Fremstad formed a couple. For Fremstad began to speak of them as one as soon as Tinka officially assumed the role of buffer. "From that time on Madame Fremstad always referred to her work as 'ours,' and frequently during ensuing opera seasons she would say something of this kind: 'Well, Tinka, we gave a good performance tonight!'" (69–70). Thus, after reading the reviews of her performance as Isolde under Toscanini: "'Now, Tinka,' she said, when all the printed superlatives were exhausted, 'you see what *you* have done!'" (120). Who serves whom? How can one tell, when the game seems to involve vying for the position of the one who serves most. Cushing refers to this ironically as Fremstad's "Martyrdom for Art" act (60) even as she aspires to the role ("dienen, dienen"). These heady exchanges of "yours" and "mine" ("see what *you* have done"; "that belongs to me") are the way in which a couple—a "we"—is constituted in a continuous struggle where mastery masquerades as submission.

Mary Watkins had entered Fremstad's service by presenting the diva with a drawing of her in her innovative costume as the *Walküre* Brünnhilde, short-skirted and athletic, and Fremstad had seized upon the young girl who had represented her as youth incarnate. On her side, Watkins began more and more, as she admits, to imitate Fremstad, even learning how to force the diva to do her bidding (always for her own good, of course). Reciprocally, Fremstad insisted that she could do nothing without Watkins, not even marry. Fremstad was ostensibly married when Watkins first entered her service, but no husband ever was to be seen; when she decided to marry again, she insisted she would do it only if Tinka promised not to leave her since the marriage depended on her. Although Fremstad further attempted to include the young Harry Brainard in the family by dubbing him with the obligatory foreign pet name (Havrah, in his case), the marriage lasted for little more than a few weeks: " 'Tinka, you must pack at once . . . I am suffocating . . . I must breathe!' 'And Havrah?' I asked. She frowned. 'And no Havrah!' she said" (292).

Finally Tinka decided that it was time to leave:

> I had become profoundly attached to this tempestuous and gifted creature for whom I had buffed through every imaginable vicissitude of professional and private life for nearly seven years. But I knew that very soon now the time would come when in justice to us both, I must step out upon my own. She had become too dependent, too inclined to shift responsibility and blame to my shoulders, whatever occurred. It was not good for her nor for me. (301–02)

Watkins announces that she is going to join the war effort and drive an ambulance. To her worry that Fremstad will be alone, the diva replies: " 'Tinka-*Leben*,' she answered sadly, 'I've been alone all my life—a solitary pine tree on a hillside, buffeted by the winds' "

(305). Tinka-*Leben;* Tinka/Livan. Separation/attachment. Buffeted, buffed, rebuffed.

In her essay on the joys and embarrassments of sapphic diva-worship, Terry Castle writes: "whether Cushing's relationship with Fremstad should be characterized as a homosexual one is question-able: there is no evidence to suggest that the two women were ever actually lovers" (215).[34] Wayne Koestenbaum answers—and moots—Castle's implied question by recalling Cushing's one explicit de-scription of their sleeping arrangements. Madame often was insom-niac, especially after performances, and if she woke she would bel-low for her buffer in tones that disturbed the neighbors, so Watkins devised the stratagem of tying a string from Fremstad's bedpost to her toe—she slept in another room—so that Fremstad could tug and she would arrive.[35] Tied on a string (once Fremstad got Tinka a dinner invitation by claiming that she—the young Watkins, that is—was her mother [211]), talking baby talk to each other, invent-ing a word for their relationship ("buffer"), all this, not to men-tion the dynamics I have been describing, scarcely count for Castle. Homosexual means genital contact, and if Fremstad and Watkins were doing it, Cushing doesn't tell.[36] Castle should know better—her essay, after all, is her "embarrassed" confession of her own love for divas, Brigitte Fassbaender in particular. Fremstad has a place in the history of women loving divas that Castle traces (the history Elizabeth Wood dubs "sapphonics") and Watkins is one of Castle's lesbian avatars.

Arguing that the appeal of the diva is erotic, Castle claims that her heavy breathing evokes "a sound-memory of one's mother having sex"; thus, she continues, "the diva awakens the infantile fantasy of having sex *with* the mother" (201). Castle's primal scene produces a one-liner to explain the object of her desire: the lure of a voice like Fassbaender's (and, she adds, Fremstad's) can be summarized in two words: "low notes" (224). Butch-femme is reconfigured thereby along heterosexual lines (for Castle, it follows that gay men must go for high notes). A more capacious account of what constitutes the erotic is needed—Eve Sedgwick's for instance—to account for the complexities of desire beyond a syntax of normativizing gender.[37] Lacan's invocation of voice as an erotic lure, detached from the standard psychoanalytic scenario of the oedipal, also provides a vocabulary for sexuality less rooted in the genitals.[38] These might better explain the appeal of a voice like Fremstad's (she had high notes too), and would support the important musicological arguments of Carolyn Abbate, who insists upon the empowerment of the diva whose vocality may run aslant the determinate gender plotting of her narrative position.[39]

The questions raised by the relationship of Fremstad and Watkins also appear in evaluations of the relationship of Cather and Lewis, usually also answered with assurances that their relationship was not a sexual one. Lewis likewise seems to have functioned much as Cushing did, as secretary, companion, buffer—though, of course, for over forty years, not the seven of Tinka's service.[40] Both Lewis and Cushing have been faulted for the reticence of their accounts (not to mention Lewis and Cather's burning of letters or the stipulations in Cather's will prohibiting citation of any that escaped the flames). Beyond the easy supposition that such destruction of evidence itself is evidence, one might note how closely Cather's piece in *McClure's* resembles Cushing's account. For both, Fremstad's life is a handful of childhood stories, a few brief facts about her European career (here there seem to be deliberate omissions), and then an account of her years at the Met. Both make much of the story of the very young Fremstad singing and mistaking the chocolate pony she was given as something she was supposed to eat rather than a reward that she was to deny herself. This last fits the Fremstad of Cather's *McClure's* piece, whose first quoted remark is "We are born alone, we make our way alone, we die alone" (42), or the Fremstad of *The Rainbow Bridge* who quotes the final line of the poem "Der Wanderer" by Georg Philipp Schmidt memorably set by Schubert (D493): "Dort wo du nicht bist, dort ist das Glück," happiness is not where you are, and imagined herself as always alone, a solitary pine tree.

These may stand as signature citations. "My name means *strange city*" Fremstad tells her buffer (46), she is the wanderer without a home. Tinka attempts to give them one, furnishing an apartment in her own hideous provincial taste, and the usual comedy ensues:

> "Tinka-*Leben!*" she exclaimed, her eyes very bright, "I simply cannot take it in . . .

"Come here child," she said, and enfolded me in one of her rare embraces. "I think it is all very splendid. You have worked hard, but you have made one mistake. It is not, as you once said it should be, *all Olive Fremstad*. No indeed, it is, I fear—mostly Mary Watkins. . . . Of course I shall put a few touches here and there, just little things you know nothing about—and presently it will be *our* home, you shall see!" (153–54).

Soon the items from an object referred to as the "homelike trunk" make their appearance—memorabilia meaningful to Fremstad, although largely opaque to her companion. After she and Watkins separated, Fremstad packed up the homelike trunk for good:

"Where is everything? . . . The Carmen shawl . . . 'Musica' . . . the leopard . . . and the others? I sent them down six weeks ago!"

"Hush," said Madame, "let them rest! I do not want them around me now. I have not touched the trunk."

"But Livan—you *have* to have them always! Why, they are part of you! They make your home!"

She stared me out of countenance. "I have no home!" she said. (309)

"She was always the foreigner—the queer one," Cushing puts it (206). "I am the woman that nobody knows" she announces early (41); "What can you know about me? Nothing!" are the words, we recall, with which she rebuffed Cather (244). Always out of place.

The denials ("I have no home"), the refusals are a way of having: to that both Watkins and Cather were drawn. The buffeted pine tree, after all, is also an image of strength and self-sufficiency. Indeed, in reviewing one of Fremstad's performances, Huneker happened to make the same comparison; Fremstad wrote to him: "I *love* the singing tree—How *did* you know that I always thought of myself as a singing tree and—always a pine!"[41] Cather knew, and her description of Kronborg's performance as Sieglinde, virtually quoting her account of Fremstad in *McClure's* ("her body was absolutely the instrument of her idea"), arrives at the same comparison: "All that deep-rooted vitality flowered in her voice, her face, her very finger-tips. She felt like a tree bursting into bloom. And her voice was as flexible as her body; equal to any demand, capable of every *nuance*" (410).

Fremstad embodied strangeness, and her practice of refusal and renunciation is key to the miracles of her performance, something of which is caught in a series of photographs of Fremstad's Isolde transformed by drinking the love potion (figs. 3–5). Cushing is as intent as Cather is on this transformation, and offers a pages-long account of Fremstad passing from being her Livan to becoming the opera singer on her way to a performance, to her arrival at the Met as "*the famous Olive Fremstad*" and then, donning the wig and costume and makeup of Isolde, her entrance into another world:

> The suspension between two worlds was the most trying period for her and for all concerned. She would stare at me and the other helpers as if we were intruders. . . . Suddenly all was calm; she had made the transition between personalities. At last she was totally the Irish Princess . . . Isolde forthwith emerged in all her majesty, glancing neither to right nor left, and marched to her ordeal with the exalted, other-world look of a queen led off to her crowning. Olive Fremstad had now cut herself off from reality with a completeness which was terrifying. (115)

Terrifying and alluring, the desire is precisely to emulate this service, to be so "cut off" as also to be crowned (Cushing's prose makes crowning sound like beheading). "To be a buffer to Olive Fremstad was suddenly all that any girl could desire" (119). Cushing's words also could be Cather's, at least in her position as fellow-acolyte; however, one must add that Watkins cast Cather in that part to secure her own relationship with Fremstad; the excision of any such relationship from *The Song of the Lark* is also the refusal of such a position.

Cather does figure her relationship with Fremstad in the novel, but through various male mentors and supporters (including Fred Ottenburg, Thea's lover and eventual husband). As I have noted, this is also a feature of Davenport's *Of Lena Geyer* with its several male narrators, one of whom, the acolyte Dave Freeman, who convinces Geyer to allow her story to be told, seems to rename Davenport in the masculine. The various strands of the relationships between Fremstad and Watkins, Fremstad and Cather that have occupied the last several pages now need to be assembled to evaluate a claim left hanging, that the crucial difference between the ways in which the

3., 4., and 5.

Olive Fremstad as Isolde.

*(Courtesy Metropolitan Opera
Archives.)*

novelists fictionalize Fremstad lies in Davenport's inclusion of a life-long female companion modeled on Mary Watkins.

In her characteristic hyperbolization, Davenport has Elsie de Haven follow Geyer from one European opera house to another (Watkins's initial fixation was much shorter and basically confined to Met performances), a solitary figure in black found night after night sitting in the same orchestra seat. She sends a floral tribute before each performance initialed "EdeH," and when Geyer finally finds out who this admirer is, she takes her up and drops the Duc de Chartres, a lover who has failed to realize that her voice counts for more than any man might (Lilli Lehmann also figures as his rival — she disapproves of the duke but gives her blessing to de Haven). When Geyer loses her voice and appears to be at the end of her career, she agrees to marry, but only if Elsie approves — and agrees to stay on as part of the household. These are but a few of the many details that match the relationship of Fremstad and Watkins. Geyer too pronounces the dictum "I have no home" (114) and also lives out of a trunk, her personal things ready to "be packed up and shipped anywhere at a moment's notice" (355). With Elsie she has a relationship characterized by a mobile dependency; if, like Watkins, Elsie realizes that the diva is "growing dependent on me" (216), she is perhaps a bit more self-conscious about the dynamic of their relationship: "I wonder now as I look back on it how I could so often turn the relationship between us from Lena as the leader and myself as the worshipping satellite to myself as preceptor and Lena as an humble child listening to me" (215). Davenport perhaps registers something of the fraught nature of the relationship through a re-naming akin to those we have noticed: Geyer dubs Elsie "Elsa" after the part in *Lohengrin* that she deplores; "*dumme Gans,*" she calls her (245), a dumb goose, alluding to and retaliating against idealistic adoration — Elsa's for Lohengrin, Elsie's for her.

This name change corresponds to a series of moments in the novel that must give pause to the claim that Davenport offers a relatively unveiled and celebratory account of a lesbian relationship. When Elsie first appears on the scene, the duke is repelled by what appear to him the clear signs of an "abnormal" relationship (197). While Leonardi and Pope are undoubtedly right in arguing that the duke's point of view is not one the novel endorses, he in fact corrects himself in a way that does find support throughout the text. He regards

Elsie's as the case of an "intensely suppressed woman who was finding the outlet for her entire emotional existence in worshipping her ideal" (197), and Elsie comes to the same understanding of herself, retrospectively realizing both "the ambiguity of [her] situation and emotions" but also assuring Dave/Davenport that "the fact remains that my feeling for Lena Geyer was childlike in its simplicity, and yet more powerful than any other emotion in my life" (208). Dave confirms these assurances too when he sums up the story, pronouncing Elsie "pathetic" rather than "sinister" (219). It is only under these conditions that Davenport allows Elsie to declare her love for Geyer, permits Geyer to seal their relationship with a kiss. "I cannot imagine what Lena saw in me," Elsie muses, likening it to the mystery that might draw a "handsome, desirable man to a homely little shadow of a wife" (237).

Leonardi and Pope endorse Davenport's representation—indeed insist that her negations only further prove that the secret tying Lena and Elsie is lesbian desire—but fail to comment on its desexualization, and seem happy to accept its marital terms as apt for describing the relationship between the women; deploring Cather's male identifications, they ignore how comfortably Davenport inhabits the voice of Dave. As they astutely argue, Lena and Elsie are joined through Geyer's voice, "united in their passion and dedicated to it without reserve. Lena's voice, Elsie says at one point, means 'as much to me as parents, a husband, children, or anything most women attach themselves to,' not, the text implies, as a substitute, but as a perfectly 'natural' if unusual object of desire" (115). In endorsing this "natural" position, a substitutive logic of a lesbian equivalence to heterosexuality is nonetheless entertained, one that downplays the erotics of the relationship through the voice. Here is how Elsie describes hearing Geyer sing Elsa for the first time:

The sensation I had was like fresh water pouring into the throat of someone nearly dead of thirst. I was quite unnerved . . . I was struck with the astonishing versatility of her voice. I think she could have done anything with it. Here she gave it a clear, pure quality so different from that of her Carmen or her Aida as to lead you to suppose that it was an entirely different woman. Yet the same physical thrill was there, that thing that gripped me and made something inside me leap into my ears and throat. (232–33)

"Elsie's orgasmic sensation suggests lesbian fetishism," Wood avers (35; voice here is certainly the petit objet a, Lacan's term for object of desire), and she finds Cather's Kronborg "Sapphonically performative" as well. The hidden truth of lesbianism for Wood, that is, is not the normative—and stigmatized—lesbianism that Leonardi and Pope endorse in Davenport and refuse to Cather; it is rather a form of desire both transgressive and transformative.[42]

Cather may deny Thea the "gynaesium" (236) that Davenport grants her diva, but she does so to refuse the kinds of substitutions and denials through which Davenport endorses a lesbian relationship which must be regarded as pure and sexless (the overt stance in *The Rainbow Bridge* as well). Cather's cross-gendered identifications are not in the service of heterosexualizing desire but of deforming it; likewise her appreciation of Fremstad's voice broaches sapphonic territory. Davenport may make diva and acolyte a lesbian couple but only after assuring the reader that lesbianism is just like heterosexuality—without sex.

Cather's representation, however, must be distinguished from James Huneker's in *Painted Veils*, his fictionalization of Fremstad as Esther Brandes—renamed Easter, the modern reincarnation of the Assyrian goddess Istar.[43] "She meant to be a Wagner singer, an extraordinary Isolde or Brünnhilde. Keep your Marguerites, your Gildas, your Juliettes, yes, even your Carmens. I must conquer Wagner," Huneker has his ambitious young singer say—mouthing Fremstad's recorded opinions (68). "The greatest Isolde since Lilli Lehmann [Huneker's attested view of Fremstad]. . . . the Great Singing Whore of Modern Babylon" (306), the novel concludes, and Easter's sex life not only includes cross-racial coupling but also stealing away the Huneker figure's female partner, a prostitute named Dora. (Another lesbian figure, Allie, "a masculine creature" [70], pays Easter's way to Lehmann's tutelage and is also her lover, even fighting a duel with a male lover of hers.) Huneker's novel is as extravagant in many respects as Davenport's in embellishing Fremstad's European career and in letting the reader know that Fremstad is the model by introducing comparisons to her in the text.[44] Like Davenport, Huneker grants his diva "versatility." But it lies less in the number of roles she sings than the parts she plays in bed.[45] Huneker may be revealing a truth about Fremstad's sex life, or may be punishing her even at this late date, twenty-plus years after the

6. Olive Fremstad as Brünnhilde *(Courtesy Metropolitan Opera Archives.)*

fact, for not agreeing to be his mistress. Or he may be offering a way to understand the appeal of the diva's voice, a heterosexual male fantasy of lesbian erotics to explain her lure and why consummation was always beyond his grasp. Cather felt the same lure, but did not translate it so literally in *The Song of the Lark*.

Cather's *McClure's* essay may suggest her occupation of the position of Watkins, even support Cushing's claim that she was its source. Like the young acolyte, Cather too was entranced by the *Walküre* Brünnhilde pictured in figure 6. "The short skirt would be a pathetic impropriety in a statuesque Brünnhilde," Cather comments, but not for Fremstad's "magnificently vital conception" in which one sees "a girl being sacrificed, not a woman being degraded" (48). In which, Cather insists, the girl has all the energy of "a boy running" as she enters. "Her body looks straight and athletic, like a boy's," she continues. For Cather, gender transformation signals Fremstad's artistic accomplishment. This is not a question of role reversal, not a matter of who is husband or wife, as it is in Davenport; it is rather a pushing of the envelope of gender as a way of finding a vocabulary for the erotic allure of Fremstad's performance. It is also a way of dispensing with the need to represent a couple.

Both Cather and Cushing find a supreme accomplishment in Fremstad's Kundry—who, of course, is nothing but transformation—marveling at her changed appearance from act to act. Both linger over the moment when the crone turned seductress kisses Parsifal. "When she reclined there on that ridiculous couch and arched her purple brows at Parsifal she was 'the Rose of Hell' incarnate," Cushing writes (141); as usual, her sense of the comic (the prevailing tone in *The Rainbow Bridge*), as well as the smear of greasepaint, defends against the power of the moment: "when she lifted a flaming curl and kissed him behind its fragrant web, sex reared its lurid head more potently than the sedate and stuffy stage had often permitted" (141; in this context it is worth mentioning that Fremstad gave the first performance of Strauss's *Salome* at the Metropolitan Opera [18 February 1907] so effectively that the work was immediately withdrawn, not to be mounted again at the Met for another quarter century). Cather gives half a column to the moment of Kundry's kiss, slowly watching Fremstad as she bends over Parsifal, the changing expression on her face as seduction becomes something "powerful because it is corporeal and sincere":

> Her right arm is about the boy; with her left hand she lifts her flowing hair and holds it before her face and his, like a scarf. Behind this she kisses him. The inclination of her head, every line of her body, contribute to the poetry of the moment. In Mme. Fremstad's performance of the part this is always a great moment;—it might so easily be a great stupidity. (47)

Where is Cather here—watching, or imagining herself as the boy Parsifal? I ask this depending on the importance of "boy" as a site of Cather's own identifications, but also recalling that moment in *The Song of the Lark* when Thea and Fred Ottenburg are engaged in a stone-throwing contest, and both "looked like two boys" (278; in fact, Davenport has something like this when the Duc de Chartres registers his desire for Geyer by noting her "virility" [89] as a lure). Fred wants nothing more than that the ferocity of Thea's stone throwing (which is a version of her ferocity as an artist) be turned on him, that she "come at [him] with foils" (279). The lovemaking scene that presumably follows this no doubt is supposed to continue in that vein. This is how Cather imagines Fremstad embracing the "boy" Parsifal; the Fremstad who, just a page later, she will see as a boy.[46]

Indeed, it might answer a critic like John H. Flannigan, who claims that *The Song of the Lark* finally abandons Thea to heterosexuality when she marries Fred (he is "her husband" exactly once in passing in the final pages of the novel [415]; many readers fail to notice it), to note that the closest Cather comes literally to naming anyone Olive Fremstad in the novel is in the name she gives Thea's eventual husband, Fred Ottenburg.[47] Moreover, it must be recalled how often Ottenburg's descriptions and estimations of Kronborg's art seem lifted from Cather's *McClure's* piece about Fremstad—or from Huneker's account of her performance as a Rhine-maiden, which he echoes (347), much as he, like Huneker, serves as the main informant about the diva's German career. It certainly should be added that Cather's fantasies of herself as a boy were also Fremstad's. Facing the dilemma of what to do about Huneker's advances—and the fact that he (like Fred) was married already—Fremstad wrote to him with this solution: "I wish I were a man, I always said it was all a mistake my being a girl."[48] That Fred and Thea are two virtually identical boys connects them moreover to the incestuous couple Siegmund and Sieglinde, and thus to the performance that marks Kronborg's arrival as a star.[49] In these (hetero)sexual relations, these cross-gendered transpositions, desires that transgress normative heterosexuality are figured.

When Cather associates Brünnhilde opening the second act of *Die Walküre* singing a treacherously high-flying battle cry with a "boy," she would seem to be challenging the view that Thea simply occupies conventional femininity when she abandons her contralto range for the soprano register. This is indeed the point made in the passage emended in 1937, when "virile" is replaced by "warm": "My dear Archie," Fred says, "that's the high voice we dream of; so pure and yet so warm and human. That combination hardly ever happens with sopranos" (365). As Elizabeth Wood has argued, it is precisely the refusal to stay in a designated proper range that constitutes the sapphonic appeal of a voice like Fremstad's—or of Lena Geyer's in Davenport's novel. As even Flannigan details, the moment when Thea unleashes her "*voz contralto*" (205) involves a cross-gender performance (she uses her lower register to sing as a man to a woman). When the scene ends with Thea abandoning the trouser role to sing the coloratura line in the sextet from *Lucia di Lammermoor,* such vocal domination is not easily read as a resolution of the scene through conventional femininity as Flannigan claims. "Then at the appointed, at the acute, moment, the soprano voice, like a fountain jet, shot up into the light. . . . How it leaped from among the dusky male voices! How it played in and about and around and over them, like a goldfish darting among creek minnows, like a yellow butterfly soaring over a swarm of dark ones" (213).[50]

Such transgression of registers—and of their meaning—is only part of the appeal, however. In the *McClure's* essay Cather turns from Kundry's kiss to what she regards as the even more riveting figure of Fremstad in the last act of *Parsifal,* in which she sings only four notes ("dienen, dienen"):

> After her ministrations to the knight, she goes to the rear of the stage and stands with her back to the audience, but there is no doubt what she is doing. She is not praying or looking into herself: she is looking off at the mountains and the springtime. From the audience one seems to see the ranges of the Pyrenees, to feel suddenly and sharply the beauty of the physical world. She moves toward the door with her bent step of "service." Before she disappears she turns again and looks at Parsifal. There are many degrees of resignation, it seems; the human spirit can be broken many times before it becomes insensate. Then only does she in truth renounce (47).

Cather looks at Fremstad, with her back to the audience, comes on her from behind, occupies her place, sees with her eyes. She sees at once life and renunciation, the perfection of sensuality and its denial. Sensate and insensate at once: like the experience of buck-fever, or the experience of not-being that marks those moments when the diva is fully inhabited by the conception, the idea that remakes her body. Cather gives Thea such a moment after her first complete performance as Sieglinde in *Die Walküre*. On the penultimate page of the novel, she offers a retrospective account that makes this first success emblematic of an entire career, Fremstad's finished career:

> Often when she sang, the best she had was unavailable; she could not break through to it, and every sort of distraction and mischance came between it and her. But this afternoon the closed roads opened, the gates dropped. What she had so often tried to reach lay under her hand. She had only to touch an idea to make it live. (410)

Commentators on *The Song of the Lark* rightly point to Thea's earlier experience in the caves of the cliff dwellers in Panther Canyon as crucial for her development. Cather's wording of this transformative experience is significant: "a persistent affirmation — or denial — was going on in her" (276). Affirmation — or denial, affirmation *as* denial: the "impossibility" of boundary-shattering transformation that at once denies the body (its mortality, its limits) and reinvigorates the body in the very act of renunciation. This is what Cather sees looking at Fremstad's back, what Fred Ottenburg glimpses by way of Thea's "vocal back" (261). It is, indeed, how Dr. Archie finally understands the haggard, aged, hoarse Thea he sees after her performance as Elsa: "she was running away from the other woman down at the opera house, who had used her hardly" (362).[51]

Ottenburg explains to Archie that Thea's Elsa does not, as other divas' do, die at the end of the opera: "She becomes an abbess, that girl, after *Lohengrin* leaves her. She is made to live with ideas and enthusiasms, not with a husband" (366). Throughout the novel Thea has been marked as "not the marrying kind" (93), as her father puts it first, as Dr. Archie thinks toward its close (304). He should know: miserably married when the novel opens, by the time he makes this comment to Fred, his wife is dead and his household is composed of three Japanese "boys" (342). Fred is not available for marriage either for most of the novel, since he is already saddled with a wife with whom he does not live. These heterosexual arrangements seem about as convincing as Olive Fremstad's two brief marriages. Fred mates Thea to "ideas and enthusiasms"; this is one way to figure

Archie's "other woman down at the opera house." Cather's diva lives for her work and nothing else, "her body . . . absolutely the instrument of her idea. . . . And her voice was as flexible as her body" (410), sentences from the end of the novel that echo the *McClure's* piece. "Who marries who is a small matter, after all," Thea memorably pronounces (401) in a scene in which she appears finally to rebuff Fred and in which retrospectively it seems she is accepting him. It doesn't matter because the diva's true "companion" is her demanding voice. This is why there is no lady companion in *The Song of the Lark,* but also why heterosexual relations are impossible. All the men in the novel are unmarriageable (Dr. Archie and Fred constitute a couple; after Thea's debut it is Fred who knows a restaurant where Thea can appear in her makeup, where all the habitués are "theatre people" and "bachelors" [381], Fred's kind too). Not only does Kronborg have no Tinka, no Cather in her life, she even refuses to return from Germany when her mother dies. Through these renunciations Cather gestures to the thing not named, to the place Fremstad cited: "Dort wo du nicht bist, dort ist das Glück." Couched only in the negative, as renunciation and impossibility, this is nonetheless what is rendered fully sensuous and embodied in the diva.

This sapphonic appeal is hardly ever conveyed, as one might expect it to be, in descriptions of Thea's voice. Thea is rarely represented when singing; or, when she is, as in the scene of Dr. Archie's "buck-fever," her voice is not amenable to description. What renders graphic the scene of Harsanyi discovering that Thea's talent lies in her voice is not a description of the sound she makes but rather his touching of her throat: "He put his hand back to her throat and sat with his head bent, his one eye closed. He loved to hear a big voice throb in a relaxed, natural throat, and he was thinking that no one had ever felt this voice vibrate before" (171). The fantasy, as we noted earlier, involves getting into Thea. Harsanyi's examination leads him to conclude "she sang from the bottom of herself" (171). It is, however, a mistake to think that the throat is "really" the vagina—or anus—though no error to see how sexual this scene is.

What is fantasized as "in" Thea does have a proper name of sorts. It is called, over and again in the novel, "It." Thus, Harsanyi imagines that there is a bird in Thea's throat: "no one knew that it had come, or even that it existed; least of all the strange, crude girl in whose throat it beat its passionate wings. What a simple thing it was, he reflected; why had he never guessed it before?" (171). The answer is in part that the bird in this passage is like the "simple thing" that Cather describes in Fremstad's performance, something so elemental that it has no name, a rhythm of life which even so to name is to misname, for it is more like the sensual insensateness glimpsed in Kundry's final moment onstage. Cather quotes: "Mme. Fremstad herself says: 'Even the voice is not a physical attribute'" (*McClure's,* 48).

Describing Thea singing Sieglinde, Cather paraphrases the text she sings as Sieglinde discovers herself in her brother Siegmund: ". . . the voice gave out all that was best in it. Like the spring indeed, it blossomed into memories and prophecies, it recounted and foretold, as she sang the story of her friendless life, and of how the thing which was truly herself, 'bright as the day, rose to the surface' when in the hostile world she for the first time beheld her Friend" (407–08). "Du bist der Lenz," the passage famously begins; Sieglinde's first name for the Friend is "Spring," and the barrenness of winter and her loveless marriage is replaced in a passage of remarkable sensuousness. "Fremde nur sah ich von je, freundlos war mir das Nahe": it is a signature moment when sung by Fremstad, describing her friendless state where all was strange ("fremde"). And then the moment of bright sunrise, striking her eye like the ringing of a resounding echo in her ear, she sings, as the orchestra builds to a climax, when in her empty frozen strangeness she beholds the Friend, "in fröstig oder Fremde zuerst ich den Freund ersah," and comes to be "the thing which was truly herself."

After Dr. Archie hears her sing for the first time, Thea reminds him of an earlier moment in their relationship—it is in fact where the novel begins. The first sound we ever hear Thea make is her "rapid, distressed breathing" (6). It draws Dr. Archie to her bedside (he is there helping her mother deliver a baby). It's clear from the start that the almost dying girl and the breath she is gulping are meant as an answer and equivalent to her laboring mother. Having a voice means grabbing in unbelievable amounts of air; the singer is this cavity (hence Thea's self-recognition in the vessels of the Anasazi). This drawing in and expenditure of breath, this gasping for life, this dying living is, I think, to be associated with what Friedrich Kittler has described through the nonce word "Weltatem" that Isolde sings at the climactic moment a few measures before the end of the Liebestod: the breath of the world. Isolde, who appears neither to hear or see, gestures to Tristan, first claiming to see his corpse alive, and then as the aria moves to its exultant climax, insisting that she hears him breathe, that she is pierced through, surrounded, lifted up and transported on his breath (lines worth comparing to the description of Thea's Lucia performance or to the throbbing that Harsanyi's fingers touch). "Tristan's extinguished breath returns as orchestral melody: the sounds he emits penetrate the listener," Kittler writes, dubbing this an "acoustic erection." He continues: "But Isolde sings all this—from the crescendo to the sound effects. Her orchestrally amplified voice thus supplements the missing voice of her lover. The voice in Wagner is so unindividuated, his acoustics so ecstatic, that to the ear of a woman singing, her own voice appears essentially as the voice of the other."[52] Kittler perhaps gives too much credit to the composer, and to the masculine. Isolde is the one having/producing the acoustic erection. The unindividuation that Kittler gestures toward undoes gender determination because it undoes meaning; the sound of the breath of the world is physiological, not psychological, and the plenitude it offers is "acoustic power beyond all humanity," Kittler writes (229), not, for example, the "mother-imago" (220) assumed by Castle, and *against* which Cather's opening scene of childbirth juxtaposes Thea's breathing. This is an altogether different mode of reproduction and of connection, sensory data so overwhelming, sound so piercing that the ego is bypassed as it heads straight for the unconscious, striking the nerves. What Wagnerian music drama embodies—and nowhere more than in Brünnhilde, Isolde, Kundry, or Elsa—Fremstad's parts—is the erotic desirability of breath itself. Fremstad liked to say she didn't have a belly, rather bellows; her favorite game with Watkins was a walking contest to see who could hold her breath longer; and her most memorable way of appearing onstage was to enter running, arriving as if out of breath, then to produce the inhuman torrents of unclassifiable sound (neither contralto nor soprano, Fremstad called it "long"[53]) that made her so entirely and impossibly cathectable.

But not, alas, recordable. As Louis Migliorini opens the standard account: "For an artist of her magnitude, Olive Fremstad is perhaps the poorest represented on records. Not only are her recordings few in number, but they manage to give only the barest outline of the range of her roles and the scope of her artistry and voice."[54] No one has ever been very happy with the fifteen selections Fremstad recorded, starting with the diva herself. Cushing reports her reaction: "'*I du meine Güte!*' she exclaimed. . . . All that work and nothing gained! When people play those things in years to come they will say: 'Oh ho, so that's the great Fremstad! Well, I guess she wasn't so much after all!'" (261–62). No one really disputes Fremstad's response, and in *Of Lena Geyer* Davenport has Geyer's recordings destroyed, offering as an explanation for their failure that "her voice was the wrong size or quality or something for those old machines" (299). No better—or more definitive—explanation of the mismatch of voice and technology has been offered, and Cushing's account of Fremstad's discomfort in the recording studio can safely be added to the reasons for failure; as Migliorini comments, nervousness must explain much. The intensity of dramatic performance was Fremstad's medium; in the recording studio she froze, can be heard to run out of breath, failing to support a tone; she often sounds constrained and lifeless.

Nonetheless the recordings do convey something, and every critic names a favorite selection or two. Cushing, for example, finds "the faintest hint of her artistic and vocal powers in arias from *Mignon*, *Tosca*, *Walküre* and *Don Carlos* as well as in her singing of "Stille Nacht" (262 n). In *Prima Donna*, Rupert Christiansen concurs in praising Fremstad's singing of "O don fatale" from Verdi's *Don Carlo*, especially for the fact that it "begins not with the attention-grabbing chesty declamation of most Italian mezzos, but with a quiet bitterness and melancholy that is arrestingly beautiful." This and her singing of "Vissi d'arte" are praised for their "introverted" power; he claims that in her singing of the aria from *Tosca* "no one— not Muzio, Destinn, Callas, or Scotto—quite captures as Fremstad does the immense sadness and essential privacy of the plaint that Scarpia is not meant to hear."[55] These are also qualities that J. B. Steane values, finding her recording of "O don fatale" "inspired," and he too is captivated by Fremstad's ability to convey "a private world of emotions" there as well as in "Vissi d'arte," in the other *Tosca* excerpt (a part of the first act love duet), and in her "Du bist der Lenz," selections also favored by Cushing. For Steane, Fremstad's greatest recorded accomplishment is "Dich teure Halle"

from *Tannhäuser,* both for the heroism and warmth of its opening, and especially for "her marvellous softening of the middle section, the dream, which becomes more and more indrawn until it
achieves a perfect stillness."[56] Steane also praises Fremstad's recording of Brünnhilde's war cry from *Walküre* and marvels that such a
heroic voice also can handle Puccini with such delicacy.[57] Indeed,
the execution of the coloratura lines in the act one selection from
Tosca is flawless.

These comments respond to the lure of an interiority insistently
sounded in Cather's account in *McClure's;* "introverted" seems to be
the word for Fremstad's art. At the core of these performances, and
not simply because of faulty technology or technique, there is something one can't see or hear. Fremstad's voice is not exactly covered,
but it is colored, so much so that it would be hard to credit her
with an identifiable sound. She can be bright, as in Brünnhilde's
war cry or the act one *Tosca* excerpt, but more often the sound is
"warm," shaded entirely by the demands of the role. While she es-
chews chest tones in "O don fatale," they are in evidence in her singing of the "Seguidilla" from *Carmen,* for instance, where the voice
is much darker and sounds more like a contralto than it does in any
of the other opera recordings, though Fremstad's Carmen is more
ferocious than flirtatious (Tosca in act one fits that description). Indeed, nothing is more startling than to go from the plangent mezzo
quality of her superb "Connais-tu le pays?" from *Mignon* to the more
toneless singing of the Wagnerian soprano parts—Sieglinde, Isolde,
and Elsa, most notably—although in both the aim seems to be the
production of a seamless sound, a legato supported by an endless
breath that finally exhausts tonality in its wake. In these recordings,
Fremstad conveys her entrance into another world—Elsa's dream,
Isolde's exalted apotheosis, the spring that suddenly bursts out for
Sieglinde and Siegmund. Indeed the A-flat on "Freund" that ends
the *Walküre* selection is one of Fremstad's most radiantly released
notes (Elsa's dream and the Liebestod seem to be working less suc-
cessfully to the same end). Christiansen's comment that Fremstad
manages in singing "Vissi d'arte" to remind us that no one is supposed to hear her is a stunning way of putting the effect of these
performances, to be contrasted only with her rendition of "Silent
Night," where a flood of sound completely unlike any other of the
recordings is released; Fremstad offstage, as it were, in a relaxed

moment letting out what supports the sounds she produced as she entered part after part.

"I do not claim this or that for my voice," Cather quotes Fremstad, "I do not sing contralto or soprano. I sing Isolde. What voice is necessary for the part I undertake, I will produce" (46). Which is to say that just as it was difficult to believe that the same body embodied "her voluptuous Venus and her girlish Brünnhilde" (to take Cather's examples [47], a claim amply supported by photographs of Fremstad, and nowhere more startling than in her appearances in *Parsifal* [fig. 7 shows her as the act one Kundry]), such must have been the experience of hearing Fremstad. No one voice, or timbre or color, no single mode of vocal production; all the "variety" multiplied in a book like *Of Lena Geyer*, was "in" her unclassifiable, opalescent voice, seamless but not self-identical, the material of transformation.

Cather's *Song of the Lark* aims to arrive at that place within toward which Fremstad beckoned. Her vocality is thus anything but "voice" and more the equivalent of that unfurnished space that Cather would later enunciate as the goal of representation, the locus of a sound "divined by the ear but not heard by it," the "thing not named" but not therefore silent.[58] This is the sound of Thea Kronborg's voice that Cather describes in the *Lucia* sextet as everywhere and nowhere, sensuous and insensate at once. As Kittler suggests, the darkened house at Bayreuth, the invisibility of the singer, first made possible a sonority that is not a stream of meaning. Hence, Cather names it only through the inexplicit "It."

"It" may be, at least at first, a bird in Harsanyi's metaphorics, but it does not stay anchored linguistically. In an earlier moment of recognition, with her piano teacher Wunsch, for instance, for whom Thea has just sung a lied from Schumann's *Dichterliebe* (a song cycle for male voice, note), he tells her "for a singer there must be something in the inside from the beginning" (71) and what he seems to know is that it is there in Thea and that she knows "what [she] will not tell [him]" (71). Thea finds herself "shaken by a passionate excitement. She did not altogether understand what Wunsch was talking about; and yet, in a way she knew. She knew, of course, that there was something in her that was different. But it was more like a friendly spirit than like anything that was a part of herself. She

7. Olive Fremstad as Kundry. *(Courtesy Metropolitan Opera Archives.)*

brought everything to it, and it answered her; happiness consisted of that backward and forward movement of herself. The something came and went, she never knew how" (72). A few lines later, the something, the It, is called her "companion." Some pages after the scene of Harsanyi's discovery of "It" Thea remembers "when she told Harsanyi that 'there had always been—something.' . . . She took it for granted that some day, when she was older, she would know a great deal more about it. It was as if she had an appointment to meet the rest of herself sometime, somewhere. It was moving to meet her and she was moving to meet it" (196). The uncanny meeting of Fremstad and Cather? Benign spirit; demanding demon. Life force; death drive.

The dictum of the cure, "Wo es war soll ich werden," where id was, ego shall be, is here reversed. For that reason an account like O'Brien's in which Cather comes into her voice in a novel like *The Song of the Lark,* and, also, comes out, as female-identified, as lesbian, seems mistaken, for what happens in the novel is rather the giving up of such consciousness, an incorporation—not without struggle, loss, aggression, and self-denial—into something that has no proper name or locus. I becomes the It—whether listening/dreaming on a stream of sound or joining with/obliterating the object. In that respect, accounts that repeat Cather's preoccupation with the transcendence of the artist as the theme of her work can be reunderstood in the powerful lure of "dienen," of abjection, of engulfment into the "strange" place—the *fremd stad*—of displaced wandering. This is the renunciation of the novel, one that is the very condition of possession. Perhaps all we need to add is Cather's remark in her 1932 preface, that her novel tells the same story as Oscar Wilde's *Dorian Gray*—but in reverse.

> It flashed across Doctor Archie that she was running away from the other woman down at the opera house, who had used her hardly. (362)

> "What's her secret?" . . . "Her secret? It is every artist's secret"— he waved his hand—"passion. That is all. It is an open secret, and perfectly safe." (409)

If, in this account, *The Song of the Lark* sounds like *My Mortal Enemy,* I have meant to signal that in my title, which puns on the aria ("Casta diva") that serves as the leitmotif of Cather's 1926 novella. In it, it remains indeterminate whether the enemy is the man Myra Henshawe had married in defiant love or Myra herself. The witness to the passion of the heroine is a younger woman, drawn in fascination to the older one. Her unspoken passion mirrors Henshawe's cryptic utterance, "Why must I die alone like this, alone with my mortal enemy!" Unrepresented but underscored by allusion, the story is a version of *Norma,* that opera about triangulated love, two women first rivals, then united; acolyte and priestess; then divided again as Norma ascends the pyre with Pollione, her "nemico fatal." Acolyte and priestess were parts Fremstad played; at the Met she sang both Brangaene and Isolde; some nights she appeared as Brünnhilde, others Sieglinde; while she sang the part of Venus more times than any of her other roles, she thought she should also sing Elisabeth in *Tannhäuser* (a part she sang only one time at the Met)—thought, that is, she should sing both parts in the same performance. Fremstad could have said, after Rimbaud, I is an Other. *The Song of the Lark* is Cather's assumption of that sentence intoned in consuming love, mortal enmity.[59]

War Requiems

Pat Barker's award-winning trilogy of World War I novels — *Regeneration* (1991), *The Eye in the Door* (1993), *The Ghost Road* (1995) — the last of which received the Booker Prize — provides me here with a route for a consideration of another award-winning World War I novel, Willa Cather's *One of Ours* (1922), accorded the Pulitzer Prize in 1923.[1] Although it simplifies matters considerably to say that Barker's writing makes explicit certain salient aspects of Cather's, it is perhaps because Barker's is a historical project that it provides terms that explicate Cather's writing situation. Moreover, Barker's novels offer metacritical leverage here precisely by including as characters real historical figures who were themselves writers whose central preoccupation was the war. Her trilogy is framed by Siegfried Sassoon's arrival in July 1917 at Craiglockhart War Hospital for treatment for shell shock (the diagnosis preferred by the military as a way of dealing with his public protest against the war, which could have resulted in court-martial, prison, and even further notoriety) and by the death of Wilfred Owen on 4 November 1918, one week before the Armistice was signed.

Like Cather's, Barker's main focus is psychological. Central to the trilogy is the relationship between W. H. R. Rivers (the neurophysiologist, anthropologist, and psychologist who treated Sassoon at Craiglockhart) and a character invented by Barker, Billy Prior, represented also as Rivers's patient, who dies at the same encounter as Owen.[2] Billy witnesses Owen's death, recorded in a painfully brief sentence: "He saw Owen die, his body lifted off the ground by bullets, describing a slow arc in the air as it fell" (*Ghost Road*, 273). Prior's appropriateness as witness for Owen's death is set up in the scene with which *The Ghost Road* opens. Owen and Prior are together waiting to be passed by the review board as fit to return to France. Owen declares his motivation: the fact that Sassoon has been wounded makes his going over "the only thing to do":

> Yes, Prior thought, it would. He remembered them at Craiglockhart: the incongruous pair, Sassoon so tall, Owen so short, the love Owen hadn't been able, or hadn't bothered, to disguise.

"*Also,*" Owen said, "I was getting pretty tired of being regarded as 'a twitching Nancy boy from a loony-bin in Scotland'." (*Ghost Road,* 14–15)

Owen's cited words are those Billy had used a bit earlier in the scene, which, he reminds Owen, he applied to himself as well. This provides terms that are crucial for me in juxtaposing Barker and Cather, the complex treatment of questions of sexuality that shape Barker's project, and not only in terms of the psychology that can be adduced from Prior's brutal, but also self-owned, phrase, "a twitching Nancy boy." The place of male homosexuality in the making of history and of literary history is Barker's continual subject, and this set of conjunctions also illuminates Cather. Moreover (this is almost too obvious to say), like Cather, Barker is a female novelist, and one aim of this essay is to consider the function of representations of sexuality—particularly, of male homosexuality—for their writing practices.

This is not to suggest that Barker provides the only way to raise these questions. It would be possible, for example, to read *One of Ours* alongside A. T. Fitzroy's *Despised and Rejected,* originally published in 1918.[3] Fitzroy was the pseudonym of Rose Laure Allatini, whose major career as Eunice Buckley, writer of dozens of romance novels, ran from the early 1940s to the late 1970s. *Despised and Rejected* is about pacifist resistance to World War I, and the central figures of the novel are Dennis, a homosexual composer, Antoinette, the woman who loves him (but who also loves women), and a younger man, Alan, whom Dennis finally chooses. In embodying the values of pacifism and art in characters whose sex lives are of crucial importance, Fitzroy operates in a terrain that Barker's novels also explore, one that, I argue, subtends Cather's writing. However, for Fitzroy, the relationship between these fields (and others, Irish nationalism and the suffragette movement, for example) is one of parallelism: various minorities—those who constitute the despised and rejected—are seen as the repositories of truth ("Being in the minority doesn't imply being in the wrong," Alan says [288]), a truth that should be brought to light in order to oppose militarism, compulsory heterosexuality, philistinism, nationalism. Indeed, the novel concludes by prophesying a time when "we shall recognize

War Requiems

in the best of our intermediate types the leaders and masters of the race" (348).

Despised and Rejected thus trades in a binaristic schema, the fantasized elevation of a despised minority into an elite. What is most interesting in this structure (beyond the protoliberationist appeal of its rhetoric, which is powerful) is also what is most disquieting: the vanguard imagined as the future "masters of the race" looks all too like the repository of the kinds of sentiment upon which invidious differences and denigration are based. The reason to read Cather beside Barker, as the citation of the scene between Owen and Prior may have suggested already, is that complicities of this sort are faced: more than a reversal is involved.

I should not begin this discussion, however, without noticing the treatment of *One of Ours* in Christopher Nealon's stunning essay "Affect-Genealogy: Feeling and Affiliation in Willa Cather."[4] There is no better set of pages on Cather's novel than his. Nealon shows persuasively that the history of the critical reception of Cather's book has been marked from the start by a refusal to recognize that its "erotic drive is homosexual" (18); he demonstrates how the idealism for which the book has often been taken to task is the very vehicle for that sexual trajectory.[5] Noting that its hero, Claude Wheeler, presents a history of repeated humiliations, frustrations, and despair only relieved by the camaraderie experienced with his fellow soldiers (and terminated by his death in battle), Nealon details the "loving and sadistic persistence" (19) of Cather's stance toward her hero. "His ignorance of his own breathtaking beauty," Nealon continues, "is Cather's continuous tenderness" (19). In this brilliantly terse and elegantly phrased observation, Nealon encompasses the epistemological grounds of Cather's novel, its author's knowingness and her character's opacity, which makes for one of the main interpretive dilemmas of the novel; for, as Nealon also indicates, this divide is breached by the love expended by Cather on her protagonist, a love that is close to refusal even in its embrace.[6] Barker manages a similar feat with her Billy Prior, as the exchange with Owen at the beginning of *The Ghost Road* intimates; the effect is to make Billy's sadism as appealing as is Claude's masochism (itself driven by Cather's loving sadism, itself a kind of masochism).[7] These erotics are not just psychological matters, however; they cannot be

divorced from the position of homosexuality in a virulently phobic society; but, even more to the point, as Nealon argues, they are also the difficult means toward the painful affirmation of alternative affiliations.

Nealon finds Cather's vision of homosexual affiliation articulated most fully in two passages in *One of Ours*. In one of these, Claude, in the solitude of an improvised outdoor moonlit bath, reaches out in his imagination to an ancient "finer race" of those who are the children of the moon rather than worshippers of the sun, a group characterized by "unappeased longings and futile dreams" (171). If this is Claude's "race," it is also, he imagines, the one to which his high school friend Gladys Farmer belongs. This formulation shares the racialism upon which Fitzroy trades; Cather does not mobilize it toward a triumphalist solution, however. Hence, in the other passage Nealon underscores, Gladys recognizes herself as one of a group of local Frankfort inhabitants "who had imagination and generous impulses" but who are all "inefficient," "failures" (129). These include an old maid and an effeminate soda jerk; she dearly hopes that the "finer strain" in Claude's nature will find realization rather than the life-in-death of these figures or, even worse, of the married man. In Claude and Gladys's formulations Nealon traces the lineaments of what he calls a "war-generated secret nationality" (21) which finds its fullest embodiment in male-male romance and a new kind of American who has escaped provincialism.

In *One of Ours* this new American is represented by David Gerhardt, the friend that Claude makes, a New Yorker and a violinist, European-trained and cultivated. Gerhardt does not entertain the conventional illusions about the war and explicitly dismisses the notion that it will "make the world safe for Democracy, or any rhetoric of that sort" (330); nonetheless, he does believe that "something unforeseen" will emerge from the war, and wonders "whether the young men of our time had to die to bring a new idea into the world" (331). In David, Claude painfully sees who he would wish to be:

In the years when he went to school at Lincoln, he was always hunting for some one whom he could admire without reservations; some one he could envy, emulate, wish to be. Now he believed that even then he must have had some faint image of a man like Gerhardt in his mind. It was only in war times that their paths would have been likely to cross; or that they would have had anything to do together . . . any of the common interests that make men friends. (332)

"The privilege of that American-European position," Nealon comments, referring to Gerhardt and through him to the long line of affiliations linking Claude back to the "race" of dreamers, Gladys to the local misfits, "compels Claude to tortured admiration and love" (23). It is along these waves of feeling that Cather communicates a secret in the novel untranslatable further, "cross-national, cross-generational, cross-familial passions too complex to name" (24). That is, Claude has no name for this feeling, and Cather does not provide more explicit terms for what he is so reticent about—what he so unknowingly knows. This is the site in *One of Ours* for "the thing not named," and it is worth noting that "The Novel Démeublé" was written at the same time as *One of Ours*. (It's also worth comparing Claude's desire to "envy, emulate, wish to be" David with Cather's fraught relationship to Fremstad.)

For Nealon the locus of this reconstituted American is France —it was there that Gerhardt trained, there that Claude encounters European culture, admiring the cathedral in Rouen, experiencing the hospitality offered to him by suffering survivors of death and devastation, finding "a new kind of happiness, a new kind of sadness" (316); it is there, obviously enough, that the war effort is greeted as a form of salvation, and not just for the French. Cather has been accused of being naive in such celebrations, although she also registers the arrival of the Americans as itself a form of "invasion" comparable to the Germans' (264).[8] Moreover, even as astute a critic of the war as W. E. B. DuBois, who understood it as another episode in imperialism and racism, a fight among Western powers over control of the rest of the globe (Barker too sees the cruel joke of rescuing defenseless Belgium from German invasion when no one had thought to save the Congo from Belgium's lethal takeover), nonetheless allows France to be a place in which black American soldiers glimpsed a version of democracy that galvanized them on their return home.[9] That is: it is not simply the case that Cather endorses

Claude's idealistic views; to follow Nealon's argument, always in question is when Cather's cherishing of his idealism is also another blow of loving humiliation.

Nealon refers in passing to Claude as Cather's "proxy son" (21), adopting a view more fully developed in Sharon O'Brien's understanding of the author's investment in her character.[10] There is certainly warrant for this, not least in the closing pages of the novel where the memory of Claude and the final understanding of his death is entrusted to his mother and the faithful family servant old Mahailey, Claude's companion and confidante from childhood on. O'Brien, however, also provides another possible mode of understanding the genesis of Claude worth further attention. As she notes, paraphrasing letters that Cather wrote to Dorothy Canfield Fisher as she was writing *One of Ours,* Claude recalls a version of herself in her 1902 trip to France in Fisher's company. Cather had felt continually like a hayseed then, lacking Fisher's excellent French and superior knowledge of the culture. As Cather herself acknowledged, the relationship of Claude and David replays hers and Fisher's.[11] Male-male romance translates a female-female plot. Cather's immediate source for Claude, as is well-documented, was a nephew of hers (G. P., the son of her beloved Aunt Franc), whose letters home inspired her precisely because in them a young man whom she had written off as a dolt suddenly appeared to have achieved levels of feeling and understanding he had not seemed capable of before. G. P. Cather's story is Willa Cather's too; the pained and abjected young man of the novel is her boyhood self, that "Will" Cather striking out to find some new version of herself beyond the confines of the "sissy" name Wilella with which she had been christened. "Sissy" is Claude's term for his own name (284), "a hayseed name trying to be fine" (16), but subject to the humiliating mispronunciation "clod" (109, 171); if Claude's name is properly French, even in its own language it is "*un peu . . . romanesque*" (283). In his (double) name, Cather names herself in the quasi-masculine, as was the case, too, in the name she chose for herself—Willa, after her uncle William—and in her double life as the naif and the sophisticate. This naming suggests that Cather's connection to Claude is not simply maternal; such a genealogy for Claude would metaphorize the route of affiliation that Nealon persuasively argues.

This connection is represented in the novel in the relationship of

War Requiems

Claude and Gladys, which could be mistaken as a failed romance, Gladys as the partner Claude should have chosen rather than his frigid wife Enid. Gladys, however, is allowed to recognize that she and Claude share a "cursed kind of sensibility" (150), and her plot runs parallel to Claude's. She comes close in the novel to marrying Claude's repellent brother Bayliss, a double in many respects for Enid. Like her, he is a prohibitionist, even lecturing his reclusive, Bible-reading mother for her use of stimulants when she takes a second cup of coffee (76). If the attraction of Claude for Enid, Gladys for Bayliss, is to be called heterosexual, then it is a heterosexuality that shows itself in its compulsory, regulatory form, rather than as a structure of desire. Even as Claude tries to convince himself that marriage "would be the first natural, dutiful, expected thing he had ever done" (122), this fantasy of marriage is punctuated by imagining Enid playing the part of a statue, while "it should be he who suffered, not she" (122). Marriage is, for Claude, one more self-inflicted humiliation. Perhaps for Enid, too; she does not want to marry him—or anyone—and decides to do so as the only way to perform missionary work.[12] In desiring a partner who is sex aversive (in one of the most chilling scenes in the novel, Enid bolts the door on Claude on their wedding night), or who is, perhaps, no more satisfied by mandatory heterosexuality than her husband is, Cather's protagonist experiences a humiliation that finds its parallel when Gladys rejects marriage, choosing the lonely status of the misfit. (Enid finally leaves Claude to go nurse her ailing missionary sister in China.) Thus, whereas the all-male world of battle companions permits Claude to recognize himself as the "least married man" (247) in the group, for Gladys there is only solitude and the projection of her desires and hopes onto Claude. She can only see herself as a sensitive misfit, another "failure."

This gendered difference is glossed over when Nealon treats Gladys's vision of the Frankfort failures as the equivalent of Claude's dream of a "race" of moonchildren; it perhaps explains, too, why Cather's novel does not offer the kind of plot to be found in a novel like Forman Brown's 1933 *Better Angel,* in which a young man from the farm finds like-minded free spirits and comes to recognize his gay identity by moving to New York and *la vie de bohème.*[13] Even if this was, roughly speaking, Cather's path, her life did not conform to a coming-out narrative, and her use of male couples who do not explicitly affirm a sexual tie always registers this in an imaginary identification with and as these men even as she simultaneously underscores by omission any such possibility for women and, by occlusion, the limits of the analogy she implies. (In *Despised and Rejected,* Antoinette, the authorial surrogate, is finally told that she is "the symbol of what has to be sacrificed to the love between man and man" [347].) Claude and Gladys are "meant for each other" not as a couple but as the male and female forms of desires that can be affiliated but can never quite be identical. Likewise, only in the projection of herself into Claude's desire for David can Cather represent how she came to be the novelist she was, surpassing the model of Fisher along the way.

If Claude has a glimpse of like-minded community before his war experience, it comes in the Erlich home in Lincoln, where his first vision of the household, of the Erlich brothers and their male friends, looks almost like a scene in a high-class male bordello: "The room was full of boys and young men, seated on long divans or perched on the arms of easy chairs, and they were all talking at once. On one of the couches a young man in a smoking jacket lay reading as composedly as if he were alone" (34). The solitude of the young man is as significant as the family scene for its suggestion that some secret life is the tie here, one that may be housed within but nonetheless exceeds such normative domesticity. This is a space of ease and largeness of spirit over which the widowed Mrs. Erlich presides. She numbers among her relatives a contralto named, significantly enough, Wilhelmina (another authorial signature); the deep-voiced singer takes an interest in Claude that may be understood less as heterosexual flirtation and more as another form of kinship. Claude is, predictably, not exactly at home in this artistic and free-spirited milieu, but this is, the novelist intimates, where he might belong were he to know himself as she does, were there a world for him. Even if he were to be at home, there would remain something *unheimlich* in such affiliation.

I use the term "unheimlich" to note an important complication to the argument that Nealon makes about a European-American secret community realized by way of French culture: the fact that the Erlichs are German-Americans (Wilhelmina translates Willa into German). Indeed, so too is David Gerhardt, modeled in fact on David Hochstein, a violinist Cather had heard play and whose letters home from the front also served her as a source of inspiration. Hochstein was Emma Goldman's nephew.[14] Changing the name from Hochstein to Gerhardt, Cather leaves undecideable whether her David is Jewish, as is also the case with Mrs. Erlich, modeled on a Mrs. Wiener, in whose home in Red Cloud the young Cather was first initiated into European culture (Mrs. Wiener, a French Jew married to a German Jew, was also the model for Mrs. Rosen in "Old Mrs. Harris"). While Claude's connections to French culture—overseas, and before too, as in the college research paper he writes about Jeanne d'Arc, the other enlivening event in his time in Lincoln—are undeniable, so too are his German attachments (in the face of virulent anti-German sentiment at home, he comes to the rescue of Mrs. Voigt, who runs a restaurant in the train station where he changes on his travels back and forth from Lincoln [200–02]). The vision of an America transformed by Europe embraces Germany as well as France. As unmistakable as it is invisible, Cather embraces the enemy. This unheimlich Heimat (homeland) is also among the novel's secrets. With it, Cather crosses the line into enemy territory, refusing the neat binarisms of a novel like *Despised and Rejected*.

One test case for this claim is a scene that Nealon does not discuss, in which male homosexuality is closest to the surface of the novel. Claude and his battalion have arrived in the French town of Beaufort; the Germans who had been occupying it seem to have fled, and as the villagers gather in the streets in celebration, shots ring out, a woman and young girl are killed. Claude and several fellow soldiers find the rifleman, Claude and Willy Katz breaking into the room from which he has been sniping. Katz dies, a bullet going straight to "his brain, through one of his blue eyes" (348). What Claude sees and hears is also mind-shattering, and provokes a blind response. Just before Claude kills him, the German calls out in "English with no foreign accent"; Claude is "unnerved" (348). What is happening to Claude here is as complicated as the strange symmetry between his being unnerved and Katz getting a bullet through his eye; indeed, the unnerving relationship is right there in Claude's German (Jewish?) blue-eyed buddy.

With his white hands and polished nails, ruby ring on his pinky, and "gorgeous silk-dressing gown," this German officer, Claude sees, is "a very different sort" from the prisoners they had previously captured (he doesn't see that the German officer belongs to that "finer race" of the "sensitive"). The officer's ring, his gold cigarette case, and platinum watch are taken as booty, although not by Claude. Gerhardt forbids despoiling his body of one other item: "Around his neck, hung by a delicate chain, was a miniature case, and in it was a painting, —not, as Bert romantically hoped when he opened it, of a beautiful woman, but of a young man, pale as snow, with blurred forget-me-not eyes" (349). Claude opines that it looks like a poet or perhaps "a kid brother, killed at the beginning of the war" (349), a response overdetermined by the opening sentence of *One of Ours:* "Claude Wheeler opened his eyes before the sun was up and vigorously shook his younger brother, who lay in the other half of the same bed" (3). Claude's eyes may be open, but he is still in the dark when the only bed companion he can imagine is a brother— or a poet, perhaps the figure of Byron in the Erlich drawing room: "This head, with the tie at a rakish angle, drew Claude's attention more than anything else in the room, and for some reason instantly made him wish he lived there" (35).

David assents to Claude's interpretation of the portrait, at any rate says he is "probably" right, but intense, and unspoken exchanges between Claude and David in this scene complicate this agreement, starting with the "disdainful expression" on David's face as he voices his seeming approval. A moment later, David touches Claude, ostensibly to point out to him the inlay work on the German officer's gun handle, and Claude notices "that David looked at him as if he were very much pleased with him" (349); he assumes that it is because he has proved his bravery. Nonetheless, he is puzzled by the way in which David acts "as if something pleasant had happened in this room; where, God knew, nothing had" (349). What is to be made of David's affect, "Gerhardt's flash of high spirits" (349)?

Commentators who have addressed this question have followed the lead of Frederick T. Griffiths, who reads the German as an exemplar of homosexual decadence, a "pervert" to be contrasted with the sublime—and sublimated—homosexuality in the bond between Claude and David.[15] Griffiths cautions that Cather is not simply to be read as endorsing sexual repression (Enid and Bayliss are hardly admirable for precisely that reason), a point that is dropped as his reading of the scene is echoed by Hermione Lee, who argues that it constitutes a denial of explicit homosexuality and serves to indicate that the relationship between Claude and Gerhardt "is meant to transcend erotic homosexual feelings" (181). James Woodress also makes this point, adding however the important detail, culled from a letter to Dorothy Canfield Fisher, that Cather had heard of just such an incident from an American captain who, like Claude, had not understood that the painting in the locket was the image of a lover. "She liked the naivete of the American officer," Woodress paraphrases Cather's letter, "and gave his innocence to Claude."[16]

David's pleasure is Cather's, the pleasure, once again, of knowing more about Claude than he knows about himself, pleasure taken at his expense, a cherishing of innocence that saves Claude from knowing what would follow were he to know himself. For David to know this is to put him in the position of the German. Even as he agrees to Claude's reading he knows that it is wrong. "Probably" is not "certainly." The disdain read on his face (by Claude? by the narrator?) corresponds exactly to the affect that Nealon argues is generated throughout the novel, Cather's loving sadism. Gerhardt agrees to Claude's interpretation and disdains it at the same time. When he touches Claude and draws his attention to the inlay work on the gun handle, this serves as a displaced site of acknowledgment, disdain replaced by a touch, the picture by the gun. Rather than gazing at the boy lover, Claude is drawn to admire the artistry of the handle. This may serve as a recoding of war (an artistic idealization); while overtly, the scene recoils from homosexuality in its portrayal of the decadent and sadistic German, the inlaid handle makes the weapon a work of art that condenses these qualities. It is a real question whether this displacement leaves much of the German behind, whether there is not a sadistic luxuriance in handling the gun. A similar implication can be read in the fact that the German speaks unaccented English; for what is disturbing is the potential for identification and recognition for Claude to which he shuts his eyes. If the German is Gerhardt's double, Claude is the boy in the picture.

What I would suggest, therefore, is that Cather's scene, which can easily be read as her very painful attempt to deflect a homosexual understanding of the relationship of Claude and David, also, and at the same time, mobilizes the very qualities of sadism and decadence for that relationship. The ferocity that Cather invites—the recognition of homosexuality as sadism—comes from knowing what could be expected if this scene had ended by Claude and David recognizing and announcing their recognition through the figure of the dead German and his boy lover: that her readers would have recoiled in the affirmation of an affiliation that crosses the battle line of friend and enemy. If Claude's innocence saves him from this, the novelist does not spare him. The release of affect—of David's weird pleasure in the scene—is not merely his pleasure in keeping Claude innocent, or in making their love a matter that can be confirmed in a touch, deflected to an appreciation of inlay, but not enunciated overtly. It is also the pleasure and relief involved in avoiding a knowledge that must remain unspoken, that is unspeakable. The release and relief is the product of a life-saving dissociation, a split, and the excess of emotion suggests how complicated this form of sadomasochistic self-saving and self-killing feeling is. It reflects the split within Cather that has her on both sides of the line: knowing with David, yet simultaneously cherishing Claude and preserving unspoken yet palpable the thing not said. Each man kills the thing he loves. Moreover, David's joy can be compared to the affect demanded by battle, an exaltation Claude experiences, and, as we will see shortly, a subject fully in focus in Barker's novels.

Cather's representational strategies here bear some comparison with *Despised and Rejected*. In Fitzroy's novel, the homosexuality of its protagonists is a secret, an open secret, it turns out at the end of the novel, when a fellow pacifist articulates that vision of a future in the hands of those "masters of the race" (348) already cited. By relegating questions of sexuality to secrecy, Fitzroy makes the opprobrium of homosexuality something suffered privately. As her Antoinette hears from Dennis about the torment of his desire, she thinks that "it was a shame that he should have to suffer so horribly from the consciousness of his abnormality," continuing to compare his situation to hers: "her own had never caused her the slightest uneasiness" (218). While this gendered difference implicitly endorses a division between men and women on public/private grounds (the unthinkableness of lesbian desire rendering it thereby unproblematic), this perhaps explains why Fitzroy represents sexual issues as personal ones. Yet the torturous silences in Cather's depictions, juxtaposed as they are to the representation of the German officer, suggest a public face for homosexuality, one that conditions her loving sadism as a response that comes close to restating the terms of abjection. Neither in its potential to establish kinship, nor in its relationship to social injunctions, is homosexuality in *One of Ours* simply a private matter. The secret lodged and claimed is, as the novel's title says, one of ours.

The kind of pressure under which Cather writes can be seen if we turn to Barker and to her complicated depictions of relationships between homosexuality and the war, a subject on the table almost from the opening page of the trilogy, as Rivers worries about Sassoon's impending arrival at Craiglockhart, a supposed "conchie" to be added to the "cowards, shirkers, scrimshankers and degenerates" (*Regeneration*, 4) already there. Rivers's terms are, of course, not his own, but represent a prevailing view about those with so-called shell shock, and "degenerate" is the coded racialized term which houses an etiology for homosexuality among its various meanings (this undoubtedly lies behind the racialized vocabulary of Fitzroy and Cather).[17] By the end of the first novel, and in the context of Sassoon's open acknowledgement of his homosexuality, Rivers worries that Sassoon's protest against the war will catch him up in a parliamentary campaign against homosexuals led by Noel Pemberton Billing. (The campaign was fueled by a book whose author claimed to know the names of 47,000 English homosexuals and lesbians who were acting as German infiltrators; and by a libel trial brought by the actress Maud Allan against those who defamed her for her part in a production of Wilde's *Salome*.)[18] *The Eye in the Door* has these events as its continual backdrop, and they enter the plot when threats of blackmail are launched against one of the characters. Barker shows that there was a war front at home, and that the campaign against conscientious objectors, socialists, and militant workers fastened on homosexuals as an easily mobilized rallying point. (This plot is not to be found in Fitzroy, where homosexuality is a secret.)

Barker's point is not simply to expose this mechanism, but to recognize its place in war mentality. That is, she sees both why this campaign was necessary for the war effort as well as its role in explaining cases of mental breakdown at Craiglockhart and elsewhere. Barker represents Rivers early in *Regeneration* thinking out these connections in terms of gender:[19]

In leading his patients to understand that breakdown was nothing to be ashamed of, that horror and fear were the inevitable responses to the trauma of war and better acknowledged than suppressed, that feelings of tenderness for other men were natural and right, that tears were an acceptable and helpful part of grieving, he was setting himself against the whole tenor of their upbringing. They'd been trained to identify emotional repression as the essence of manliness. (*Regeneration*, 48)

In *The Eye in the Door*, Rivers puts the connection to sexuality speculatively and succinctly in answer to his patient Manning's question why his homosexuality is the lightning rod for blackmail: "In war there's this enormous glorification of love between men, and yet at the same time it arouses anxiety" (156). While this could be taken as granted, the thin line between the acceptable bonds of male homosocial relationship always being policed for the possibility of transgression into forbidden territory, it could also be said that war exacerbates this ordinary situation of terror.[20] Or, that it brings to a breaking point the mechanisms of control; this is Rivers's paraphrase of the "strict Freudian view of war neurosis": "the experience of an all-male environment, with a high level of emotional intensity, together with the experience of battle, arouses homosexual and sadistic impulses that are normally repressed. In vulnerable men—obviously those in whom the repressed desires are particulary strong—this leads to breakdown" (*Eye in the Door*, 158).[21] Rivers sees that war demands a splitting even as it fosters precisely the affects it wishes to repudiate. And he also sees, perhaps here too following a strict Freudian view of the necessary discontent of civilization, that the most prized accomplishments—of scientific detachment, of anthropological observation, of the maintenance of the line between the doctor and his patient—demand just this same solicitation and dissociation. It is this dissociation that allows men to kill each other on the battlefield and at home, and it seems ultimately impossible to draw the line of distinction between the value of civilized restraint and the unleashing of mass destruction.

This recognition guides Rivers in an early conversation with Sassoon, in which he urges him to retract his protest against the war as a way of safeguarding his sexuality. Sassoon replies:

"What you're really saying is, if I *can't* conform in one area of life, then I *have* to conform in the others. Not just the surface things, *everything*. Even against my conscience. Well, I can't live like that." He paused, then added, "*Nobody* should live like that." (*Regeneration*, 205)

Rivers, whose most important contribution to the literature on war neuroses Barker succinctly represents in his thoughts about derepression (he sought to make it possible for his patients to remember and work through rather than to deny the trauma), at the same time counsels if not exactly repression, then the necessity of the regime of the closet. Barker interprets this, in fact, to imply that Rivers himself was homosexual (he lives the life of outward conformity that Sassoon disparages), and that his success with his young male patients had everything to do with that. (Rivers was also similarly successful with his male students.) Just as dissociation is a saving and killing solution, Rivers's success at "curing" is the same technique that produces the problem, here again brought to crisis, since what Rivers aimed to do was to make it possible for men to return to battle. This dilemma is represented in the "cure" of Billy Prior, who arrives mute at Craiglockhart (the hysterical symptom part of the way the trauma has been repressed), and who leaves split in two; taking up a position in military intelligence, which he consciously subverts, his other half ruthlessly does the job. That part of himself remains totally unavailable to consciousness until Rivers intervenes.[22]

For Rivers, Barker implies, what remained unspeakable (and perhaps unknown) was the homosexuality that enabled him. This rings true reading Rivers's writing, which departs from a strict Freudian view on several counts. Rivers, for example, believed that the function of dreams was to provide, at levels unavailable to consciousness, solutions to present conflicts; acknowledging the Freudian tenet of the centrality of sexuality to the unconscious, Rivers, however, insisted that this was not a general truth, claiming that sexuality was not central to the war neuroses suffered by his patients; nor was it to be found in his own unconscious (his dreams, he claims, mainly concern professional difficulties [*Conflict and Dream*, 110–11]).[23] Barker's writing thus performs a complicated reading of

Rivers, leaving tacit and protected just what he protected (his sexuality), and recognizing why this remained necessary to keep him from breaking down. Or, rather, the breakdown is depicted at the level of consciousness at which even Rivers came to recognize it, as he found himself in the "humorous" position, as he put it in *Conflict and Dream* (168), of being converted to pacifism even as he convinced Sassoon to return to the war. In this book, Rivers represents Sassoon as patient B, someone who "was not suffering from any form of psycho-neurosis, but was in the hospital on account of his adoption of a pacifist attitude while on leave from active service" (167), and ponders what would result if his "task of converting a patient from his 'pacifist errors' to the conventional attitude should have as a result my own conversion to his point of view" (168).

This is the context adduced in the analysis of Rivers's own two-part "pacifist dream" in *Conflict and Dream,* to which I turn now. In keeping with the notion that the dream solves a conflict, Rivers reads the pacifism in the dream as an ego-driven expression of his desire to renew scientific work and contact with German colleagues. The analysis of the dream accords to Sassoon nothing more than the circumstantial trace, the daily residue of their discussions. It insists that an umbrella and bowler hat in the dream are not phallic symbols, but rather signs of the civilian status that Rivers wishes to resume, a desire to put off the uniform that requires him to do the conventional work of returning his patients to war. Scrutinizing the dream, Rivers worries the question of how he is clothed, an issue that arises for him particularly through the figure of someone in the dream who he insists is German, although he speaks English, a man, otherwise unrecognizable, bandaged, and with his arm in a sling, whom Rivers encounters after climbing a stairway and entering through a portal marked "Physiologisches Practicum" (165–66).

It is, of course, impossible to analyze this dream thoroughly along strict Freudian lines, but tempting to try. Who is the bandaged figure at the top of the stairs? Might it be Henry Head, with whom Rivers conducted physiological experiments that involved cutting a nerve in Head's arm and the years-long tracing of its path of regeneration? The figure in the dream has his arm in a sling, after all, and the primary scene of Rivers's English physiological practice were the experiments with Head. In these experiments in nerve regeneration, Head's penis served as the locus for testing normal responses. Might the choice of this spot have been overdetermined by Head's name? (Rivers "explains" the choice by arguing that the glans penis has only primitive neurological responses, a rather loaded "scientific" characterization.) [24] Can Rivers's physiological practice be entirely shielded from an erotic component? or his dream from a sexual reading?

What, moreover, is to be made of the confusion in tongues in this dream? What does it mean for a figure in a dream to *be* German but to speak English, if not, as in *One of Ours,* to be making a kind of connection and disconnection at once, perhaps in this instance from Rivers's English physiological endeavors to his German psychological ones, a mind-body connection of the kind that Rivers sought to unfold as a psychologist. Could the room at the top of the stairs be a scene of psychoanalysis? If so, might not the "German" be the English-speaking Siegfried (with his overdetermined name)? What is it that pacifism codes in the dream? Why does it speak two languages at once? Why is it, in analyzing the dream, that the one symbolic detail Rivers does puzzle is the question of what he and the other figures in the dream are wearing? Could Rivers's answer—the desire to return to civilian status, bowler and umbrella included—not disguise and clothe another desire: to remove his clothes?

In *Conflict and Dream,* and in greater length in *Instinct and the Unconscious,* Rivers presents an aspect of his psychology, also represented by Barker, that seems of significance here: his lack of the capacity to visualize. Rivers was certain that he had not been born that way since he could recall in exact visual detail the home in which he spent his earliest years. He could remember everything except the upstairs where, he assumes, he saw something so frightening that it caused him to lose the ability to visualize. Rivers has no clue what the trauma might have been (Barker supplies a scene in which he sees the portrait of his wounded namesake—a scene of threatened castration [*Ghost Road,* 96]). The pacifist dream culminates in a room at the top of the stairs in which a wounded man, German and English at once, awaits a Rivers who has doffed his uniform. This does not tell us what Rivers saw as a boy, but it seems likely to add to the homosexual aspect that I have been adducing in his dream of pacifism, whether we suppose that Sassoon was the wounded man, or take the desire to return to scientific work to have a phallic route back to Head. My point is not to declare some private truth about Rivers, but rather to see disclosed here lines of affiliation like those that Nealon reads in Cather and which are also to be found in the complex associations Barker traces of a war effort opposed by "an unholy alliance of socialists, sodomites, and shop stewards," as one of Barker's characters puts it (*Eye in the Door,* 48). The avowed (and dissociated) aims of the return to collegial relations with Germans, or the resumption of scientific work, let alone the comedy of changing places with Sassoon (Rivers is, in effect, having his patient's dream; Sassoon assiduously took Rivers to be a father figure, an equally convenient way to translate the erotics of the relationship[25]), are not unrelated to sexual impulses or to the possibility of a secret community that imagines some alternative mode of social organization to war.

These speculations prompted by Rivers's pacifist dream could be put beside the logic of the converging plot lines in Barker that involve Rivers and his two patients, Sassoon and Prior. Rivers worries over and again about returning Sassoon to the war front, fears that in arguing Sassoon out of his pacifist protest—and thus safeguarding his homosexual secret—he will also have given Sassoon no reason to live; he is producing the split, demanding repression and its displacement into aggressivity directed at Germans and at himself, endorsing the joy-in-battle that can be compared to David Gerhardt's weird exaltation over the corpse of the German homosexual officer. Thus, after Sassoon returns wounded by a shot to his head from a British soldier who mistook him for a German, Rivers attempts to get Sassoon to see that his reckless behavior on the battlefield is suicidal, a reading that Sassoon refuses:

> "You stand up in the middle of No Man's Land, in the morning, the sun rising, you take off your helmet, you turn to face the German lines, and you tell me you weren't trying to get killed."
>
> Siegfried shook his head. "I've told you I was happy. . . . Yes I was happy most of the time, I suppose mainly because I've succeeded in cutting off the part of me that hates it." (*Eye in the Door,* 222–23)

Rivers protests this, although this joy is necessarily a part of the cure, and, alone beside the sleeping Sassoon, he takes further stock of the situation:

Siegfried had always coped with the war by being two people: the anti-war poet and pacifist; the bloodthirsty, efficient company commander. The dissociation couldn't be called pathological, since experience gained in one state was available to the other. Not just *available:* it was the serving officer's experience that furnished the raw material, the ammunition, if you liked, for the poems. More importantly, and perhaps more ambiguously, that experience of bloodshed supplied the moral authority for the pacifist's protest: a *soldier's* declaration." (*Eye in the Door,* 233)

There seems no way out of the impasse when self-destruction is also life-saving.

Parallel to this, Billy Prior's unconscious half (the part of him that announces "I was born two years ago. In a shell-hole in France. I have no father" [*Eye in the Door,* 240]) betrays a pacifist he had promised to protect; once Billy consciously regains this side of himself and the dissociation is healed, he returns to war; two days before he is killed, he sends Rivers a note: "My nerves are in perfect working order. By which I mean that in my present situation the only sane thing to do is run away, and I will not do it" (*Ghost Road,* 254). Healthy and divided, dissociated, and knowing the dissociation: the Rivers cure is mockingly, sadistically turned back on the doctor with whom Billy openly, aggressively flirts in this letter, as he always had in person. Sexually, Billy lives a double life; engaged to Sarah Lumb, a woman he loves, he continues to have sex with Manning, the married man whose closet has been penetrated. ("For somebody like Manning, profoundly committed to living a double life, the revelation that both sides of his life were visible to unknown eyes must have been like having the door to the innermost part of one's identity smashed open" [*Eye in the Door,* 155]). Billy's closet is the secret self that must destroy his pacifist friend; likewise, Billy's homosexuality is always lined with sadistic impulses. But so too is Rivers's; his eye penetrates Manning, and his loving sadism drives his relationship with Sassoon and Billy Prior.

Although Barker is explicit about Sassoon's homosexuality as well as Owen's, she never actually represents either of them having sex. Their erotic spheres include Sassoon's intimate relationship with Rivers, Owen's with Sassoon as they collaborated on drafts of his poems, or the homosexual/literary circle of Robbie Ross in which

Sassoon moved and to which he gave Owen entrée. Sex between men is represented only through Billy Prior. Fittingly, he translates Rivers's perceptions about war into a more graphic register; "the whole bloody western front's a wanker's paradise" (*Ghost Road,* 177) he notes in his diary. A few days before he dies, Billy has sex for the last time: a French boy catches his eye; meeting him later, their communications reduced to gestures (Billy's schoolboy French is not up the French boy's slang), when Billy doesn't immediately respond to what appears to be a request for cigarettes, the boy says something in German. "I suppose it should have disgusted me," Billy notes in his diary, about being mistaken for the enemy, but "it had the opposite effect" (*Ghost Road,* 247). The boy leads him into a wooded area, bends over a tree, Billy tongues his asshole and imagines his tongue reaching "on the other side of that tight French sphincter, German spunk" before he fucks the boy and sucks him off (248). Billy also finds this a comical scene, knows there is no German semen still lodged in the boy's rectum, just as knew he ought to have been upset at being misrecognized as a German, and yet was and is excited. If Billy imagines that in fucking the boy he is fucking the German who had previously fucked him, his aggressivity also turns upon himself (as a boy Billy had been paid to bend over); the German he is fucking through the boy is also himself, as the boy (mis)recognized, addressing him in German; it is also the pacifist friend whom he betrayed.

The recoils in these texts—in Rivers's dream, in Barker's depiction of Rivers's relationship to his patients, in the saving/killing dissociations of Billy Prior—could be compared to Cather's treatment of the German officer. Rather than returning there, however, I would recall another scene in *One of Ours.* In France, in the midst of war, "four young men, all more or less naked" are bathing in a muddy shellhole (295). Claude joins them. This looks like it might realize the moonlit bathing scene with its revery about a finer race; instead, as Claude "slid[es] into the pool beside Gerhardt" (296), he hits "bottom," disturbing a German graveyard which sends fumes bubbling up to the surface. The innocent bathing scene has turned in the direction of Billy Prior's sex-scene, and the men in Claude's company put up a mocking sign, "No Public Bathing! Private Beach/ C. Wheeler, Co. B 2-th Inf'ty" (296): this dirty hole is only for Claude. Yet the sign erected might be compared to Cather's explanation for the title of her critical essays, *Not Under Forty*, "The title of this book is meant to be 'arresting' only in the literal sense, like signs put up for motorists: 'ROAD UNDER REPAIR,' etc. It means that the book will have little interest for people under forty years of age. The world broke in two in 1922 or thereabouts . . ." (v).[26] 1922 is, of course, the year *One of Ours* was published; the dissociation toward which Cather points, as well as the road she hopes to repair, connect the doubled necessities of the unsayable. If she, like Barker in her representation of Billy caught in the loop of sadomasochism, could appear to be endorsing the strict Freudian view, lining up homosexuality and sadism, she also reveals that this equation is not the truth of homosexuality—not, that is, the explanation why homosexuality should be stigmatized, extirpated—but is nonetheless (im)properly recognized as an undoing of the social order. To the question that Leo Bersani poses in *Homos*, "Should a homosexual be a good citizen?" (113), Cather responds, like him, in the negative, not so much in a programmatic or ethical way, not in answer to a "should," but rather to a "could."

To close the comparison I've been making between Cather and Barker, I recall a previous citation—the conversation that Rivers has with Manning—this time to complete what was left suspended:

> "In war there's this enormous glorification of love between men, and yet at the same time it arouses anxiety. Is it the right kind of love? Well, one way to make sure it's the right kind is to make public disapproval of the other kind crystal clear. And then there's pleasure in killing—"
> Manning looked shocked. "I don't know that—"
> "No, I meant civilians. Vicarious, but real nevertheless. And in the process sadistic impulses are aroused that would normally be repressed, and that also causes anxiety." (*Eye in the Door*, 156)

Homosexual sadism, so-called, is, in fact, homophobic sadism.

The context for Rivers's conversation with Manning is a performance of *Salome* sponsored by Ross; in the men's room afterwards, Manning meets the man who claimed to know of the 47,000 homosexual/lesbian pacifist infiltrators unmanning English society, followers of the "cult of the clitoris" headed by Salome-performer Maud Allan. The scene offers a reading of the play, and the question

of why the sadistic Salome is the site of Wilde's authorial investment. Manning's wife had opined that the attack on Allan was to
use her lesbianism as a cover for anxieties about women in general,
especially women entering the workforce during the war. Barker
endorses this (Rivers agrees to this interpretation), but she also sees
(and allows Manning to articulate) Wilde's cross-gender "identification with Salome" (*Eye in the Door,* 156), one based on the understanding that misogyny and homophobia go hand-in-hand. More
than that: Salome is the product of the hatred unleashed upon her,
the specter of the awful phallic woman at the same time as she represents a killing love for men. This reading underscores Barker's own
identifications with the male-male relations that are central to her
novelistic enterprise, a point which must remind us of Cather as
well. It prompts further consideration of Barker's relationship to
the two writers in her novels, Sassoon and Owen, who provide her
narrative frame.

An older but prevailing view on the question of the homosexuality of these writers can be extrapolated from Paul Fussell's influ-
ential and much-cited *The Great War and Modern Memory.*[27] Noting,
for instance, the importance of the figure of the "dream friend," the
"ideal companion" in *Memoirs of a Fox Hunting Man,* the first volume of Sassoon's autobiographical trilogy, *Memoirs of George Sherston,* and valuably connecting this figure with Rivers, Fussell pauses
knowingly to comment that Sassoon's books might as easily be
titled "Men Without Women" (102).[28] This all-male world is fueled
by what Fussell calls homoeroticism, which he defines as "a sublimated (i.e., "chaste") form of temporary homosexuality" (272; the
kind Robert Graves said he had); when Fussell comes to consider
authors whose homosexuality seems something more than situa-
tional—Owen, for example—he praises his poems by saying that
they "finally transcended his leanings towards mere homosexuality"
(296). This is odd praise in a book that wants to see through literary
depictions and tropes to the real, as in the exemplary vocabulary
list that Fussell offers: generalizing prevarications like "*blood, terror, agony, madness, shit, cruelty, murder, sell-out, pain* and *hoax*" covering over such realities as "*legs blown off, intestines gushing out over his
hands, screaming all night, bleeding to death from the rectum,* and the like*"
(169–70). Fussell's list houses an evident plot: the truth of war is
castration and the sodomization of soldiers, covered over by a situa-

tional homoerotics as eviscerated as the prettifying language of Sassoon's nostalgic and retrospective recountings of his life; when a poet starts telling the truth, as when David Jones drops the language of chivalric romance in *In Parenthesis* to focus on " 'that shit Major Lillywhite' " or " 'that cissy from Brigade,' " then, Fussell opines, "the humanity of the poem seizes the reader" (154). Nothing so human as a good dose of homophobia; nothing so fine as a poet who gets past his "temporary" or "mere" homosexuality. Let us not recognize that Sassoon's entire writing practice after the war was a sustained act of unresolved mourning.

More recently, homosexuality has been seen as fully consequential for Owen and Sassoon, but as a problem. Thus, in a study recently adduced as the "notable exception" to the failure of criticism to consider the place of homosexuality as a necessary part of the analysis of the work of Sassoon or Owen, Adrian Caesar's *Taking It Like a Man* paints a picture of the intense discomfort of Owen and Sassoon with their homosexuality, and regards the writing of war poetry as the means through which they worked out their conflict.[29] For Caesar the conflict takes the form of an assumed passivity/femininity (of homosexuality and of poetry making) compensated for by the masculinism of war making. The poet is riven by a passivity/activity divide that Caesar reads as a sadomasochistic one, and the war poem is a solution in which sadism is vented upon the enemy (or upon those who send the poet into war and death) while masochism is embraced by the valuation of suffering. "Fighting is the means to glorious suffering, to the 'greater love' of martyrdom and to homo-erotic solidarity" (155), Caesar paraphrases one of Owen's poems (in fact, this is his reading of every poem he considers). Caesar finds some of these poems "vicious" and "sinister" (terms he uses in discussing Sassoon's "The Kiss"), especially when women are targeted as unthinking supporters of war (as is certainly sometimes the case); here the poet's lashing out at his own femininity (i. e., homosexuality) takes women as an object, Sassoon's "The Kiss" displaying "self-hating fear of male sexuality and a fear and hatred of women" (78). If Caesar is correct in the reading he offers, it is difficult to see how anything more than self-hatred could motivate Cather or Barker to be interested in male homosexuality.

Barker points out, however, in a fictionalized conversation between Manning and Rivers in which they discuss Sassoon's "The Kiss," that his disquieting lines about the bayonet, gendered female, and savage ("Sweet Sister, grant your soldier this:/ That in good fury he may feel/ The body where he sets his heel/ Quail from your downward darting kiss"[30]), could easily be drawn from phrases from the handbook of training: "It's one long stream of sexual innuendo. *Stick him in the gooleys. No more little fritzes*" (*Eye in the Door*, 159). War activity, the use of the bayonet in particular, is sexualized, sadistic, aggressive. The plot of emasculating men through the phallic female bayonet is misogynist and homophobic and well within a heterosexual arsenal, even as it is the case that sadistic and homoerotic energies are mobilized.[31] Indeed, if, as Leo Bersani writes in *Homos,* it should be possible to trace "a theory of love based not on our assertions of how different and how much better we are than those who would do away with us (because we are neither that different nor that much better), but one that would instead be grounded in the very contradictions, impossibilities, and antagonisms brought to light by any serious genealogy of desire" (108), what must be emphasized in recognizing a shared ground of desire is the difference Bersani merely notes in passing: between us and "those who would do away with us." This is something lost when Caesar assumes that Sassoon's depictions of women kept ignorant about war, or Owen's supposedly invidious comparisons of homo- and heterosexual desire or his depiction of women, as in "The Kind Ghosts," taking pleasure in piling up male corpses, are simply examples of misogyny rather than attempts to move women to question war ideology (most of the poems usually cited are ones Owen regularly sent to his mother, and it is from his letters to her that his most explicit misogynist statements are gleaned) — and that such aims are congruent with attacks on civilians in general, whose violence Caesar also deplores. These are not antiwar poets, he claims, because they are so bellicose. "Owen is not a pacifist and his poems aren't either," he declares (158). Sassoon wasn't protesting conditions on the Somme, he was bewailing the death of David Thomas (74; Thomas was one of those embodied dream friends, the Dick Tiltwood of the Sherston books).

It's hard to see how one could have been a pacifist under the conditions that Caesar stipulates, although one might find his critique pertinent to a novel like *Despised and Rejected,* which, in making absolute the difference between pacifists and warmongers, falls readily into an endorsement of suffering as well as into a heroicizing of that position that depends upon the very militancy it deplores: "you are always my comrade in battle, my comrade in love," Alan says to David (289). It could be argued that the pacifism of Owen and Sassoon, soldiers both, or Cather's or Barker's writing of war novels, insists upon complications lost on Caesar, who claims for himself the only possible moral position, one that decries protest that becomes "bellicose," or that faults Sassoon and Owen for their unresolved homosexuality. Aiming to be sympathetic, Caesar comments on how difficult it was to be a homosexual then (as if it were simple now), and seems to think there must be some way to be a proper and contented homosexual, rather than one riven by sadomasochistic impulses. It would seem that there is here somehow a belief that heterosexuals are immune from these impulses, as when Caesar contrasts "the creativity of Eros" to the greater love of Owen's poem of that title, which, he claims, glorifies through male-male erotics an ethos of suffering and violence, a "morbid" sadomasochism (154). Such a point manages entirely to fail to recognize the place of homosexuals in a phobic society, and seems close to the view in Dominic Hibbard's studies of Owen, which simply collapse homosexuality into sadomasochism.[32] These critics seem to have forgotten the kinds of facts about the psychology of desire to which Bersani alludes and which any page in Freud chosen at random might remind them is never unfraught. Who ever desired without there being an element of aggressivity involved? Who ever felt love without also feeling pain? As Freud says, concluding his 1915 essay "Reflections upon War and Death": "It might be said that we owe the fairest flowers of our love-life to the reaction against the hostile impulse which we divine in our breast."[33] If Freud is to be faulted here, it is not for his recognition of the inevitable twinning of love and aggressivity, but for his collapse of desire into the singular; "we" are not all the same in this, and social positioning has everything to do with that. A woman or a lesbian or a gay man might well recognize that Freud's universalizing "we" is tilted in favor of heterosexual men, as is apparent in the metaphorics of the defloration of "the fairest flowers of our [sic] love-life." And, as Freud does not say, it is that plot that gets transferred onto "aggressive" women and "passive" men.

In denouncing the sadism and violence of war poetry, and laying the blame for it on sexual conflict, Caesar makes a psychological reading that is blind to crucial distinctions: the real sadism of a war, which can scarcely be said to have been launched by or for homosexuals, is slighted in favor of the role of sadomasochistic fantasy; the aggressivity of representation is taken to be more reprehensible than the violence of "normality"—the moral fervor of campaigns against homosexuals, lesbians, pacifists, the entire war effort *at home.* Caesar seems blind to the overwhelming pain of loss and to the erotics of melancholia. Sadomasochism is not simply a pathology; not only can it be "explained," at the level of sexual fantasy it needs no excuse. Indeed, were one to follow Leo Bersani, it could be argued that such refusals of community standards pose the most radical rejection of sociality and *its* lethal energies.

Take, for example, Sassoon's relations with one of his men, Jowett. "I wrote a poem about Jowett," Sassoon tells Rivers in *The Eye in the Door.* "Not that he'll ever know. He was asleep. He looked as if he were dead.' A silence. 'It's odd, isn't it, how one can feel fatherly, not exploiting the situation or even being tempted to, and yet there's this other current. And I don't think one invalidates the other'" (230). What Sassoon doesn't add, of course, is that he is also forbidden to connect these two currents (this road must remain under repair, dissociated), that to be caught having sex would end his military career, that it's dangerous even to be looking, safe only when the boy is asleep. In *Sherston's Progress,* Jowett, renamed Howitt, is one of the "dream companions" embodied. "Handsome Howitt asleep on the floor, with his moody sensual face and large limbs. (As usual he looks as if he were dead.)" (172). Dream companions: first, like Claude Wheeler, he thought such a figure would never be possible except in dreams; then he saw all of them die, and thought he would never find another (Cather has Gerhardt die along with Claude; Billy Prior dies a moment after he watches Owen die):

The Dug-Out

Why do you lie with your legs ungainly huddled,
And one arm bent across your sullen, cold,
Exhausted face? It hurts my heart to watch you,
Deep-shadow'd from the candle's glittering gold;
And you wonder why I shake you by the shoulder;

Drowsy, you mumble and sigh and turn your head . . .
You are too young to fall asleep for ever;
And when you sleep you remind me of the dead.
(*War Poems,* p. 129)

It is possible, perhaps inevitable, to assume that the beloved object
is dead in this poem before we discover that he is only asleep; it
is possible, too, to find that the pathos of the poem is driven by
sadism, that the beloved is made dead as part of the act of cherishing. But it is impossible to ignore that handsome Howitt may well
soon be dead, lying sullen, cold, and exhausted; that the speaker has
seen and will never forget having seen young men killed in the war;
that he has been forbidden any touch beyond the one he offers here
(unless we imagine in the ellipsis of the poem that forbidden contact has taken place); that the war that promotes such tenderness
also forbids it. That war goes on all the time, everywhere, even in
the sympathetic ministrations of a doctor like Rivers or a literary
critic like Caesar. The candle glitters gold, but this is in the shadows;
it has already, always already been assigned to death; nonproduc-
tive sex. In memorializing this love it is shaken into life, valued and
cherished; this is not to embrace sacrifice, but to acknowledge sacrifice as the condition under which this love exists. This poem holds
out for its readers, any readers faced with the denial of the value of
their lives, the possibility of an affiliation which must protest these
conditions of existence.

There is one further supposition that a reader like Caesar might
bring to a poem like "The Dug-Out," and it is answered in *Regenera-*
tion, when Barker has Rivers refuse the notion that male tenderness
necessarily involves feminization, and that such supposed feminization represents an aggressive usurpation of women. "He distrusted
the implication that nurturing, even when done by a man, remains
female, as if the ability were in some way borrowed, or even stolen,
from women—a sort of moral equivalent of the *couvade.* If that were
true, then there was really very little hope" (107). If it were true,
it would be impossible for Barker to write as she does, living inside her most introspective characters, almost all of whom are male,
ventriloquizing Rivers's thoughts, writing Billy Prior's diary. Impossible for Cather to assume her position of loving sadism toward

Claude in *One of Ours*. Commentators, however, have been quick to diagnose Claude's "problem" (what is the matter with me, he asks over and again in the novel) as feminization, his passivity faced with Enid's missionary zeal (she tends him through illness), his assumption of a feminized position as he nurses men struck down by influenza on the ship crossing the Atlantic.[34] One limit to this kind of reading is noted by Frederick Griffiths: that there are a series of women starting with Jeanne d'Arc, and including a female pilot—a German—who do not fulfill the "feminine" role, and who may well be sites of admiration for Cather, indications that she does not assume conventional gender. The marriage most in focus in the novel is that of Claude's parents, a bullying sadistic father, a suffering mother. Almost the first we see of Claude, he is nursing a wounded mare, abused by one of the rough farmhands his father so likes (mainly, it seems, because they pain Claude). Claude certainly suffers with these suffering females and identifies with them. But it would be impossible to say that Cather endorses their situation, or that she faults Claude for this mode of identification.

Indeed, she seems to go far in the opposite direction, almost to be endorsing the very misogyny that it is claimed inevitably accompanies male homosexuality. Among the men with whom Claude bonds is the womanizer Victor Morse; after dinner with him, Victor proposes that they go out to look for dates, but Claude wants to return to the hospital to see how Fanning, the young man he had nursed aboard ship, is doing. Fanning . . . "that ass!" Victor exclaims (267), making clear what Claude is choosing instead of "girls." Claude does not get to the hospital because his eye is drawn to a one-armed man in the street and the woman with whom he walks arm-in-arm; he watches them as they cling together "in an embrace so long and still that it was like death" (270). The next day at the hospital, Claude discovers who this man is—a victim of shell shock, "a psychopathic case" (272), he has forgotten one aspect of his past entirely, the women in it, "even the girl he was going to marry." "Maybe he's fortunate in that," Claude replies (273), no doubt envying and identifying with the wounded man's dissociation. Dr. Trueman (what's in a name?), who had prescribed Claude's nursing regime with Fanning, turns to him "affectionately" and urges him not "to talk like that the minute you land in this country" (273); he shouldn't be saying such scandalous "French" things.

War Requiems

His worry is that Claude is coming close to articulating the secret that must remain secret. Yet what is being repudiated here is not women per se, but women with missions like Enid, those who want to make whole men like the amputee with his shell shock—men like Claude—by making them straight. That is not Cather's mission either.

To draw some threads of this essay together, a fortuitous conjunction. Sassoon, after the war, found another of his dream companions and, from 1927 to 1931, had his only sustained sexual relationship with another man. The man was Stephen Tennant, twenty years his junior, a rich aristocrat who lived a life devoted entirely to pleasure, a model for Evelyn Waugh's satiric picture of 1920s youths, their party-going and play-acting and endless posing. While his biographer insists that Tennant was a witty man, the wittiest thing he records him saying is perhaps his response as a child to his father asking what he wished to be when he grew up. "A Great Beauty, Sir," Tennant supposedly replied.[35] It was the only thing he worked at; a gifted but desultory draftsman (he doodled endlessly in the margins of his voluminous diaries), writer of an unfinished Firbank-inspired novel, constantly redecorating his house, Tennant spent most of his time on his clothing, his costumes, his hair, nails, and makeup. He was, in a word, an outrageous queen. But hardly, simply passive. Here is the scene as he disembarked from the *Berengaria* in New York in 1934, orchids in hand. " 'Pin 'em on!' shouted a tough customs officer. 'Oh, have you got a pin?' exclaimed Stephen. 'What a wonderful welcome! I've searched the whole ship for one.' Quite out of his stride the burly customs man fumbled behind the lapel of his coat and handed Stephen what he wanted. 'You're a darling!' cried Stephen. 'What a lovely start to my visit! You kind, kind creature!' " (191).

A year later, Tennant arrived in New York again, this time at the invitation of Willa Cather. He had begun corresponding with her in 1926, sending her a letter of admiration to which she had responded. At the end of the first round of visits, before she sent him off to the Shattuck Inn, Cather gave him what she identified as one of Tom Outland's turquoises. Her parting gift was a copy of *One of Ours*. Tom Outland, like Claude, died in the Great War.

What is to be made of this strange conjunction? It is easy enough to imagine what Sassoon saw in Tennant, but what of Cather, especially the Cather usually assumed to find effeminate men repellent and supposedly so secretive about her sexuality? What can this warm welcome suggest if not a meeting across gender, an identification of an effeminate man and a masculine woman?[36] It was one furthered even after Cather's death when Edith Lewis took up Tennant, paying for extravagant vacations for them together financed by her legacy from Cather. It was presumably Lewis who commissioned Tennant to edit a collection of Cather's critical essays for which he supplied an introduction (virtually the only prose of his ever printed).[37] In it, he takes up the figure Cather used to describe *The Professor's House,* the view beyond the confines of a room so often found in Dutch paintings of interiors. For Tennant, the novel démeublé had these secret vistas, and it was there that Tennant found himself as well, at the site of "unspent feeling" shared with the author (xiv): "The seemingly trivial events and emotions — these, by some oblique method never apparent on the surface, she makes momentous—vivid, more than our own disguised and uncharacteristic lives. That is why her readers adore her; she restores to the ravaged ego its sense of unity—shall we say of *some* unity?— of a scheme, a final design in the rich, desolating chaos we call life" (xii–xiii). Flamboyance meets spareness, union, but not quite ("shall we say of *some* unity?"). Strange meeting, but perhaps equally strange is the fact that Tennant kept Cather alive for Lewis; he sustained the connection through his identification with Cather (ROAD UNDER REPAIR). While, for Sassoon, he embodied a dream companion from his prewar youth. Differentially—and simultaneously— Tennant occupied both places in their "affect-genealogy," to recall Nealon's argument.

Another thread drawn. The title of this essay signals its end. Throughout, I have had in mind Benjamin Britten's *War Requiem,* that divided, dissociated, and intensely felt work. In it, the Latin text of the requiem mass is juxtaposed to settings of poems by Owen. The forces of the work are divided too: a distant choir of boys, usually accompanied by an organ; the chorus assigned the Latin mass text, and often joined by a soprano soloist, a full orchestra behind, in settings that are operatic, ferocious laments, fervent prayers, frequently recalling Verdi's *Requiem*.[38] The poems by Owen are assigned to the tenor and baritone soloists, accompanied by a chamber ensemble. Britten wrote the work to express his pacifism, and assigned the solo parts to singers of the European nations devastated by World War II: England, Germany, and Russia. These divided forces meet in all kinds of juxtapositions, too complex to be discussed here, overlappings of instrumental forces, eerie echoes of conventional consolations against their deformations in Owen.[39] Once, in the closing bars of the *Agnus Dei*, the tenor sings a line in Latin, although it is extraliturgical. Only in the final section, as she sings "In paradisum," does the soprano sing along with the male soloists. In the final measures, at the bottom of her range, and almost entirely on one note (an E), she sings the line, "et cum Lazaro quondam paupere aeternam habeas requiem," and with Lazarus, once a pauper, may you have eternal rest, while the English tenor (the part was written for Britten's lover, Peter Pears) and the German baritone exchange in an always unsynchronized and harmonically unresolved duet the final line from Owen's "Strange Meeting," "Let us sleep now" (the tenor line resolves on the same E as the soprano line does, while the baritone ends dissonantly on a D). In that poem, the speaker in a state of dissociation, buried and alive, meets a man who laments the waste of war and discovers that he is a man he killed in battle. "I am the enemy you killed, my friend."[40] Britten's work celebrates with Owen the greater love, but it offers for this no easy consolations; the strange meetings—of Latin and English, of male and female—remain estranged. There can be no peace, not even in this pacifist *War Requiem* ever alert to ongoing antagonism and agony.

On the closing pages of *One of Ours*, the memory of Claude is left to his mother. Throughout, she has been a figure of conventional religious belief; to Enid, Claude is no Christian, and with his mother he presents a view that might justify this, claiming that the only interesting characters in the Bible are sinners, to which his mother reluctantly agrees, but adds that Jesus is the exception. "Yes," Claude concurs, "But I suppose the Jews were honest when they thought him the most dangerous kind of criminal" (72). Owen writes to his mother: "Christ is literally in 'no man's land.' There men often hear

His voice: Greater love hath no man than this, that a man lay down his life—for a friend. Is it spoken in English only and in French? I do not believe so. Thus you see how pure Christianity will not fit with pure patriotism." These are the sentences that Edmund Blunden, in the memoir that prefaces his edition of Owen (the text that Britten read), refers to as his "creed" (25).[41] At the end of *One of Ours,* Evangeline Wheeler accepts Claude's death because she knows that had he lived and seen that the war had accomplished nothing he would have been likely to have committed suicide. And so "she feels as if God had saved him from some horrible suffering, some horrible end," saved because she knows that Claude "could ill bear disillusion" (370). This is the shattering close to Cather's novel, the only way to save Claude is to kill him. Each man kills the thing he loves. Cather does this, but she also has written the novel, and so this is not quite the end.

In one of the war-ravaged sites in France where Claude finds himself at home, he enters a room made habitable again; nothing much more than a few pictures on the wall, "a shelf of books, a table covered by a white silk shawl embroidered with big butterflies." This is where Mlle. de Courcy lives with a young man named Louis, her brother's orderly, another one-armed man, wounded by the same shell that killed her brother. "The sunlight on the floor, the bunches of fresh flowers, the white window curtains stirring in the breeze, reminded Claude of something, but he could not remember what" (311). It's not his home or any place he had ever been. It is, rather, a description of Cather's apartment, where he might have had a place, like the wounded Louis, joined in a couple: a single woman and her dead brother's lover. Where he has a place, as Cather's alter ego.

Willa Cather=Claude Wheeler

Anagrams, all that is left over is Cather's "I," Claude's "U." I and you. I am you? Strange meeting. I am the enemy you killed, my friend. Oh my friends, there is no friend.[42]

> All that was strongest in Wilfred Owen survives in his poems; any superficial impression of his personality, any records of his conversation, behaviour, or appearance, would be irrelevant and unseemly.

The curiosity which demands such morsels would be incapable of appreciating the richness of his work.[43]

He saw Owen die, his body lifted off the ground by bullets, describing a slow arc in the air as it fell.

(The Ghost Road, 273)

Strange Brothers

The others in this chapter are two contemporaries of Cather's, women she could have known but almost certainly didn't. Blair Niles, like Cather, was born in Virginia and eventually resided in New York. Laura Gilpin, a westerner who briefly lived in New York when she studied photography with Clarence White (1916–1918), was hosted, as was Cather, by Mabel Dodge Luhan in Taos; more to the point, as I detail below, she imagined that her photographic projects had affinities with Cather's writing.[1] These contingencies of place and profession, paths that could have but probably never crossed, barely begin to speak to the (non) relationships between these figures. They may emblematize my project here, which, as in earlier chapters, has to do with the dense transfer points and occlusions around race, gender, and sexuality that link these figures. Cather's *Professor's House* (1925) is the hinge of this chapter, and I will be considering the strange brotherhood that links the more explicit treatment of male homosexuality in Niles's 1931 novel, *Strange Brother,* to Cather's far less sexually explicit project. Nothing necessitates this comparison beyond a certain close chronology, the fact that in each instance a woman writer has found male homosexuality for her subject. Yet something like these contingencies are more properly the subject in the second part of this chapter—Gilpin's unrealized project of joining her photographs to Cather's text.

While *The Professor's House* is the central text here, the overarching nexus for the comparisons between Cather, Niles, and Gilpin's attention to questions of sex and gender lies in their relationship to race. Gilpin, a WASP, is best known as a photographer of the Navajo. Niles opens her story of male-male desire in Harlem, which affords a particularly crucial site for its realization; similarly Cather locates hers in the ruins of the Anasazi as well as in the professor's house. As Peter Burton observes in the introduction to a 1991 reprinting of *Strange Brother,* "Niles's approach to Harlem (and to the homosexuality which is after all her main theme) is that of an ethnographer," and as he adds, she brings an anthropologist's eye consistent with most of her nonfictional travel writing.[2] These books, to which I now turn briefly, were most often set in Caribbean, Central and South American locales, and Niles came more and more to address the very subject matter that also preoccupies Cather's professor, the Spanish in the New World, a subject of interest to Cather herself throughout her career. Niles dedicated one of her last books, *Passengers to Mexico: The Last Invasion of the Americas,* "to faith in the freedom of mankind." The book takes as its subject nineteenth- and early twentieth-century attempts to bring Mexico under European sway; as the subtitle suggests, Niles writes in the hope that the conquest might someday really be over.[3]

Niles's earliest writing was undertaken in tandem with expeditions in the company of her first husband, C. William Beebe, a noted naturalist. As Mrs. C. William Beebe she appears as the author of the final chapter of *Two Bird-Lovers in Mexico* (1905), which is devoted to practicalities and offers advice to women to show the right "spirit" of adventure—but also to make sure to have a cook, so that camping will be a matter of pleasure, otherwise one won't really be able to enjoy nature.[4] As Mary Blair Beebe, she is named as the co-author of *Our Search for a Wilderness* (1910), contributing as her solo piece in that volume chapter 3, "A Woman's Experience in Venezuela."

One route from journeys like these to *Strange Brother* is suggested when, in the introduction to an anthology of texts she gathered on Europeans in the New World, *Journeys in Time,* Niles queries why a woman who grew up on what she terms a "plantation" in Virginia (she was born in 1880) should have felt so strong an affinity with Spanish America. Her ultimate explanation lies in the fantasy of some ancestral memory (a male progenitor of her family had first lived in Spain before migrating from England to the United States), but a more plausible and proximate source is "one of the Negroes of my childhood world . . . named Pizarro; 'Uncle Zarro,' we called him."[5] Niles imagines that some family member "interested in the conquest of Peru" was responsible for this name, the conquistador now naming the conquered, a "gentle, serene old man." Beside this cross-naming (and its suspect nostalgia and its euphemized "interest") might be placed another crossing that Niles recalls, retelling her childhood in a volume she wrote on the James River for the *Rivers of America* series. There, "the education of a plantation child begins with the dark people . . . ; the earliest impressions are from the more primitive race which thinks in terms of proverbs and drama, the race which, like the child itself, lives close to nature."[6] Athwart this all-too-familiar equation of child and primitive stands the more stunning memory of "Mary's first feminine playmate . . . a small colored girl named Milly" (13), and of the two girls reading *Little Women* and acting it out, Milly playing blond Amy, pine shavings coating her "black frizzy hair" (13).

The zigzags in these early memories—between views whose nostalgia almost occludes a history of slavery and conquest, which is nonetheless registered; between the embrace of an unexamined notion of primitivism and clear indications of intimacies and possible identifications that must call these automatic prejudices into question—also characterize the early travel writing. *Our Search for a Wilderness*, for example, is for the most part a description of birdlife in Venezuela and New Guinea. Yet birds are described in a language more apt for the native inhabitants, while the latter figure (insofar as they do) as less interesting flora and fauna: "There were populous villages of Hoatzins and great wandering tribes of Scarlet Ibises and Plovers; Herons much occupied with their unsocial and taciturn calling as fishermen, stood silent and solitary in secluded pools."[7] Next to these vivid accounts, a native is "so much a part of nature, that one hardly felt any difference between him and the forest folk"; indeed, when a boat appears, in it is "a fisherman, as silent as the Herons themselves" (81), and apparently not worth the extended description afforded the villages and tribes of birds. These passages from "A Woman's Experiences in Venezuela" depend upon an assumption spelled out later, that the native is "the creature of Nature" (152), a view we have seen also in Niles's account of Blacks in her childhood. Natives are dehumanized, naturalized. Specimens are more interesting—only once does Beebe transcribe human songs (p. 265), something she repeatedly does with bird melodies.

Yet, even in this book sympathetic observation remains possible. Early on, in the midst of a sustained pages-long description of the sounds of monkeys, howling in a storm, a boat appears filled with "several screaming women" (22); later, however, when they are described in the chapter offering a woman's view, the demeaning equation of these women and monkeys is suspended. They are no longer merely "fools" making noise; their perilous journey has a purpose—to find husbands. Explanation—thereby according these women the right to be depicted as persons—is short-lived, however. Their chance of finding husbands, given the large number of single men employed in the tar pits, is high: "there was hope, even for adventuresses so black and uncouth as these" (104). Throughout the book, this tone of amused condescension prevails as "childlike" inhabitants are befriended (see, e.g., 94), although the text is perfectly capable of noting and pitying conditions of disease, poverty, and displacement that are to be attributed to Western conquest (see, e.g., 103). Yet, as is suggested by a passage explicitly offered from "the woman's point of view" (195) on the advantage of being able to wear trousers—"one realizes as never before with what handicaps woman has tried to follow in the footsteps of man" (196)—these early experiences in the wilderness may have disrupted some conventional gender identifications even if they solidified other racial stereotypes. Indeed, they may have facilitated the ability to hear and recount a story of a missionary weeping for the death of one of his Indian boys: "He used to talk to me. He was not like other Indian boys. . . . It is a lonely life sometimes, you know" (231). As Mary Blair Beebe perhaps knew too when she divorced her husband in 1913 on grounds of "cruel and abusive treatment."[8]

When she resumed writing as Blair Niles a decade later (she had married Robert Niles Jr. shortly after divorcing Beebe), she continued the project announced in the opening pages of *Our Search for a Wilderness,* the pursuit of locales "abounding in romance" (ix). " 'It's romantic!' the purser would say, speaking of Ecuador, 'romantic!' " are the opening words of *Casual Wanderings in Ecuador.*[9] Here, however, are no bird sightings, although landscape takes precedence over inhabitants. For Niles, the history of Ecuador is simply told: defeat of the natives by the Incas, then the Spanish invasion. A hundred years of independence from Spain have scarcely moved the land out of the inanition that is its historical legacy, or the "bewildered stolidity" (112) characteristic of its inhabitants. Niles finds one group of natives who escaped this history living in and as jungle inhabitants with all "the eager alertness of untamed animals, with no consciousness of man." Against these people, who, she concludes, "are—the past" (227; this despite the fact that she encounters them on their way to market to sell dyes), futurity rests only with *cholos,* those who have some white — Spanish — "blood" in their veins:

> Servile man is an abnormality, a monstrosity. Man was not made to bear poverty or humiliation, but to press forward toward the distant goal of a superman. He was destined to power; to overcome, not his fellow-man, but himself and his environment. And when that destiny is frustrated he becomes but a poor patient thing like the trotting Indian of Ecuador, whose spirit was long ago so broken that it seems now to raise its head only when it has been stimulated by an infusion of the blood of its conquerors. (102)

This is a "spirit" that seems only to be male. Upper-class Spanish American women Niles finds baffling, "without curiosity about abstract things," lacking "intellectual outlet" (158) and mesmerized by family and religion. While one can find an identification with the natives in these views, perhaps facilitated by the racialism of the "spirit," there is only disidentification with the white women who might otherwise be Niles's counterparts.

The view here, as Joseph Boone has noted in a discussion of *Strange Brother* in the context of other modernist works in which questions of sexuality are placed in the highly charged atmosphere of 1920s Harlem, is typical in its deployment of primitivism: "Despite her celebratory intentions, Niles's use of primitive language to uphold the black race as more 'natural' than the white race thus occasionally reveals the unconscious racism involved in the frequent modernist association of blackness with sex and primitive civilization."[10] The repetition of a white supremacist plot that Niles quite overtly deplores in lamenting the history of the Ecuadorian native and yet seizes upon in advancing the "paradox" that "it is in the *cholo* that he, all unconsciously, achieves a partial resurrection" (113) points, at least, to the self-consciousness of questions of race in Niles's writing; even her brief attention to the limits possible to white womanhood in Latin America fractures white power along gendered lines (this in turn invites Niles to a cross-gender identification). In *Black Haiti,* which appeared just a few years after the book on Ecuador, such issues come to the fore — as the title of the book immediately suggests.[11] While the usual forms of primitivist belief abound in the text — as when native drumming and dancing are characterized as "sweeping back the tide of life to the beginning of us all" (27) and "the gift of the drummer to the world is the precious and imperishable faculty of imagining" (189) — Niles also knows that drumming has been outlawed precisely because of its political uses. Indeed, for her, Haiti, far more than Ecuador, is a place in which an ongoing history is crucial (at the time of her writing, U.S. forces were in occupation), and a place whose history needs to be recovered and retold to counter falsely prejudicial views. This is quite unlike the romance of Ecuador, a locale presented as a blank slate ready for inscription.

Black Haiti moves along several divided paths. Opening with an anecdote about her New York elevator man, once a sea captain, and his belief that Haitian blacks are cannibals, Niles understands why blacks, in response to a history of enslavement and torture by whites, might delight in tormenting their former tormentors with such impressions of them. The first episode of the book set in Haiti involves an old "mulatto" who stops Niles (and her photographer husband) from snapping a picture of a seven-year-old black boy picturesquely intent upon a book. " 'I will not have the child put on a post card and labelled a "monkey"!'," he exclaims (10). In a sense, Niles spends the entire book attempting to understand and to justify this outburst, which she does largely in terms of the history of Haiti. She never quite sees, however, that her own photographing (and writing) activity might be as capable of the charge, instead blaming the "mulatto" for instilling "race animosity" (11) in the black boy; nor does she pause for a second to question the racial taxonomies that supposedly measure amounts of "blood" that she deploys and which I have highlighted in recounting the episode.

Black Haiti is torn between two Haitis, as Niles admits, a real historicopolitical entity, whose revolution is seen as inspiring and is fully embraced, down to the discomfort of reporting and justifying the intense hatred of whites of Jean-Jacques Dessalines, for example; and a "dream Haiti" (21) whose primitivism and resistance to history is preferred. Although this is a Haiti of projection, Niles is also fully committed to the real. She seeks out texts written by Haitians (a full chapter is devoted to the poet Oswald Durand, while long chapters detail the histories of Dessalines, Toussaint Louverture, and King Christophe), even as she values what she regards as the "inarticulate" (52) persistence of Africa. She is as capable, in her embrace of primitivism, of unthinkingly repeating evolutionist views as she is of endorsing modern decouplings of race from questions of intelligence, culture, or levels of civilization (280; indeed, she thinks that such progressive views explain the ideological program and intellectual contribution of King Christophe). Even the invidious taxonomies of amounts of "blood" are deployed to depict a society that is pointedly far less racialized than in North America, as signs of the understanding that "black" is not a monolithic category. The American occupation of Haiti is given only limited endorsement by an author "who, generally speaking, disbelieves in Marines" (167) but not in the value of Western science and order supposedly necessary to secure Haitian progress.

At their most heightened moments, these conflicted views, which can all be attributed to Niles's liberalism, provide passages, crossings, and complications that lead to what she regards as a primordial level of consciousness and identification: "I found myself remembering Haitian ancestors as though I had actually known them" (200). We have seen Niles elsewhere reaching back to ancestors who lived in Spain, to blacks in her childhood whose very naming implicates them in histories that run parallel, and yet athwart, their own. Niles's anthropological projects—and projections—can therefore plausibly be connected to her work as a novelist—and not only in *Strange Brother*. Of Niles, one could say, as has also been observed about Cather, that the line from ethnography to fiction was not so straight.

"Not all that straight" is David Harrell's characterization of the relationship of Cather's fictionalized version of the "discovery" of the Mesa Verde cliff dwellings by Tom Outland in *The Professor's House* to the December 1888 sighting of the ruins of the Cliff Palace by Richard Wetherill and his brother-in-law Charlie Mason. "The creative route from Richard Wetherill to Tom Outland was not all that straight," he observes.[12] Harrell's "not . . . straight" says more than he means to say. His aim is simply empirical, to measure passages in *The Professor's House* against other tellings offered by Cather (both in a 1916 piece of journalism and in the letter she published on *The Professor's House* in 1938[13]) and to detail factual slips: such things as Cather's description of the thirty-year-old Wetherill as a "young boy"; or of her 1916 informant, in all likelihood Clayton Wetherill, as "a very old man," when he was only forty-seven when she spoke to him; or the misspelling and misnaming to be found in Cather's claim simply to have built upon the facts:

> The Blue Mesa (the Mesa Verde) actually was discovered by a young cowpuncher in just this way. . . . I myself had the good fortune to hear the story of it from a very old man, brother of Dick Wetherell. Dick Wetherell as a young boy forded Mancos River into the Mesa after lost cattle. I followed the real story very closely in Tom Outland's narrative.[14]

Harrell chalks up the divergencies (in this telling, for instance, Wetherill is as unaccompanied as Cather's Tom is) to some "private myth of discovery" (140). In a footnote he records the fact that while Cather is not alone in misspelling Wetherill's surname, "he was never known to anyone as Dick" (141 n. 6), an error neither he nor an expert he has consulted can understand as anything but "curious."

Harrell seems accurate in his claim that Richard Wetherill was always "Richard" to those who knew him, but it is not quite true that he was only Cather's "Dick." He was also Laura Gilpin's, a point that may suggest the logic of the failed convergence studied below, and not least if one has Judith Butler's essay on Cather or "The Lesbian Phallus" in mind.[15] Edith Lewis also has him "Dick" in *Willa Cather Living,* as she tells the story of how Cather heard from "a brother of Dick Wetherill . . . the whole story of how Dick Wetherill swam the Mancos river on his horse and rode into the Mesa after lost cattle."[16] Lewis follows Cather here, not only in making Wetherill the sole "discoverer" (Lewis uses the scare quotes) of the Cliff Palace, but also in naming Wetherill "Dick." Yet to say that she follows Cather is too easily to grant her the secondary, behind-the-scenes status she often has. Her narrative here, as in other moments we observed in "Cather Diva" earlier, moves in and out of a position in which "we" (she and Cather) go to Mesa Verde and spend a week there, passing an entire day alone in the Cliff Palace; telling how, on the way out, they got lost and waited to be rescued for four or five hours, sitting on a rock as the moon rose on the canyon before them. Lewis describes events participated in by a couple, but registers their effect in her second-hand understanding of Cather's response to them. "The four or five hours that we spent waiting there were, I think, for Willa Cather the most re-warding of our whole trip to the Mesa Verde" (97). The syntactic complications of that sentence perhaps can be read alongside the folie-a-deux of their shared Dick, an overdetermined instance, to be sure, of the masculine name. As Lewis joins and separates with the person she always calls "Willa Cather" (never either one or the other name, always both), she presents as her thought her hypothe-sis about what Cather felt. Not explicit in this passage is the very "personal record" that Lewis claims to present and yet for whose ab-sence she is often blamed.[17] There is no narrative of how this "we" operated. There is, rather, the movement of identification and dis-tance, of displacement and overlapping. "Dick" is one of the sites where Cather and Lewis meet, the shared misnaming that makes Cather's Dick also Edith Lewis's or perhaps the other way around. "Dick" is a (mis)naming of their relationship.[18]

If the route from Richard Wetherill to Tom Outland was not "straight," it is, in part, because it passed through this couple, and through the misnaming instanced here. It is, moreover, I would argue, the relationship with Lewis that needs to be read as a sus-taining condition not only of Cather's life but also of her writing. Lewis writes that "*The Professor's House* is, I think, the most per-sonal of Willa Cather's novels" (137), interpolating and ventrilo-quizing Cather in just the way in which she described their Mesa Verde experience. Lewis's allusion to the personal meaning of the novel for Cather might be a way here, as in the passage I discussed in "Cather Diva," for her to occlude and yet allude to the role of Isabelle McClung in Cather's life, and a compelling case has been made by Leon Edel for thinking that the elegiac, despairing tone of *The Professor's House* is rooted in Cather's loss of McClung, newly married to Jan Hambourg (the likely prototype for Louie Mar-sellus).[19] The professor's rejection of the backyard study at Outland that Rosamond and Louie are building finds a parallel in Cather's similar refusal in 1923 of McClung's offer of a study in Ville d'Avray. But one must also recall that Cather, unlike the professor, had un-threatened places in which to write; in the Bank Street apartment or the cabin on Grand Manan that she and Lewis shared, the locales where *The Professor's House* was written; indeed, the summer after the novel was completed, Lewis reports, "we decided to build a small cottage on Grand Manan" (130). Critics like Doris Grumbach who assume that Cather's loss of Isabelle McClung signaled the kind of terminus that she finds in the professor's condition—"The tragedy of St. Peter's love for Tom is that it is private, unconfessed, sublimated," and that Cather is similarly letting go of something she never had—too easily conflate Cather and her professor, and in treating McClung as Tom, ignore the existence of Edith Lewis, the houses they shared and built together.[20]

What makes *The Professor's House* so personal? Lewis, characteristically, fails to say, indeed stresses the symbolic nature of the novel as a sign of its personal import, an evasive tack which nonetheless resonates with Cather's sense of the secret self most people carry unknown within. Harrell thinks the novel conforms to a "private myth of discovery" found as early as in Cather's 1909 story "The Enchanted Bluff," which he describes as concerning "a group of boys" who "dream of conquering a legendary mesa where ancient Indians once lived" (138), ignoring in this summary the crucial fact that the narrator of the story is an unnamed boy who forms part of the group and hence a site for authorial transportation to a primordial self. Grumbach finds a precedent for *The Professor's House* in an even earlier story, the 1902 "The Professor's Commencement," in which a delicately feminine bachelor professor who lives with his masculine sister humiliates himself at his farewell party as he had when he had graduated years before; in this professor's bleak life of retreat and overrefinement, the one moment of life had been a stunning student, dead in his early twenties. These stories suggest that whatever was "personal" in *The Professor's House* went back further than McClung's marriage. But however much they express Cather's early anxieties they do not lead "straightforwardly" to *The Professor's House*. Tom Outland lives on the mesa; Cather wrote his story on Grand Manan. The awful fear of having missed the chance to love—the overwhelming sadness of the professor in his recognition of and resignment to what has been lost—is, arguably, not entirely Cather's position. This is not to deny the point that many critics have made, that Cather's identifications in the text extend both to the professor and to Tom; they are versions of the old man and the boy that also structure her account of the route from "Dick" Wetherill to Outland. The two coalesce, condensing the double trajectory of identification, in Godfrey St. Peter's belated discovery of his earlier self, the boy with whom "he had meant . . . to live some sort of life together" (239).[21]

That boy might well have been Tom. "Tom Outland's Story," the central section of *The Professor's House*, Tom's telling of his discovery of the Blue Mesa and its ancient ruins, is not the interpolated and autonomous central episode it appears to be, but is woven throughout *The Professor's House*. Dead, Tom continues to exert his influence on the living; St. Peter and Dr. Crane, his one valued colleague, are at odds, for instance, because the money realized in the work that Tom did in Crane's laboratory has found its way into the professor's family. Indeed, it is impossible to describe the tensions and difficulties of the family—and of the initial section of the novel, which bears that name—without seeing how Tom is at the core of all of them. There is scarcely a character in the first part of the novel who fails to come into Tom's orbit after he arrives at the professor's house, while in the final section of the novel it is Tom above all who is on the professor's mind. The money that divides the professor and his colleague also is a sore spot between the professor's daughters; Rosamond had been engaged to Tom and has married the man who capitalized on Tom's invention, Louie Marsellus. But even before there was a legacy, Tom was between the sisters, and it is difficult not to believe that Rosamond's announcement of her engagement to Tom triggered Kathleen's acceptance of Scott McGregor (53), a precipitous marriage to someone her father finds unworthy of her, however decent Scott is in himself (something of a question). Kathleen's marriage registers her disappointment at losing Tom to Rosie.[22] Indeed, when the professor and Kathleen bond together in the novel against Rosamond it is through their shared possession of that earlier Tom: "Our Tom is much nicer than theirs" (113). Moreover, it is arguably this position of identification that inflects the professor's wife's misunderstanding of St. Peter's position. "You didn't get the son-in-law you wanted" (38), she opines; but the professor's critical attitude toward Rosamond seems more straightforwardly jealous. Tom only saw her as others do, as a ravishing beauty (47); had he seen better, he would not have chosen her. If, within a heterosexual logic of choice, this means that the professor wanted Tom for Kitty, their bonding over Tom could as easily suggest how the professor wanted Tom for himself, how the animus against Rosamond is motivated not only by her having forgotten Tom, but by her having gotten him in the first place.

One sign of this can be seen in the relationship Tom had to Rosamond and Kitty when they were girls. They were his confidantes, and to them he told the story which only belatedly he relates to the professor (as "Tom Outland's Story"), the story of the "discovery" of the mesa that is entangled with Tom's friendship with Roddy Blake. Their response to his narrative was to identify with its protagonists, "to play at being Tom and Roddy" (105). This means that in desiring Tom they took up the place of the male partner. It implies, too, that in shaping themselves through Tom's stories their desires were formed through same-sex ones, and that their gender identities are similarly inflected. Kathleen bonds with her father through Tom; it is her father's face, no one else's, that she can capture in her drawings—a sign of her identification with him. So, to the professor, Rosamond is his wife's daughter, especially after she marries Louie Marsellus. However, these questions of identification are more complex; in looks, at least, Rosie resembles her father. Perhaps in erotic choice as well.

Mrs. St. Peter's mistake about the professor's desired son-in-law brings up the vexed relationship to Tom's successor, Louie Marsellus, the man who turned Tom's scientific discovery into cash. Lillian's relationship to Louie is a close one, and in part registers her former aversion to Tom. He is a kind of substitute lover for her. Louie obviously lives in the shadow of Tom, and his gauche decision to name the new house he and Rosie are building "Outland" is one sign of this. Much else in Louie is repellant: his need to dominate social situations, his miscalculated attempts at intimacy and generosity. While the professor expresses aversion and resentment over Louie's appropriation of Tom ("I can't bear it when he talks about Outland as his affair" [36]), he also allows himself to acknowledge him as "magnanimous and magnificent" (149), as he exclaims when Louie is even willing to forgive Scott if he has blackballed him, and asks him for forgiveness for the mistreatment he has received from the family. Louie is clearly trying to live up to an impossible ideal. Found to be in possession of Tom's fortune without, unlike the others, having had any direct knowledge of Tom, he is the illegitimate inheritor who is scorned for having what is not rightly his.

(Even McGregor can score a point of resentment against Louie precisely on the basis of the fact that he at least knew Tom at school.) His outsider status is registered too in the Jewishness that emblematizes it, but which also accounts for the desperation of his attempts to please and to ingratiate himself. He overdoes it, and one recognizes in his flamboyance something which raises Cather's hackles as well. His is the sin for which she had so much earlier lambasted Oscar Wilde, in a gesture that is readily seen as both self-protective and self-hating.[23]

That sins of the Oscar Wilde sort attach to Louie must be remarked. He loves to shop; he sits over a jewel case with Lillian, whom he always calls "dearest." He embodies the "florid style" (36). Louie is marked, as a Jew, as an outsider, as distinctly effeminate and effusive. But these are also signs of identifications with Tom even as they also register as attempts to deflect that identification. Tom, too, was an outsider, an orphan who comes from nowhere. "He departs leaving princely gifts" (103), and Louie is similarly generous, also "princely" (141). And, as Lillian points out, invidiously, jealously, Tom also was "highly coloured" (38). Moreover, Louie knows against whom he is being measured, and that he can never quite measure up. Significantly, Cather allows him to speak the words she chooses for the book's epigraph, a recognition of value in a locus of indistinction: "A turquoise set in silver, wasn't it? Yes, a turquoise set in dull silver" (90). Ostensibly a description of a gift from Tom to Rosamond that she wore when Louie first met her, it also evokes the shimmering value found in the dull setting, the thing not said glimmering in Cather's deliberately understated prose. These are qualities she attributes to Tom's diary: "To St. Peter this plain account was almost beautiful, because of the stupidities it avoided and things it did not say. . . . Yet through this austerity one felt the kindling imagination, the ardour and excitement of the boy, like the vibration in a voice when the speaker strives to conceal his emotion by using only conventional phrases" (238). Louie is the flaming version of Tom, easy enough to be scorned; he is the protective flare that draws off from Tom the signs of a flamboyance that otherwise might be all too legible. If Rosie and the money are the most visible signs of Louie's inheritance, the recognition of the bracelet points to the secret path of their identification and makes plausible Louie's thinking of Tom "as a brother, an adored and gifted brother" (145). It is not just the money that ties Louie to Tom or made him a substitute husband for Rosamond.

St. Peter himself posts the warning that is meant to safeguard his relationship with Tom and to ward off the making legible of such secrets: "My friendship with Outland is the one thing I will not have translated into the vulgar tongue" (50). (By the vulgar tongue, the professor means cash; hence the figure of Louie and his translations of Tom are implicated.) Readers sympathetic to Cather's work who balk at finding sexual meanings in her texts might be said to follow this injunction against "vulgar" translation. Hermione Lee, for one, points out that the professor's final remembrance and recovery of the boy that he meant to make his lifelong companion is couched in explicitly asexual terms, the recognition of a primitive, original self replaced with maturity:[24]

> The Professor knew, of course, that adolescence grafted a new creature into the original one, and that the complexion of a man's life was largely determined by how well or ill his original self and his nature as modified by sex rubbed on together. (242)

"Sex" in this formulation is almost unnatural, a social grafting; sex here is also explicitly heterosex. "After he met Lillian Ornsley, St. Peter forgot that boy had ever lived" (240), and his life has been shaped by the demands of marriage and family, the demands of the "secondary social man" (240). So, earlier, he insists to Rosamond that while her bond to Tom was social (and therefore monetary, a matter of property and possession), his was not (50).

If the professor's ultimate state of resignation involves a refusal to live in these social terms and a regrasping of an elemental self, the question remains of where and how Tom fits into this reordering, whether he can really be cordoned off to a nonsocial, nonsexual state of the self, or whether the social-sexual state by being heterosexual leaves open other sexual possibilities for the asocial state of the primitive boy. The "secondary social man" would seem to be related to the "accidental" chance elements of life, which the professor regards as having shaped his existence ever since he lost touch with the original boy. Even in these terms, Tom cannot be so easily allied to the primitive condition since he represents "a stroke of chance he couldn't possibly have imagined" (233), and one that changed everything—gave shape to the professor's work, imbricating itself in every domain of his family; but also—and far more importantly—Tom came close to filling the role of the imagined boyhood companion. As the professor reflects back upon his past, his happiest moments are vacations away from his family shared with Tom, trips to the mesa, to Mexico, and the projected trip to Paris never accomplished. This undoubtedly explains why at the end of the novel the professor refuses to go to Paris with his family, choosing instead to be alone with his memories. Remaining in the study of the old house, he returns to the place where, when the family had been on vacation, he had been a bachelor again, the "back garden" (5) where he and Tom had spent summer evenings together, the very place where Tom finally narrates his story:

> Over a dish of steaming asparagus, swathed in a napkin to keep it hot, and a bottle of sparkling Asti, they talked and watched night fall in the garden. If the evening happened to be rainy or chilly, they sat inside and read Lucretius.
>
> It was on one of those rainy nights, before the fire in the dining-room, that Tom at last told the story he had always kept back. (155)

Tom ends his story back in the garden—"I landed here and walked into your garden" (229)—just as it was by its "green door" (95) that he first entered, "the hottest boy" the professor had ever seen (100). The professor's French garden is a seemingly sterile place where "trees . . . don't bear not'ing," as his landlord puts it (40), a site of barren shrubs, devoid of grass. "It was there he and Tom Outland used to sit and talk half through the warm, soft nights" (7). The back garden is Tom's site, outward reflection of his inner nature: "The boy's mind had the superabundance of heat which is always present where there is rich germination" (234). What he makes grow are the professor's "sons," his books (144). While the professor acknowledges this as a romance of the mind, this abstracted translation conflicts with the heat and generativity of this backdoor site of unnatural graftings. "Nature's full of such substitutions, but they always seem to me sad, even in botany" (165); this sentence, pronounced by Tom on Roddy's failure to have children, Hermione Lee takes as Cather's most explicit acknowledgment of her own sexuality. The sad substitutions are nonetheless within nature. Just as Outland's story runs throughout the narrative, so too his relation to the professor cannot be stabilized on one or the other side of the divide (natural/unnatural, natural/social, sterile/germinative, asexual/sexual). Tom's position is continually belied by the doubling most explicit through the figure of Louie. He is both inside and out; the homosexual lining of the heterosexual as well as the homosexual irritant to the heterosexual; the Lucretian rub of chance that might be nature or might be nature as written and grafted:

> It struck him that the seasons sometimes gain by being brought into the house, just as they gain by being brought into painting, and into poetry. The hand, fastidious and bold, which selected and placed— it was that which made the difference. In Nature there is no selection. (61)

If the professor's legacy from Tom is memory, it materializes in a diary written in his hand, even more in the hand itself as the focus of the professor's interest and revery. At first, when Tom arrives with his princely gifts, turquoises in his hand, St. Peter looks instead at "the muscular, many-lined palm, the long, strong fingers with soft ends, the straight little finger, the flexible, beautifully shaped thumb that curved back from the rest of the hand as if it were its own master. What a hand!" (103) Contemplating what would have become of Tom had he not been killed in the war and had had the opportunity to profit from his invention, it is the desecration of "his fine long hand with the backspringing thumb, which had never handled things that were not symbols of ideas" that the professor regards as what Tom has avoided by dying (236). If this is the choosing hand— the hand that refuses to be natural, the artistic hand—it is also evidently a sexual hand. The translation out of the vulgar and into the ideal and the symbolic is a sign of that, as Lewis teaches us by remarking how Cather registered the most personal through the most symbolic.[25] "Nice hands" (36), the professor comments to Lillian: the hand in Cather is not necessarily attached to a body of either gender; the professor's responsiveness to Tom and to Lillian focuses on an organ they both share.

Tom's hand or his manuscript (read only by St. Peter) in its anything but "florid style" are not the only sites for the transmission of the unspoken. There is also the blanket Tom gave the professor, Rodney Blake's blanket in which Tom had been wrapped when

Roddy nursed him through pneumonia. Kathleen reads it as a symbol, like the cups passed between "*Amis* and *Amile*" (111), a token of identity that is also a sign of identification. The blanket functions as this legacy, and not simply in these immaterial terms. Louie characteristically seizes upon the purple blanket as a costume (144), but the professor wraps himself in it when he is chilly. "Nothing could part me from that blanket. . . . It was like his skin" (111). Like the token that passes between friends, the blanket doubles Tom's body. This is how the professor sleeps with Tom, beneath his blanket/skin, or inside his book, divining the lode between the plain words on the page, phantasmatically grasping or being penetrated by the hand, the flexible thumb, springing in the back garden. Tom embodies these forms of transmissions. Tom-the-boy, the Tomboy of Cather's enchanted mesa. The blanket takes us from Tom and the professor to Tom and Roddy and to the scene of discovery.

As in "The Enchanted Bluff," with its "big red rock" that "no white man" has ever been atop, and which is the site of "a village way up there in the air,"[26] so, too, the "tantalizing" (170) sight of the Blue Mesa draws Tom and Roddy; they similarly plan to "be the first men up there," and "climbing the mesa" is their "staple topic of conversation" (166). The dream proves realizable after Tom has his unforgettable first sight of the cliff dwellings, a moment literally breathtaking:

> In stopping to take breath, I happened to glance up at the canyon wall. I wish I could tell you what I saw there, just as I saw it, on that first morning, through a veil of lightly falling snow. Far up above me, a thousand feet or so . . . I saw a little city of stone, asleep. (179)

Tom's first impulse is to keep secret what he has seen, and part of the powerful effect of the mesa and its city in the sky has to do with its being the locus of the kind of numinous secret to which Cather's art is devoted. The city is a site of perfect geometry, modernist harmony organized around a red tower. The symbolic architecture is, thus, one place toward which Cather's Dick drives. The ensuing rupture with Roddy is likewise to be explained by what the city in the cliffs keeps secret: "I never told him just how I felt about those things we'd dug out together, it was the kind of thing one doesn't talk about directly. But he must have known; he couldn't have lived with me all summer and fall without knowing" (216). The "things" are meant to be like the cups by which Amis and Amile recognized each other as ideal friends.[27]

As the symbolic site of the unspoken relationship between Tom and Roddy, it is the Blue Mesa that makes "gorgeous" their homo romance (to recall Sedgwick's description [68]). This is not to say that in itself traces of romance cannot be read in Tom and Roddy's relationship. It can be seen in the way in which Tom opens his narrative of the discovery and the friendship by reporting himself entranced by this surly stranger in their midst ("I'd been interested in this fellow ever since he came on our division; he was close-mouthed and unfriendly" [161]); drawn back in fascination to rescue Roddy from a poker game threatening to turn nasty, Tom follows him from behind to his room where he strips him of the gold pouring out of his pockets and lying around his hips (162), finally seeing to the money being safely deposited in a bank. This friendship is reciprocated, as is evident in the reversal that follows, as Roddy now tends the ailing Tom who had watched over him. Roddy quits his job for Tom, does his work for him, finally selling the "curios" (the artifacts excavated on the mesa) and setting up an account in Tom's name so that he will be able to afford to go to college. If they are at first in a quasi-filial relationship (Blake calls Tom "kid" [163] and "son" [163], and Tom himself is the sad substitute he remarks [165]), they become a pair of "boys" (175), age difference erased by fraternity and friendship in an all-male family in which Henry Atkins does their cooking, cleaning, and interior decoration. From the start, Tom is drawn to Roddy by his strong silence, and they bond together over the unspoken mystery of the mesa. Roddy's antisociality makes for an alternative sociality on the mesa. When Roddy effects his vulgar translation, turning the mesa artifacts into cash, the rift is opened. Cash makes the mesa a social site couched in terms of property and possession. Yet, once Roddy disappears down the hole, Tom comes into "possession" of the mesa (226), living in the cliff dwellings, doing his Latin. The contradiction here between the avowals of disinterest and the luxuriance of Tom's summer and fall "feeling that I had found everything, instead of having lost everything" (227) is perhaps built into the mesa's symbolic function as the site of unspeakable desire. It may remind us of the similar disavowals around Alexandra Bergson's relationship to the land in *O Pioneers!* and, more generally, to the ways in which desire cannot be separated from disavowal and sacrifice, the point that Judith Butler makes, and which has stood behind the analyses offered in previous chapters of this book. On the mesa Tom comes into himself, without Roddy, much as the professor will come into himself alone in the closing pages of the book; the mesa is the locus of a series of sad substitutions and sublimations, not least in its lure of self-possession after betrayal and loss.

For it must be remarked how transitory that exultant moment of possession is; Tom remains haunted by the need to make restitution to Roddy; indeed, this sense of guilt has been passed on to the professor and to the family who keep up the search for Roddy. When Rosie and Kathleen play Tom and Roddy they play a version of the relationship in which Roddy was "noble. He was always noble, noble Roddy!" (106). It is, of course, the Roddy that Tom has depicted for them. His betrayal of Roddy is perhaps a deeper betrayal than Roddy's—for Roddy had treated the "relics" as things to be sold for the sake of his friend; and his friend had insisted on a panoply of symbolic meanings—many of them, as he admits, invented on the spot (219)—to place the mesa and the ruins above their relationship.

This excruciating moment in the story—anything but adequately described as "nothing very incriminating, nothing very remarkable; a story of youthful defeat, the sort of thing a boy is sensitive about—until he grows older" (155)—suggests, I think the "double life" of this text, divided between what flashes out as gorgeous in the mesa and the deliberate understatements of the novel, covering those traces of desire and ferocity more deeply painful than the surface bickering in the family. One cue to this doubleness is named in the "two lives" (19) of the professor, the division between his teaching and his writing that only begins to name the divides: between his upstairs and his downstairs life, between Tom and his family, between past and present with its strong homo and hetero cleavages. Even more to the point is the fact that "double life" is a recognizable term for gay life in the opening decades of the twentieth century, as George Chauncey has shown.[28] If the professor lives a double life, Cather's text could be said to be written in the kind of double language that Chauncey describes, one in which "common words" are given "a second meaning that would be readily recognized only by other gay men" (286). Cather's double language is perhaps a bit more private (the "personal myth" that Harrell invokes), but not entirely so, and such "coding," as I suggested earlier, is only the beginning in plumbing the resonances in Cather's language. If the mesa and the lost civilization resonate so deeply for her, they do in part because of a classical echo (Anasazi pots are said to be identical to Greek ones). The organizing red tower almost requires no comment; nor, perhaps, the "back court-yard" with its wall "like the sloping roof of an attic" (186). That rear space connects the Cliff City to the professor's study, his "shadowy crypt at the top of the house" (94), with its window and its view of Lake Michigan always inviting like an open door; it connects thus to his back garden — and to Tom: "one seemed to catch glimpses of an unusual background behind his shoulders" (112). Guarding against the drift of this reading is the remarkably pure water deep in the cave. Or, perhaps, that purifies these dark desires. The cave is on the divide, a "twilit space"; "there was perpetual twilight back there" (186), Cather repeats. In the end, the professor comes into the "twilight stage" (239) he had not had before.

"Twilight" is a key term in describing the allure of the mesa, seen over and again in the purple and gold of the fading sun, and it is also the term that leaps out as a recognizable piece of the double language that Chauncey details. Andre Tellier's *Twilight Men* (1931), for instance, makes explicit the code, just as the title of Lillian Faderman's *Odd Girls and Twilight Lovers* draws on it as well.[29] It is, moreover, the code that provokes the title and lexicon of Blair Niles's *Strange Brother*. I turn now to Niles as a fiction writer to pursue the comparison promised at the opening of this chapter.

Strange Brother locates its twilight man, the "half-man" Mark Thornton, in a "shadow world" (the phrase recurs) in which he lives half of his double life. Its most recognizable inhabitants he refers to as a "tribe" (one, moreover, that makes him sick, he avows [50]), a population of rouged and marcelled boys with names like Pansy or Nelly or Lilly-Marie. It is the feminine part of these half-men that makes them recognizable and, for Mark, a site at once of recognition and aversion. Seeing himself in them, he also sees the possibility of being seen as one of them, something that would blow the cover of his double life. Nonetheless, they are the latest indication that "the thing had existed always, everywhere," that this modern "tribe" connects to Native Americans, who had a word for it, "*burdash,* meaning half-man, half-woman" (307); from such evidence he draws solace, as well as from defenses of gay love by Carpenter and Ellis that go back to the Greeks. While these connections recall those Cather makes between Native Americans and the classics, Niles does not write a mesa romance; instead Mark can be more natural and open among the "citizens" of Harlem where a number of scenes of the novel are set, and where he is first seen, with two black friends: "Above their white shirt fronts there seemed only shadows, blacker and more tangible than the shadows of the corner" (15). Although Mark is a "Nordic" (16), fair and Grecian in his good looks, Niles presents him in this shadow world to suggest that he inhabits a subculture all but hidden to ordinary view, "Mark's furtive world, unrecognized by the forces which raised the skyscrapers of New York. Yes, there were the underground lavatories of the subway, as well as the shining eminence of the Chrysler Tower" (324).

Mark belongs to an invisible minority, but he is linked to other minorities, most emphatically Blacks, who give color and visibility to his shadow world; he identifies with them specifically on the basis of persecution and suffering: "the Negro had suffered and that bound Mark to him" (234). Mark and his black companions discuss the difference between their visibility and his invisibility, and one aim of Niles's novel is to uncloset the homosexual and to align him with the "Negro," a project effectively realized when, for example, Mark recites Countee Cullen's "Heritage" and weeps. The point of contact is made as well by regarding straight "Nordic" males as the embodiments of a puritanical law, while Blacks, Jews, and Latinos are proclaimed to be "natural about sex" (184). This pronouncement is made by Irwin Hesse, a Viennese scientist accorded a position of authority in the text. On the basis of his observation of "the number of sex forms existing among the social insects"—ants and termites, for instance—he insists that there are "more than two hard and fast sex forms in man" (173), a point that the novel endorses. "Abnormals" (a term used throughout the novel) are therefore as natural as Cather's "sad substitutes"; indeed they are offered by Hesse as "Nature's great experiments" (178). Through them, an alternative to the straight Anglo world is imagined and embodied, the shadow world.

Hesse's "more than two . . . sex forms" translates in the novel into the double sex form that provides a way of understanding Mark and his ilk: "It's as though I had the body of a man and the psychology of a woman! I'm what you might call a half-man" (153). Mark explains himself in this way to June Westbrook, the white journalist who is the central figure of the novel (and an obvious stand-in for Niles). June is remarkable for a sympathetic ability to get under the skin of other people, not only homosexual Mark but various black women, one explicitly lesbian. If the novel, on the one hand, is committed to a kind of minoritizing view of sexual difference (to use Eve Sedgwick's crucial terms), in which homosexuality is confined to a small group of people whose affinity to other minorities is based in persecution, it is also, by way of its arguments about a natural multiplicity of sex forms, advocating a universalizing view. Both meet and cross in the novel's various cross-gender and cross-racial configurations, and it is through them that *Strange Brother* launches its attempts to understand a "brotherhood" that crosses the homo/heterosexual divide.

This is mainly done through the association of June and Mark, a woman and man who bond over their love problems. Or, rather, through June's sympathy for Mark's problems, which she recognizes as her own, for she never tells him that Palmer Fleming, her first husband (a kind of Gilbert Osmond figure), was gay—something she discovers in the course of the novel when she sees him at a Harlem drag ball clothed in Venetian garb with a companion "in the dress of a woman of the Turkish harem" (217). Nor does she tell Mark about her sexual frustrations with her current lover, Seth Vaughan, who dies in an airplane crash, their affair remaining unconsummated. From Beulah, her Caribbean maid, June comes to understand that Seth was the kind of man who could have a heterosexual relationship only once in his life; she has come to him too late. If Seth, in these ways, seems a bit like St. Peter, the explanation for his sexuality lies in the novel's depiction of a homo/hetero continuum that ranges from the confirmed queer cases like Mark along a sliding scale that includes Palmer Fleming and Seth. As Mark explains to June, "there are any number of degrees of normality and abnormality with very many border-line cases, men who emotionally are on the border between normality and abnormality" (155), a view June hears again from an artist friend late in the novel (265).

This continuum offers one way of understanding Mark's situation, why he and June both have the same object of desire, and the same trouble finding it. With June's support, Mark embarks on assembling an anthology to be called *Manly Love,* citations from which appear in the novel to make the case for the acceptance of homosexuality as on a continuum with the masculine norm. Having the same desire as June, however, places Mark on the extreme feminine edge of the continuum, and this explains his aversion to his own kind, the worry that he will betray himself socially by being perceived as effeminate. Mark thus repudiates feminine identification, even as the novel depends upon the cross-gender identification that identifies him as a half-man. Like *The Professor's House, Strange Brother* can scarcely imagine for its hero the possibility of a sustained male-male relationship, and it is similarly less than fully persuaded about the possibility of heterosexual relations. Neither Mark nor June can get a man, although the extremity of Mark's situation leads him to suicide. Mark falls for June's cousin Phil, who is virulently straight, outspoken in his antipathy to queers. "Sex is for the purpose of reproduction," he avers. "Anything else is a farce. . . . There's no such thing as any third human sex. When such cases aren't actual degeneracy, they are retarded mental development" (178; June on the other hand falls for gay or impotent men).

Through June, *Strange Brother* extends liberal sympathy to homosexuals. Against this it offers a world of prejudice and, even worse, one where a law that brands Mark's sexual choices as "crimes against nature" hands out unjust punishments for acts that harm no one and that are moreover natural. As Mark sees, the law is one of entrapment, and it encourages blackmail. In presenting the situation this way, the design of *Strange Brother* follows the novels Niles had written previously. She had shaped her journalism on the French penal colony in Guiana to which Dreyfus had been sent into *Condemned to Devil's Island* (1928), her first novel, a fictional biography. The aim of the novel, more or less announced in an opening section, "In Explanation," and reiterated at various points, is to condemn the system as inhumane, and to insist on the humanity of those condemned. This is first posed as showing that the hero does not have a "black" soul, that rather it is prison that shows "the dark places of our civilization."[30] This implicit racializing of humanity is even more evident in *Free,* written the year before *Strange Brother,* which follows a prisoner released but forced to remain in exile in Guiana. Niles is taken with the seeming paradox that French Guiana is a reverse world of imprisoned whites and free blacks, while in *Condemned,* Michel, the hero of the novel, knows that it will only be a black who will help him escape—because they share a history of mistreatment, although this cannot be depended upon, since the prisoner is white. The bond possible between the black man and the white prisoner is made insofar as both "had renounced white civilization" (106). In *Free,* criminality is seen as an alternative to repressive sociality, criminals being either "not strong enough to fit into life the way it's organized" or "too strong to shape themselves to it" (249).

These alternatives of strength and weakness are plotted in part in sexual terms. *Condemned* often has in focus male-male sexual relations in the prison world, what the preface to the novel refers to as the "strange tragic world" (xiii) of men without women. Weak men in this world are the "girly-boys" (330); "brats" is the usual translation of *mômes,* and Niles writes in a footnote: "In the womanless world of the Guiana prisons the men who satisfy Adam's desire for Eve are called *mômes*" (53). As in *Strange Brother,* male-male sex is understood through a third-sex model, but also in a syntax capable of being absorbed by heterosexuality (much as June's normal desires match Mark's abnormal ones). Just as humanity can be figured as properly white, same-sex desire can be seen as natural insofar as it looks like heterosexuality. Niles is capable of making the relations between men and *mômes* romantic; she is also capable of seeing them as the unfortunate result of prison life, one more way in which prison makes men inhuman. Her hero, at any rate, is not involved in the system: " 'There are only three sorts of men in prison,' Michel often said, 'the men who keep brats, those who become brats, and those who learn how to relieve themselves . . . I have decided which I will be' " (133).

Michel's strength lies in self-sufficiency, a refusal of the system. If this implies masturbation, it also takes shape in the *plan,* receptacles in which prisoners hide whatever cash they can hoard as they plan their escape—the desire for freedom is the sign of humanity—receptacles that they hide in their anuses. Self-sufficiency takes that form. *Free* offers a kind of parallel, for in order for its protagonist to win true freedom he must resist the allure of a woman. He expresses his fantasy in this way: "I'd like to try every kind of life there is! I want to experience everything. I'd like to live a thousand incarnations. I'd like to be born often as a woman, as well as living the lives of many men."[31] This fantasy, of course, defines Niles's phantasmatic writing position, the sympathetic transports of her June, the liberal extensions of the white woman to blacks, homosexuals, exotics. The hero of *Free* is finally saved when he is accepted as a "mascot" on board a ship on which he has stowed away, one of numerous male-male forms of sociality that the novel offers (including the church, prison, school) as borderline sexual institutions. The woman that he resists winds up marrying a Haitian black; she is the child of two prisoners, and throughout the novel she is insistently marked as black even though she is white. "I don't think blood is everything. She's pure white blood allright. But she thinks black" (187–88). The racial back and forth here measures the double force of having white parents who were convicts and who remain as *liberés,* the name which says "free," but which in fact marks the status of those permanently exiled in Guiana.

Niles's fictional projects are consistent with (the contradictions in) her travel writing. Certainly her liberal advocacy is admirable, when, for instance, she lets June Westbrook be corrected by her artist friend when she opines that the sheer number of abnormals means they are due consideration. "If there were only one, he should be considered, according to my way of thinking," he responds. "A fact is a fact and has as much right to exist as any other fact. And anyway, however people may feel, a fact is going to exist. There's no getting away from that. Intolerance gets us nowhere" (266). "Tolerance," however, is scarcely the same thing as social transformation, and the recognition that the novel seeks does not carry with it any hope for or plan for widescale social transformation since it is tied to a minoritizing view. A few liberals and artists as well as blacks (but only if Harlem manages to survive white incursion) are assumed to be sympathetic; women like June will keep Mark's secret, and share it. The most that can be done is advocacy of the kind *Strange Brother* or Mark's projected anthology represents. Mark learns that he can never have sexual satisfaction; his boyhood mentor tells him that he must pursue his art (Mark draws) as a way of overcoming and sublimating his desire. "Put into your work all that you feel—all that you suffer. Make something beautiful out of your pain" (141). Writing as "outlet" (157): this is how Mark can transcend the debility of abnormality, June (and Niles) of female gender, in a world where straight men are homophobic and misogynistic, and sympathetic men are not straight.

Mark's Midwest mentor is named Tom Burden, Cather's Tom and her Jim Burden (the narrator of *My Ántonia*) conflated. This is not the only possible connection between Niles and Cather; did Cather choose to name Marsellus after the hairstyle of pansies? Or to dress him à la Turque in the professor's little pageant for much the same reason that Palmer Fleming's date is so attired? Or to think of Louie as black (as Othello, the "extravagant and wheeling stranger of here and everywhere") when the professor, in the position of Brabantio, imagines he has lost his daughter (or, more likely, his Tom) to him? [32]

In asking these questions, I mean merely to indicate some of the ways in which Niles's "knowing" novel could be read as a kind of vulgar translation of Cather's. No doubt a sufficiently complicated mapping of the possibilities afforded by the crossing of minoritizing and universalizing understandings of sexuality and gender could be drawn to plot the complex relationship between the representational strategies of Niles and Cather. It is a nice question, of course, whether Niles's primitivist, naturalizing association of male homosexuals and African Americans is more suspect than Cather's mobilization of the Anasazi. The programmatic liberal defense that Niles offers is certainly not Cather's position. Not only because she was no liberal, but also because she did not enjoy the distance that allowed for Niles's sympathy (however much Niles's June identifies with Mark, she is also insistently "normal" in her desires). Cather has been faulted for her supposed lack of interest in live Indians and for representing Native Americans as extinct, but had she represented living Native Americans as sites of alternative sexualities (in the manner in which Niles presents the citizens of Harlem) that would not have made the matter any less vexed. Cather does not represent the homosexual per se as a minority; not given such existence, he is not aligned with other recognized forms of minority existence, nor is he the object of sympathetic understanding or vicarious inhabitation. Rather, the homosexual is indistinct from the heterosexual, as is the case with St. Peter or Tom, not because he is closeted but because forms of desire are not assumed to be absolutely distinct. Or rather, if a closet is involved it is not one that contains a certain group of people, but a certain capacity in all people, the secret self that Cather posited in her essay on Katherine Mansfield. Cather like

Niles can be assumed to suppose that this is not a part the world chooses to see, but she can also be supposed to have something other than a tourist's relationship to its inhabitation. She knows—and not just because, like June, she has been unlucky in love—that this world exists. The shadow world is not for her somewhere else and not to be translated into something else. Not an alternative, not simply a pocket of difference, it is rather the difference within the same, the nonidentity of identity. Social conformity seeks to block it out; most people choose that path of least resistance. But it nonetheless is the lining of the normal and its irritant. Niles remains a valuable point of comparison with Cather because she is so explicit, and so inconsistent in her minoritizing/ universalizing views of gender/sexuality—and of racial differences. Hers is always a syntax that needs the poles same/different. In Cather this is not so evidently the case, and it is this that allows Cather's transportation of herself in the masculine not to be a matter of disguise or false consciousness, of self-hatred or self-repudiation.

The alterity of homosexuality is given its most realized form of social embodiment in *The Professor's House* in a site that must seem rather unexpected in terms of the ways in which Cather's politics are usually discussed, through a figure who bears another form of the overdetermined masculine name, Rodney Blake—Roddy, for short (Blake, as I remarked in the initial chapter of this book, is a nominally displaced "black"). If the professor sees in Tom the embodiment of "the dream of self-sacrificing friendship and disinterested love down among the day-labourers" (151), those are qualities he derives from Roddy, as Tom insists in his descriptions of him as a typical working man (161, 164). Blake's radical politics—his support of the Chicago anarchists massacred in the 1886 Haymarket Riots and his Dreyfusard position—are not Tom's, however, but may well have been Cather's (an early piece of journalism was pro-Dreyfus).[33] While Cather was certainly never someone who stood up for the worker, she may well have known what George Chauncey argues in *Gay New York,* that the most vibrant instances of gay culture (or, more accurately, of the acceptance of same-sex desire) flourished in working-class culture in the early twentieth century. Cather could have known this first hand from a favorite bachelor brother, Douglass Cather, who (like Tom when he met Roddy) worked on the railroad. The same-sex family on the mesa is composed of the derelict

Henry and the railroad workers Tom and Roddy. When Roddy puts his friend above his country, he enunciates a working man's ethos, or speaks from a position of disenfranchisement that might also attach itself to unjustly condemned Jews like Dreyfus (or Louie?), or to excoriated "abnormals" (anarchists were, of course, associated with free love if not usually with same-sex couplings).[34] "Queer," Tom muses, thinking of his observation of those in Washington, D.C., who work for the U.S. government, "how much more depressing they are than workmen coming out of a factory" (213). So, when Tom attempts to link the artifacts of Anasazi civilization to his ancestry (he is, pointedly, an orphan without familial ties) or to his country (his surname suggests he has none), he seeks various forms of legitimization for and sublimations of the meaning of those objects in his relation with Roddy, social sanctions for a relationship that cannot be imagined to have its own minoritized form of existence; indeed—as his sacrifice in the Great War conveys—Tom articulates these values *to his death* as a denial of the bond of friendship and love with Roddy.

Tom's ultimate understanding of what he "did that night on the mesa" when he drove Roddy away is formulated in terms of their relationship: "Anyone who requites faith and friendship as I did, will have to pay for it" (229). Roddy here is condemned—and Tom himself finally as well—for not realizing that their friendship could not be translated into commercial terms. His ominous expectation that he will be "called to account" when he least expects it points to the sacrificial logic that the professor unfolds when he imagines how Tom's death saved him from marriage, the management of a fortune, from social existence, duties to his "town and State" (236). "He had escaped all that" (237), and it is of such an escape that the professor dreams at the end of the novel, a "falling out of all domestic and social relations, out of his place in the human family, indeed" (250).

Rodney Blake's experience with Tom is not the first time that he has been "unlucky in personal relations" (164); it is, rather, his life's story, "skinned" by his friends, "double-crossed" by the girl he was to have married (164). The latter double cross is writ large across the mesa, with its presumptively adulterous mummy dubbed Mother Eve, and across Cather's novel with its misogynist hostility so often on the lips and in the thoughts of the professor. It is that which has made *The Professor's House* difficult for many of its readers, and which might give pause to the kinds of translations that I have been suggesting, the routes of painful identification across gender and sexuality to the nomination of Cather in the masculine. I don't know whether it helps to recall that the professor has a moment of almost inarticulate bonding with Lillian in the novel—"You, you too?" (78)—that suggests that she was as unsuited to the heterosexual life as he was (and which would make just a bit less malignant his fantasy of being shipwrecked in all-male company [79]); or to note that the professor thinks of his lifework as a piece of weaving not unlike that of Queen Mathilde (85); or to recall that when Tom meets him for the first time and recites his Virgil, he speaks the words of Aeneas to this demanding Dido; or to note that at the bottom of his box-couch the seamstress Augusta's patterns and his manuscripts "interpenetrated" (13). I do think it worth pausing over Augusta, too often treated as a figure of maternal rescue and reconciliation in the novel since she is there at the novel's end to save St. Peter from his Ophelia-like suicide. Augusta, when she first appears, is called a spinster (8). So would Cather have been called. About the only thing St. Peter wants to know from her is about the Magnificat, a piece of female writing (or so Augusta claims) celebrating pregnancy without having sex with a man. It might be the fantasy form that solves the question of natural and unnatural graftings in the novel; it attaches them in this instance to the rough, unsentimental hand of Augusta, and to the Virgin's pen. At any rate, it suggests that the animus against women in the novel is (as in *My Ántonia* or *One of Ours*) more pointedly against married, procreative, heterosexual women, against the "cruel biological necessities" (13) they embody even when abstracted to the dummy forms of the professor's attic space shared with Augusta. The professor's female-identified moments, or his bonding with Augusta, arguably hint at a potential movement across gender and sexuality, and in the direction of Cather and Edith Lewis.

For if one had to name the scene that lies behind or that translates the romance of the mesa, its "bluish rock" as seen "under the unusual purple-grey of the sky," as the valley turns "lavender and pale gold" (178), that perpetual backlit twilight scene, the "sunset colour" dousing the valley while "the mesa was one great ink-black rock against a sky on fire" (171), perhaps it is here, in Edith Lewis's understated yet gorgeous prose:

The four or five hours we spent waiting there were, I think, for Willa Cather the most rewarding of our whole trip to the Mesa Verde. There was a large flat rock at the mouth of Cliff Canyon, and we settled ourselves on this rock. . . . We did not talk, but watched the long summer twilight come on, and the full moon rise up over the rim of the canyon. The place was very beautiful. (97)

We will have occasion to recall this scene (which itself echoes many moments in Cather when the landscape serves as the locus of the thing not named) when, toward the end of this chapter, something like its double appears in Laura Gilpin. I turn now to the collaboration that failed to materialize between Cather and Gilpin, an eminent photographer of the American Southwest who made that her subject for more than fifty years until her death at the age of eighty-eight in 1979. While representations of Native Americans by Anglos and the kinds of suspicions that these practices have often justifiably occasioned remain as problematic issues, in pursuing this failed meeting, I am most concerned to detail a range of representational difficulties that relate to gender and sexuality, with measuring these as they are enabled by and therefore, to some extent, must occasion more nuanced explorations of racialized relations. Above all, and without privileging personal experience as an unproblematical category, I wish to detail affective links (affect-genealogies, to recall Christopher Nealon's term), as these lines of identification are also and necessarily occluded and redirected. The failed collaboration of Cather and Gilpin is a sign of these fraught relations, the fact that the solicitations of an alternative world of secret selves is lodged in and obscured by more overt ties.

According to Martha Sandweiss, my guide to this episode, sometime late in the 1920s Gilpin had the idea of providing photographs for an edition of *The Professor's House* (1925).[35] Gilpin, as it happens, had made two trips to Mesa Verde at the same time that Cather was writing and publishing her novel; nineteen of Gilpin's photographs of the site appeared in her 1927 book, *The Mesa Verde National Park*.[36] Whether or not these images were considered already to be illustrations for Cather's novel, Sandweiss claims that "Gilpin thought her pictures of the majestic, sculptural ruins compensated for Outland's shortcomings" (*Desert,* 66). The "shortcomings" Sandweiss has in mind presumably lie in Tom's remark that his "small kodak" images of the ruins he and Roddy had discovered were not very likely to impress the officials in Washington he had hoped to persuade to support their further investigations of the site. "They gave no idea of the beauty and vastness of the setting," Tom continues (*Professor's House*, 204). Whether Gilpin actually meant to declare that her photographs could do what Tom's couldn't is not clear; the project apparently never proceeded far enough for Gilpin to clarify her intentions. As Sandweiss explains, Gilpin approached Cather "indirectly" through an intermediary, the photographer Alice Boughton, whom both she and Cather knew (*LG*, 44); but her "efforts to contact the author failed" (*Desert*, 66). Sandweiss does not explain the nature of this "failure"; Cather was not at home when Boughton came to call, but it is unclear whether or not they had had an appointment or whether Cather knew what brought Boughton to her apartment. (A 1929 letter from Boughton to Gilpin is, apparently, the sole document recording the existence, and failure, of Gilpin's project.) Hence, Sandweiss concludes, "Laura . . . did not get the opportunity to compensate for Tom Outland's photographic shortcomings" (*LG*, 44).[37]

Sandweiss's story stresses the "compensatory" nature of Gilpin's project. If it was presented to Cather in these terms (if Cather ever heard of the project, which remains uncertain), it would be entirely plausible to suppose that she would have had no interest in the planned edition. Except for some Benda woodcuts that she had commissioned for the first edition of *My Ántonia*, Cather's novels never were illustrated. (*A Lost Lady* was filmed in 1925, however, and again in 1934; Cather's response was to stipulate in her will that her novels were never again to be filmed or dramatized.)[38] It is unlikely that Cather would have welcomed Gilpin's illustrations even if they bettered Tom's work. Presumably Cather depended on her words to do what a "kodak" could not.

Sandweiss opines that Gilpin saw her photographs of Mesa Verde as having the same aims she recognized in Cather's depiction of the Blue Mesa in *The Professor's House*, that, like Tom, she regarded the ruins as "fabulous sculptures by a brilliant and long-gone people" (*LG*, 44). Further connections can be drawn, as Sandweiss does, between Cather's novel and the text Gilpin provided for her Mesa Verde photographs when she republished them in *The Pueblos: A*

Camera Chronicle (1941).[39] Not only do both authors treat the site as a kind of national monument or originary moment in U.S. history, they also stress the peacefulness of the former inhabitants and the high level of their artistic accomplishments (*LG*, 67). "Perhaps more than any other place in the United States," Gilpin writes, "one gains a feeling of antiquity at Mesa Verde. The warm, brilliant sun of the Southwest imbues these ancient buildings and creates a lasting sense of peace" (*Pueblos*, 38); her sun-infused shots create this impression as well. So, too, Tom's first description of the sculptural city seen through the snow stresses its "immortal repose," "the calmness of eternity" (*Professor's House*, 180), a past preserved in amber. Gilpin's description of the ruin at Betatakin, whose buildings, made of the same stone as the cave in which they are set, produce "an extraordinary semblance of unity, as though it were all the work of a giant sculptor" (*Pueblos,* 62), guides her composition and has its echo in Tom's estimation of the Cliff City: "It was more like sculpture than anything else" (180), a characteristically laconic statement that takes in canyon, cave, and buildings, held together in a symmetry that "made them mean something."

Gilpin's statements and, indeed, her sharp-edged, close-up photographs of the ruins at Mesa Verde correspond to Cather's writing, sharing the modernist aesthetic that regards them as timeless sculpture.[40] Moreover, the "chronicle" of Gilpin's book parallels Cather's plotting. Gilpin moves from soft-focus distant shots to geometric compositions in order to "first place the ruins in the landscape, then move in to show the design effects of changes in light and shadow on the architecture" (7), as Vera Norwood comments; in much the same way, the narrative of Tom's "discovery" moves from his distant view of the city in the cliffs to his more precise architectural account, a sequence repeated as the story progresses from these initial views to Tom actually scaling the walls and taking possession of the ruins. Gilpin's view of Shiprock, "floating full sailed in a sea of mist" (*Pueblos*, 44), the closing shot in the Mesa Verde sequence, offers a Whistleresque study of tones and shapes that resonates with the insistent twilight scenes on the mesa in Cather, or with the veil of snow that she provides as Tom catches his first heart-stopping sight of the city asleep in the cliffs.

Such similarities in description or aesthetic valuation do not mean that Gilpin's photographs somehow compensate for Cather's shortcomings (as if her text were also a kodak image). However much Gilpin's photos may have called up Cather for the photographer, they in fact illustrate quite another text, the one Gilpin herself provided. If we attend to the generic dimensions of these projects, a point of contact can be drawn across media (actually, of significant noncontact, for in beginning with this failed collaboration I seek to understand the terms of meeting beyond what might literally have been possible). The Blue Mesa is not literally Mesa Verde, Tom Outland not "Dick" Wetherill. However much a real place and history lie behind Cather's text, renaming signifies that fiction-making is going on. Central to this fiction is the question that occurs to Tom immediately upon seeing the Cliff City for the first time: whether he should tell Roddy about it or keep it "secret as the mesa had kept it" (*Professor's House,* 180). Secret sharing, secret withholding, constitutes the significance of the mesa as the site of meanings untranslated further by Cather.

Gilpin, too, saw Mesa Verde in terms of secrets; for her, however, at least at the most explicit level in her heavily fact-based text, "scientists have done so much in solving the mysteries of past ages that it is easy for us to visualize what life must have been seven hundred years ago among these peaceful, home loving, agricultural Indians" (*Pueblos,* 38). It is to such "visualization" that Gilpin proceeds, and not only in the sentences that follow; if, as she insists, we can see "bronze, black-haired figures moving about, busy at their various tasks" (38), it is because these figures have been pictured already (on 29, 31, 33) and will be again as the Mesa Verde sequence closes (42). In fact, the final shot in *The Pueblos* (124) is another of these Mesa Verde images, which show Mesa Verde inhabited by contemporary Native Americans posing as ancient inhabitants. Whereas Cather repopulates the Blue Mesa with Tom and Roddy, who live together in a romance ultimately broken by betrayal, Gilpin provides a pseudonative population, living Navajo dressed up as ancient Anasazis. Gilpin's imaginative project in her Mesa Verde photographs is as much a fiction as *The Professor's House;* her genre, unlike Cather's there, is historical romance.

Gilpin's use of Native Americans posed as ancient cliff dwellers, which might be compared to Niles's primitivism, has been an object of criticism (much as Cather has been critiqued for being far more interested in dead Indians than living ones). In interviews given close to the end of her life, Gilpin herself came to disown the photographs with "natives" in them, or at least to find them embarrassing; this embarrassment has perhaps licensed Gilpin's critics to temper their admiration for these images.[41] Sandweiss is not alone in finding them "backward-looking" and guilty of "romanticism" (*LG*, 68). In this she follows an essay from the early 1950s by John Collier Jr., which plots Gilpin's career along a familiar evolutionary, progressive model from the undoubted racialism in her images of "picturesque" Pueblo inhabitants (Collier thought these images looked "more like museum sets than breathing human beings") to the more informed, documentary, and "realistic" images in *The Rio Grande: River of Destiny* (1949). Collier in fact is more generous to Gilpin than some of her more recent critics, commenting that while Gilpin clearly *felt* the Indians in *The Pueblos* (he italicizes), in her earliest photographs she did not have "the concepts and techniques for accurate social observation."[42]

In this context it is disturbing to note how two of the essays in the catalog of the dazzling 1996 show of Southwest desert photography at the Whitney Museum, *Perpetual Mirage*, both take Gilpin to task. Evan Connell, in a brief discussion of Mesa Verde images, links Gilpin to a tradition of syrupy romance (these are his terms); he extends Sandweiss's remarks concerning Gilpin's embarrassment about her posed images to all of her Mesa Verde photographs. Perhaps even more perturbing is John Chavez's "Gilpin's Rio Grande as Seen by Another," in which Gilpin's 1949 book tracing the course of the river from its source in the Colorado mountains to its end in the waters off Mexico is set against 1970s Chicano representations that "remind us that the Rio Grande remains a contested landscape" (151). Through this juxtaposition Chavez implies that Gilpin should have anticipated these current attitudes, that representations of places where Chicanos live are best left to Chicanos. In Chavez's account Gilpin is made to stand for the failings of her race, despite the fact, as he briefly notes, that for her, as a woman, it was not easy to marshal the resources to practice as a landscape photographer and make these images.[43] It is possible, too, to consider whether the optimism that Gilpin often expressed (and which Chavez criticizes) simply tallied with her own experiences. Her faith in American democracy must have existed in a complicated relation to her situation as a relatively unprivileged and economically disadvantaged woman attempting to make a career in a field dominated by men.

Chavez does not comment upon the photographs in *The Rio Grande,* and represents his damaging textual citations as adequately conveying Gilpin's project (similar limitations can be found in Judith Fryer Davidov).[44] It is thus difficult for a reader who does not know Gilpin's book (copies of it are rare) to be aware that as Gilpin follows the river downstream she organizes her account in terms of such topics as "The Indian Pueblos and The Prehistoric Relics" (pp. 85 ff.) or "The Heritage from Spain" (pp. 107 ff.). Moreover, after the first third of the book (in Colorado), virtually every inhabitant photographed is either a Native American, Spanish American, or Mexican. It is true, as Davidov notes, that Gilpin writes as if her readers are only Anglos, and as an advocate for the "American Way of Life" (68), but not as unreservedly as has been claimed. She thinks that Catholicism, for instance, is an "addition" to native religions which retain "fundamental force" (97), a view that echoes Cather's in *Death Comes for the Archbishop;* that Spanish American *retablos* and *bultos* "hold a high place in the folk art of our country" (114); that the real history of the Southwest begins with natives and Hispanics. In the final paragraph of the *Rio Grande,* Gilpin lambastes modernization that may have improved agricultural output but has also led to soil erosion, deforestation, and drought. "Will present and future generations have the vision and wisdom to correct these abuses, protect this heritage, and permit a mighty river to fulfill its highest destiny?" she asks in closing (236); the faith that this text expresses is finally centered less on the United States and more on the possibilities of "the close relationship of three cultures" (70) which have produced a "blending of peoples unique in the Western world" (xii).

It is difficult not to believe that Chavez and Connell critique Gilpin for downplaying the tensions in such a vision of harmonious relationships in part because they expect her, *as a woman* who undoubtedly had to overcome prejudices based on her gender, to be sensitive to every political need at every time. She is made to bear the brunt of a critique more cogently launched against privileged male photographers whose work in the West accompanied the destruction of the landscape and the exploitation of resources and people. Nonetheless, Gilpin's images can also be seen to arise from highly "contested" struggles; they serve as sites of conflict that have much to do with her gender and sexuality. That these sites of oppression and enablement crisscross unevenly and produce some regrettable representations of Native American or Chicano cultures—regrettable in terms of what Gilpin included and excluded and especially in terms of the manipulations and falsifications involved—needs to be registered in an interpretive framework that engages these complications.

This is not to suggest that a "political" critique of Gilpin (or of Cather, for that matter) is totally unwarranted. Gilpin did, for instance, make unfortunate statements about the childlike quality of Indians. But the question remains how far such explicit attitudes govern her photographs. Assuming that they do allows critics to avoid some difficult questions; surely there is more to do than to deplore Gilpin's work until it tallies—as it is claimed her final book, *The Enduring Navaho* (1968), does—with current senses of politically progressive or artistically sophisticated, supposedly realistic documentary work.[45] This "progression," to which, admittedly, Gilpin's remarks in her final years contribute, obscures continuities between her early and later work.

Similarly, Cather's many outrageous statements about the exalted status of the work of art, along with her dismissive remarks about the programs of the New Deal and other issues, have led critics to take her political conservatism as a given rather than to recognize that it might conflict with other impulses in her work. Her disinclination to write socially engaged, activist texts does not mean that the politics of her representations can be dismissed as retrograde in every respect. The "secret" energies of her writing, the complex routes from male-male to female-female sexual relations are not necessarily politically progressive, but they do not follow in any simple way from Cather's "politics." There is a similar case to be made about Gilpin.

To see that Gilpin's photographs may operate at some distance from her prose (whether soberly descriptive or disturbingly "naive") involves more than recognizing the genre of her images (which links her to such writers of historical romance as Helen Hunt Jackson in *Ramona* or Oliver LaFarge in *Laughing Boy*). Take, for instance, Gilpin's first image of a "native" in *The Pueblos:* "Long ago some Cliff Dweller maiden may have leaned from this very window," she writes (28). The photograph she offers, however, already has a

8. Laura Gilpin, *House of the Cliff Dweller, Mesa Verde, Colorado.* Platinum print, 1925. (© 1979, Amon Carter Museum, Fort Worth, Texas. Bequest of Laura Gilpin.)

woman within it (see figure 8). "Long ago" is right now; Gilpin's soft-focus lens makes available such a past. Indeed, the woman in the window, with her illuminated bare shoulder and her otherwise darkly wrapped body, is a study in shadow and light akin to the surfaces of the building that surrounds her; she is similar in her modulation to the only other rounded object in the image, the pot placed diagonally below her. This initial image draws attention to something that the text does not mention: that all but the last of the Mesa Verde inhabitants in *The Pueblos* are women. This fact is almost disavowed by the text that accompanies the next photograph, also of a woman in the shadows, in this case looking intently at a round object. The text is about the religious practices of "old medicine men" (30), a dying knowledge lost on "the young men" of the present. The text dwells on this male tradition, but the image silently visibly "compensates" for and contradicts it. The woman pictured, and the woman taking the picture, are not in the situation of male debility.

I would suggest, therefore, that the fictional choices of Cather and Gilpin, however much they diverged, and however unlikely of realization Gilpin's project of illustrating Cather might have been, may yet meet in their cross-purposes, that Cather's dead Indians and male-male couples speak to her desires much as Gilpin's staged "living" Indians are projective sites for hers. Access to same-sex female desire occurs along these highly conflicted routes. Cather's path is doubly displaced by gender and by race; while all of Gilpin's Mesa Verde Indians are not female, most are, and it is in the possibility of gendered identification that I would trace sexual desire. The "bad politics" of Gilpin's (non)relationship with these women thus may be a site worth valuing for its representation of desires that cannot be written off as simply exploitative of native bodies.

The Indians in Gilpin's *Pueblos* photographs were paid models; it is usually claimed there is nothing of the "deeply personal" relationship always adduced as the element in *The Enduring Navaho* that redeems its images from the charges of decontextualization, aestheticization, dehistoricization, and generalization leveled at the earlier work.[46] There are more than a few questions to be raised by the supposed distinction between soft-edged and hard, pictorial and "straight" photographs (to use Stieglitz's terms),[47] between images thought to be romantic and regressive and those praised for their individuality and realism. Gilpin, however much she viewed her career as a progress away from pictorialism, is nonetheless a guide to a further complication when she insistently denies the commonplace assumption that the purpose of a photograph is "to record a scene."[48] Rather, she wrote, what photographers want to do "is record the emotion felt upon viewing that scene, and consequently a mere record photograph in no way reflects that emotion" (1987). If this is the case, something beyond the distinction between falsifying and truth-telling is needed. In this regard it is worth emphasizing the continuity within Gilpin's *The Pueblos* from the initial section that includes Indians posing as Anasazis to the final set of images of "Historic" Pueblo Indian culture (74–124), almost every one of which includes figures.

Throughout *The Pueblos,* the continuity between ancient and modern is insisted upon in text and in images. To make her point that native culture has "endured" (the final word of the book and the linking term to her study of the Navajo), Gilpin risked falsifications of all kinds. The frontispiece, for instance, shows a group of Pueblo women at the watering hole at Acoma (figure 9). These women are "traditionally" costumed; that is, they are wearing clothes most Pueblos do not habitually wear now and did not usually wear when Gilpin was photographing them in 1939. The watering hole is a severe geometric study of light and shade that cuts shapes and patterns; indeed, the planes of the image imitate the design of the geometric Acoma pot in the foreground. Imitation and reflection are arguably the keys to this photograph, both formally (in its use of reflecting images in the pools of water) and thematically (in the ways in which the image cannot but recall the well-known studies of Edward Curtis that lie behind it).[49] Women in this picture are reduced to geometry; yet, for all its formality and modernist abstraction, the image must register in its very reflectiveness the emotion felt by the photographer. Geometry is rendered female, and, given the poolside reflections, the picture reads as narcissistic, autoerotic, and potentially homoerotic.

But not entirely self-reflexive: the Acoma pot is a key to the image, just as it is central to Gilpin's belief that the endurance of the Indians is registered in their art. The Pueblo women whom Gilpin photographs—and women predominate in the historical section of the book, as they do in the antique shots—include mothers, wives, and brides-to-be; they are usually posed alone (occasionally in a manner as staged as the Mesa Verde shots) and sometimes in groups performing religious ceremonies or household tasks, but they are more often shown as potters or in proximity to pots. These "vessels" may register as obviously feminine, as in the water scene at Acoma, but this is not how Gilpin's text reads them. The final image of a

9. Laura Gilpin, *Acoma Watering Hole, Acoma, New Mexico.* Gelatin silver print, September 1939. (© 1979, Amon Carter Museum, Fort Worth, Texas. Bequest of Laura Gilpin.)

male "native" is placed above a concluding text that summarizes the contribution of the Pueblo Indians:

> They have left monuments of great beauty and interest, fashioned with the crudest of tools. . . . They have an inherent sense of beauty. As artists they are aware of the great rhythm of nature and are keen

observers of her forms. They have given us in their art a virility and beauty of design beside which much of our own becomes weak and somewhat insignificant.

Above all they have endured. (124)

What is one to make of this conclusion? The continuity from ancient art (the "sculpture" of Mesa Verde) to modern Indian culture is assumed, but the final art, praised for its "virility," is clearly the art of the potter, the Pueblo woman's art, and the art of the photographer, whose admission of weakness and insignificance goes hand in hand with the kind of generalization of the Indian character that one must question even when, as here, it aims to value Pueblo Indians above Anglos. The gendered complications here, the anachronism, the falsifying generalizations, and the aestheticism are undeniably suspect; uncomfortable as they are, they also enable Gilpin's work, sites of pockets of value and of possibilities that cannot be contained by ideological critique. These are the terms for Gilpin's sympathetic identification and "personal relation," across all sorts of barriers and limits, with Native American women and their culture; moreover, these relations, which I have characterized as "projective," were, in fact, reciprocated.

To take the question of cross-gendered representation first, I would note that just as *The Pueblos* ends with a picture of a staged native male, the first figure photographed in the book is also male, an Anglo scientist: "Here is a noted archaeologist, Dr. Frank Roberts," the book begins (13). Throughout, Gilpin's text seems to rely on a male science to deliver the secrets of this culture. This reliance also may serve as a cover for aspirations for a place among landscape photographers, a male preserve, a profession supposedly too strenuous and dangerous for a woman to undertake. One risk avoided may be seen in comparing Gilpin's photographs of Mesa Verde with the precedent-setting images of Cliff Palace by Gustaf Nordenskiöld.[50] His are in many respects far more conventionally romantic than hers. The roughness of the stones and the inclusion of rubble and decay make them appear cruder ruins than in Gilpin's modernist view; but his distant view offers an image far more mysterious and "feminine" than any Gilpin took, one in which the Cliff Palace is barely discernible within its darkened cave. If the secret of the cave dwellers in Nordenskiöld's image is feminized, while

Gilpin favors the more hard-edged, sun-illuminated views of architecture as sculpture, her approach may suggest a desire not to have her landscape work seen as in any way feminine. So, too, one might say that the allusion to Curtis and the severe geometry in the Acoma watering hole protect the picture from the reading that I offered above, much as Cather's focus on males and her abstraction might also seem remote from her gender or desires. Like Cather, then, Gilpin produces representations recognizably within a "male" tradition but also resistant to certain forms of mastery and specularization in order to forestall another understanding of these conventions. Such complicities could be understood as part and parcel of the supposed "bad politics" of this work, but I hope I have suggested enough now about the complex relations between the politics and the gendered and sexual aims of these images to dispel this view as the last word about them.

Gilpin's insistence on the emotion of the photographer even in "straight" work suggests, moreover, the continuing legibility of her images within the aims of the pictorial school in which she trained. Her work might be compared to some early photographs by Alice Boughton, the emissary to Cather she chose in the late 1920s. By then Boughton was a well-known portrait photographer. In the opening decade of the century, she, like many fellow pictorialists, provided allegorical titles for her photographs. "Dawn," "Nature," "The Seasons," and "Sand and Wild Roses," for instance, are the titles of photographs by Boughton in Stieglitz's avant-garde *Camera Work* (1909); all of them feature nude female children and adolescents. "Nature" includes an older woman, clothed, embracing a girl whose genitals are visible. The backdrop to the scene is an imposing tree. No doubt these images are meant to be read as displays of femininity, generativity, motherhood, and the like (commentators point out that some of the naked girls are Boughton's daughters), pictures of "Nature," in short. But nothing guarantees that that is how they were seen or even were intended, whatever their titles.[51]

Boughton's images and Gilpin's views of an "enduring" native tradition can be read within an essentializing view of gender and to some extent invite such readings. Gilpin's work is understood this way, for instance, in Rina Swentzell's essay on "The Pueblos" in *Perpetual Mirage,* which repeats the familiar complaint that Gilpin failed to see "the Pueblo people . . . as full and complex human beings" but then seeks to redeem her work by emphasizing its "domestic moments," instancing a photograph in *The Pueblos* of mother and child (137). Swentzell's domestic affirmation follows from the way she reads Gilpin's investment in the land as a mother, the guiding assumption as well in Vera Norwood's essay on the organic relationship between landscape and figures in Gilpin's work. The collapse of the landscape into mother earth has its risks, among them effacing the kinds of political problems raised by Chavez (for my point has not been to deny these issues but to relocate them within a sufficiently complex point of view). Moreover, to pick up the thread guiding my remarks throughout this discussion, an emphasis on maternity (as if that alone constituted womanhood) invites a treatment of Gilpin's gender in entirely normative, heterosexualizing ways.[52] In this context it needs to be emphasized that there is only one image of a woman and child in *The Pueblos* (87). In fact, the figures are not a mother and child but a grandmother and child, and the text the photograph "illustrates" includes the quite suspect remark that "Indians are a simple and childlike people" (86).

To summarize: Gilpin's aspiration to be a landscape photographer is not a normative one for her gender but an incursion into a male domain; and if the desert is no lady, to recall the title of an important anthology of essays on women and landscape in the Southwest, what is she? The frontispiece to that volume provides an answer: it offers a 1971 photograph of Gilpin taken by Fred Mang Jr. (figure 10). Well past eighty, betrousered, a man's hat in one hand, Gilpin stands, her left arm raised to the level of her tripod. Behind her is the desert; she is on level and bare ground littered with a crutch she has thrown aside as well as other pieces of photographic equipment. (When Gilpin began to need a crutch in old age, she remarked that the third leg made her a natural tripod.) Squinting into the sun, Gilpin rises heroically above the landscape she is about to capture on film. A wind is blowing, but she is unmoved and firm. The camera on the tripod has replaced the woman with her crutch; the camera lens, her squinting eye. These prosthetic extensions, instruments of artistic realization, move Gilpin beyond any normative definition of her gender. Whatever this picture implies about Gilpin, how this woman becomes a photographer of the desert would seem not to

10. Fred E. Mang Jr., *Laura Gilpin photographing along dirt road.* Gelatin silver print, 1971. (© 1971, Amon Carter Museum, Fort Worth, Texas. Gift of the artist and Laura Gilpin.)

be legible in terms of maternity or heterosexual reproduction. Nor, I think, would one want to read the masculinization of this image to mean that Gilpin simply occupies male gender.

My aim thus far has been to affirm Gilpin's connection with Cather, to seek to understand how the two offer quite different homoerotic translations of and relationships with the Southwest and its native inhabitants. In the remaining pages I want to think further what it might mean to label Gilpin's work, especially *The Enduring Navaho,* a lesbian project, and to consider why this is a topic barely broached by her critics. (When Gilpin's sexuality is mentioned at all, it is treated as a personal matter best taken no further.) Indeed, if Cather and Gilpin are worth thinking about together, it is not only because their relations to the Southwest resonated sexually but also because such vibrations are so refused by critics who otherwise admire these artists in valuable ways.

It is in this context that I would mention an essay by Robert Adams, alluded to earlier, which is included in *Why People Photograph* in a section called "Examples of Success." Adams's admiration for Gilpin is warm throughout the essay. In line with his estimation of her "deeply personal" relation to the Navajo (95), he labels as "most important" her "sharp-focus portraits . . . of Navaho women and children" (91) but also commends something "that Gilpin did particularly well, and in this case right from the beginning, . . . distant landscapes" (93). Adams's views echo familiar ones in their assumptions about when Gilpin succeeded with photographs of native people and which ones represent her best work. While there are a number of images of women and children in *The Enduring Navaho,* once again a domestic image is substituted for the range of depictions offered, for in this book, as in *The Pueblos,* images of women predominate, though by no means only in a maternal setting. When Adams praises Gilpin's landscapes, "whether in soft or sharp focus," he adds immediately that "they are 'straight' in a way that gives that word its full meaning" (93). That "full meaning" is not further specified, and the claim is more than a bit baffling. In the strict sense of the photographic term, it would not seem to apply to all of Gilpin's images, some of which are manipulated. One suspects that they are "straight" in the way images of women and children are presumed to be.

The need for this insistence is clear when Adams turns to review Sandweiss's *Laura Gilpin: An Enduring Grace,* praising the book for its "tact" (94) in its handling of Gilpin's lesbianism, as Adams all but says. Like Sandweiss, he is content to note Gilpin's more than fifty-year "friendship" with Elizabeth Forster, to praise it for the loyalty and patience shown during times of great difficulty. "If we are curious about more," Adams continues, "by what right do we inquire?" Not saying "more," Adams nonetheless tells all. One might compare this to Sandweiss's remarks as she concludes her narrative about Gilpin and Forster's 1945 decision to live together:

> After a close and supportive friendship of almost thirty years, the two were finally able to set up house together. In Santa Fe, a city long tolerant of unconventional living arrangements, the fact that Laura was a photographer with a keen interest in the culture of the Southwest and Betsy was a nurse who had worked on the Navajo

Reservation was of more interest to people than the fact that they were two women sharing a household. (*LG*, 77)

Women often share houses; Sandweiss goes out of her way not to say what she is saying: that they weren't simply two women living together, but a couple. Assuring her readers that even the "tolerant" residents of Santa Fe couldn't have been less interested in this couple as a couple, Sandweiss clearly projects her own sense of the proprieties. As Adams says, Sandweiss "describes the outward signs of the friendship"; as he does not say, both he and Sandweiss are fascinated by what they don't tell and yet want their readers to know and not to know. They open and shut the closet door.[53]

There is no reason why personal life need be made public, and it is certainly the case that Gilpin's photographic work does not advertise itself as lesbian or seek to make sexual freedom its cause. Yet the reasons for inquiring about Gilpin's sexuality are not the prurience that Adams supposes. When he mentions "the fact that the friendship helped Gilpin's work with the Navaho" (94), he scarcely says what is needed: Gilpin only came to have a "personal" relationship with the Navajo because Forster lived among them as a nurse in 1932–1933. Gilpin's "personal" relation to the Navajo was based in her relationship with Forster. One of these relationships is praised as responsible for the very best work she did as a photographer; the other is treated as a secret. So, again, I would stress that the nature and value of Gilpin's accomplishment demands attention to her gender and sexuality. In the pages that follow I will be looking at *The Enduring Navaho*, but I also want to suggest ways in which that work, conducted from the 1930s through the 1960s, continues some of her earlier aims and achievements in *The Pueblos*. Finally, Cather will not entirely have been left behind as this chapter draws to its close. (At this point, it scarcely needs saying how the occlusion of Gilpin's lifelong relationship with Betsy Forster matches the way Cather's relationship to Edith Lewis and, with it, the question of her sexuality, is made not to matter in so much writing about Cather.)

The Enduring Navaho is dedicated to Elizabeth Warham Forster, R. N. "Dear Betsy," it begins, "This is as much your book as mine."[54] Gilpin's page-long dedicatory letter details how she and Forster came to find themselves in Navajo territory, how listening to

Forster's "tales" during her two-year stint as a nurse on the Navajo Reservation served to whet Gilpin's "interest" as she became "impressed by their rugged character and mode of life." From this acknowledgment of Forster's role in making her work possible, Gilpin turns immediately to praise Forster in terms suggesting that what she came to see in the Navajo she also saw in her friend:

> From time to time my visits revealed the work you were doing, your understanding, and your generosity, for you literally gave of your substance as well as your knowledge and nursing skill. I saw the response of the Navaho People to your attitude toward them, your willingness to go anywhere at any time when a call came for help. I know, too, the lives you saved and the succor you gave. (v)

It's a handsome tribute, and it continues to the end of the letter, as Gilpin recalls the day of Forster's departure from Red Rock, six of her best friends watching and then, in unison, bowing their heads and weeping; as she remembers their trips back to find old friends and the new ones made as well; and, for the dedication is not as maudlin as my summary may suggest, as it insists on the "fun" they have had all these years together: "What fun we have had evolving this book." And again, in closing, "As a tribute to our long and happy friendship, this is your book."

At the very least, Gilpin's relationship with the Navajo was mediated and facilitated by her relationship to Elizabeth Forster. The undoubted depth of relationship often to be seen in Gilpin's portraits has much to do with the fact that so many of her subjects were friends of Forster's, that often what we are seeing in the photographs is not merely Gilpin's sympathetic knowledge of her sitters but their response to "Betsy," as she says in the dedicatory letter. "The People knew Miss Gilpin through Miss Forster," Harry Walters, museum director of the Navajo Community College, comments in a film made to accompany *An Enduring Grace: The Photographs of Laura Gilpin*, the 1986 retrospective show organized by the Amon Carter Museum.[55] Nor is it an overstatement when Gilpin insists on *The Enduring Navaho* as Forster's book as much as her own, for the project as first planned was to use her photographs to illustrate a text made up of Forster's letters home to Gilpin and to several of Forster's women relatives and friends. Various difficulties—the war, a life-threatening illness of Forster's, financial exigencies that led Gilpin to go to work in the Boeing factory—interrupted the plan, and when it was resumed in the 1950s Gilpin wished to extend her 1930s project to include more up-to-date photographs. Still, the original plan for the book is felt throughout *The Enduring Navaho;* virtually every story told in the initial section on the Navajo People (the Dineh [20–40]), for example, is culled from Forster's experiences. Gilpin echoes her critics in refusing to offer a generalized account, but her specificity is attributed to a quite specific person: "But generalities are not enough; one must know the individuals. My first acquaintances were made when I visited Elizabeth Forster" (23).

This is a note sounded throughout the text; countless times paragraphs begin, "when we were visiting," "we made a trip" (68), "we found" (72), "Betsy and I heard about a road" (77), and so on. Whatever other narrative structures organize the book—and it has a quite deliberate "public" structure detailing "The Navaho World," "The Way of the People," "The Coming Way," and "The Enduring Way," a four-part structure resonant with Navajo religious belief and cosmology—the narrative of Gilpin and Forster recurs; the very end of the book, for instance, details a ceremony that "Betsy and I" had often seen (237–38), while the brief epilogue focuses on one of those six best friends of Forster's, Mrs. Francis (247–50).

In an attempt to recreate the original project, Martha Sandweiss has edited a version of Forster's letters with Gilpin's photographs as *Denizens of the Desert.* This volume further reveals the ways in which the relationship between the women is fundamental to an understanding of Gilpin's photographic relations with the Navajo. The book begins with a prologue by Gilpin that tells the story of their arrival in Navajo territory and of the desire of her "intrepid friend" to live and work among the Navajo.[56] Gilpin gestures toward the "remarkable place [Forster] made for herself in the lives of the Indians in this region" (34), and it is this remarking that I have tried to note above in the triangulated relationships among Gilpin, Forster, and the Navajo photographed. Gilpin provides some further terms for this relationship that may resonate strangely with the language of her work on the Pueblos, or, rather, that suggest further some of the continuities between that work and the photographs of the Navajo. She points to how Forster "mysteriously understood [the

Navajo] in spite of a language barrier, her remarkable psychological understanding of them . . . , and above all the feeling the Indians had for her" (34). I don't mean to suggest in any vulgarly reductive way that this "mystery" was simply a sexual one, but I do wish to draw attention to currents of unspeakable "feeling" (or at least feelings that no shared language could turn into words) as productive of a remarkable sympathetic identification. If in *The Pueblos* Gilpin counterpointed male penetration of native mystery with photographs of native women, shadowed and mysterious, the mystery now begins to take on a human form and moves from a generalized and suspect characterization to a particular embodiment.

This relationship with the Navajo resonates with Gilpin's earlier project with the Pueblos. Forster, for example, writes in her initial letter about the "peace and protection" that she has come to associate with "desert life" (37), and we might not only recall Gilpin's emphasis on peacefulness in the text accompanying her pictures of Pueblo ruins but also note now how often she characterizes the cliff dwellings in terms of their inaccessibility and the protection they afforded (see, for example, page 68 for a particularly emphatic statement, in this case about the Canyon de Chelly, the subject of Gilpin's final, incomplete photographic book project). Forster's letters describe a life of hardship, brutal weather, disease, and death, yet the serenity insisted upon here, as much as in Gilpin's often upbeat texts, has everything to do, I think, with what two "intrepid" and "unconventional" women found in native culture: a place of unquestioned acceptance. "They said," Harry Walters reports of the Navajo who came to know Gilpin and Forster, that "they were two fearless ladies." There may be "tact" in this acknowledgment, or it may be that there are ways of not saying that still say it all.

Describing a visit to ruins, Forster puts into words what I think for her, as for Gilpin, was one basis for the response to native cultures, to "extinct" as well as living Indians:

Once within these caves, surrounded by relics of a forgotten past, things of today faded from immediate consciousness and imagination played irresistibly with a long dead, primitive civilization. I cannot tell you how completely one loses one's sense of familiar identity and becomes imbued with the romance of ancient life which is suggested on every hand. (43)

This description of loss of identity sounds a bit like Jim Burden registering his arrival in Nebraska in the well-known sentence in *My Ántonia* ("Between that earth and that sky I felt erased, blotted out").[57] Some of this wonder of loss and fulfillment is suggested in a letter from Forster to Gilpin describing her attendance at a native ceremony, its "strangeness and mystery" (49), and the need to record something she is in danger of losing because she has no terms for it.

This need to record might also describe the aim of Gilpin's photographs and the way in which they manage to "catch" their subjects without seeming either to impose on them or really to come from them. The figures in Gilpin's photos invariably keep their reserve even as they communicate their acceptance of the photographer. This ease recalls the moral Forster draws from her experience at the religious ceremony, as she withdraws from it a bit to reflect "at the consternation some of our friends would doubtless feel if they suspected our 'whereabouts.' But never for an instant," she continues, "were we made to feel uncomfortable by the strangers whose celebration we had invaded uninvited" (50). If even friends might have wondered what Forster and Gilpin were up to, this description registers the kind of place they had found. Their acceptance in this place was possible because Forster never acted like the condescending and unknowing missionary whom she scorns in a letter (51), nor with a belief that her medicine was there simply to replace native knowledge: "the idea that I am a medicine man and at their service is a source of kindly amusement to them always" (125)—and to her as well. In the repertoire of Forster's communication skills, Gilpin points in *The Enduring Navaho* to her humor, telling a story about how she threatened to rope one of her recalcitrant patients and how, when her remark was translated for his wife, she led her husband out on a leash and handed him over to Forster, laughing all the while (30–31). Of this "uneducated" woman ("she has never been to school and doesn't speak English," Forster writes to Gilpin), Forster simply says, "I have fallen in love with her" (*Denizens*, 80). One can imagine a shocked "political" response to this declaration of "love" for a woman with whom Forster cannot exchange a word, but the story of the roping and the witty translation of it by the unnamed woman suggest that Forster's love was returned.

It is left to Timothy Kellywood, the young Navajo man who served as Forster's translator and helper throughout her time among the Navajo, to "translate" something otherwise unstated. After one of Gilpin's visits, Forster writes: "Dear Laura, It was a rather doleful party which left you in Santa Fe. When Timothy remarked pathetically 'We sure are lonesome' I roused myself to cheer us as best I might" (74). Kellywood and Forster change places here; he voices her feelings for Gilpin, she cheers him up. After he departs, thanking Forster for taking him to Santa Fe and "for treating us so nice," and after Forster "thought he was gone" for the night, he runs back and says to her, "Don't be too lonely, Miss Forster" (74). Writing to Gilpin a few weeks later, she remarks how "Timothy voices the belief that you would enjoy this or that" (77). In his job as translator, Timothy ventriloquizes "Miss Forster" and "Miss Gilpin," one to the other. This is the remarkable place, I would argue, of the Navajo between these women in Gilpin's photographs and in Forster's life.

Robert Adams, like so many estimators/domesticators of Gilpin's work, praises her portraits of women and children. There certainly are some of these in *The Enduring Navaho*, and some of them are enormously powerful images: the one on the cover of the book, for example, of a mother with four children, or several of the opening shots in the sequence on "The Dineh," including two of the volume's best-known images of the Navajo family in a wagon (21) and of the woman and child and sheep (28). Overwhelmingly, however, the images of women that dominate this book, as they do *The Pueblos,* are portraits or images of women at work as weavers, basket makers, potters, secretaries, teachers, even as politicians. (The only full-page image of a politician is that of Annie Wauneka [170], first chair of the Tribal Council, and it is followed by a smaller picture of her taken ten years later, after she won the Freedom Medal [171].) Again, Gilpin does not present women simply as mothers or caretakers, nor does she emphasize that role. And among the photographs Gilpin had on her mantle in her last years in Santa Fe (images not included in *The Enduring Navaho*) there is one of Elizabeth Forster with child and lambs that looks much like the famous shot of mother and kids; another shows Forster standing looking over the shoulder of a woman at the loom. These images insistently connect Forster with photographs in *The Enduring Navaho*. Another image of Forster standing between two Navajo women also needs to be added to this group (unfortunately, the negative for this photograph is too damaged to be reproduced here). In it, Forster flashes

11. Laura Gilpin, *Portrait of Elizabeth Forster,* ca. 1930s.
(© 1979, Amon Carter Museum, Fort Worth, Texas.
Bequest of Laura Gilpin.)

Gilpin a smile radiant with love as in a portrait of Forster that Gilpin made at about the same time (figure 11). The two Navajo women retain their composure. Forster, standing quite literally between the Navajo women, is also between the photographer and them; she enabled Gilpin to photograph those women.

It has to be noted, moreover, that many of these images date from the 1930s, that is, from the same time as some of the "posed" photographs in *The Pueblos,* and that in both cases it is rare for the women photographed to interact with the camera. If the posed shots do this to make the Pueblo women mysterious, the images of the Navajo suggest a camera looking on as life takes its course. Thus, mothers are engaged with their children and weavers with their looms; even figures with no visible activity appear, in most instances, reserved. It is arguable that this reserve is what attracted Gilpin and Forster to the Navajo, a secret keeping that goes deep. It explains why Forster, however personal her relations with the Navajo were, did not know the names of many of the women with whom she spent time and shared meals; "the Ute woman" or "Mrs. Francis" (wife of Francis Nakai) are her names for them. This reserve is the equivalent of the respect shown in Gilpin's photographs, but also the privilege they display, as Gilpin was admitted into hogans and allowed to witness religious ceremonies usually off-limits to whites. Indeed, the only photograph in *The Enduring Navaho* that includes Forster, the shot in the hogan of Hardbelly as Forster administers digitalis to him, speaks exactly to Gilpin's position as an outsider permitted in, an outsider who does not violate what she has been allowed to see (figure 12). Hardbelly's wives stare impassively at him while Forster looks at her syringe; no one looks at the photographer, who is there but is not simply making a documentary record. She is there thanks to Forster, thanks to the personal relationships that bind these figures together.

Fittingly, in *The Enduring Navaho,* Gilpin follows the 1932 photograph taken in Hardbelly's hogan (31) with a sequence of "The women . . . as we found them in" 1955 (35–37). The theme of "endurance" in her work encompasses not only aspects of traditional Navajo life that survive into the present but also the relationships established in the 1930s that are still vibrant years later. As Gilpin tells, often it was the act of showing her 1930s photographs that reestablished connections or made new ones. And often tears flowed in recognition. It is impossible to separate the aims of this photographic project as documentation of a way of life becoming ever more precarious, of mortal subjects preserved by the camera, and of the ties founded in reserve and respect that allowed this couple to find themselves so welcomed and accepted by the Navajo community, in particular, by its women. One of Gilpin's most memorable images is undoubtedly the two-page spread of the summer hogan of Old Lady Long Salt (70–71), a picture of a group of women intent upon their domestic labors: "we were soon to learn, to our astonishment, that we were in the presence of five generations of daughters" (69). That astonishment, shared by Gilpin and Foster, is the meaning of the image, the quiet, unremarked presence of an embodied his-

12. Laura Gilpin, *Hardbelly's Hogan, Arizona.* Gelatin silver print, 1932. (© 1979, Amon Carter Museum, Fort Worth, Texas. Gift of Laura Gilpin.)

tory stretching back into the century before, of activities that might have been done then in a setting that would still have been familiar. One can, if one wishes, complain that such an image is more committed to the past than the present, that it fails to do the political work that documentary photography is meant to do. But there are reasons, I believe, to suspect those aims and to question the assumption that they represent the only possible progressive politics. Gilpin rarely photographs her subjects in modern houses; nor does she document poverty, criminality, or alcoholism (though the latter is certainly mentioned in her text). I believe that one can argue that these "failures" cannot be separated from Gilpin's continued, persistent valuing of native difference and that the unobtrusive respect shown in her photographs and in the Navajo's relationship with her and Forster is reflected in the kinds of images she produced, early and late. Before labeling Gilpin as lamentably conservative for not producing images with recognizable documentary aims, it is worth pondering whether the humanitarian goals of documentary work, to reveal squalor, for example, do not often impose upon their subjects' normative bourgeois views of how people ought to live that obscure other ways in which people make their lives, that is, whether documentary photographs don't have a suspect missionary aim that devalues native resources and obscures the relationship between the economic arrangements that produce poverty and the government-sponsored forms of "amelioration" that often also ensure the perpetuation of disadvantaged status within capitalist society. The "fun" that Gilpin insisted on as the essence of her life with Forster, and of *The Enduring Navaho* as its emblem and embodiment, might be her word for registering the value of Navajo life that resonated with her own; "fun" is declared essential alongside all the undeniable financial and medical difficulties Forster's letters reveal in their long life together. And the unmentioned difficulty of being a couple.

I don't want to make Gilpin sound Pollyannaish, and so I close by pondering the images in the epilogue to *The Enduring Navaho.* These feature a 1930s photograph of Mrs. Francis, in Navajo blanket, her eldest son beside her (248). Characteristically for Gilpin, the warmth of Mrs. Francis's gaze is not directly caught by the camera, and the boy, too, looks aslant; mother and child are together insofar as their shared locus of attention is elsewhere, though where they are looking is unseen by the viewer/camera, perhaps at Elizabeth Forster, standing beside the photographer. Below is a picture of Francis Nakai taken at the same time, more frontal but not completely so; he is half smiling, half shadowed. On the facing page is a photograph of the Nakais taken upon Gilpin and Forster's return to Red Rock in the 1950s (figure 13):

> It was seventeen years before we saw them again, and we found many changes. Still living in the same little house, they then had two daughters, much younger than the boys we had known. The oldest son had been killed in the European theatre of World War II, and almost the only object in the room in which we were sitting was the flag that had been over the boy's coffin at the time of his burial in France. Both Francis and his wife seemed dejected and we were distressed by the change. (247)

13. Laura Gilpin, *Navaho Family (Francis Nakai and family, Red Rock)*. Gelatin silver print, 1950. (© 1979, Amon Carter Museum, Fort Worth, Texas. Gift of Laura Gilpin.)

Gilpin's words begin to give a sense of the devastation caught in the image; here, for once, eyes meet the camera, and except for a certain reserve in Francis Nakai's face (perhaps explained by the alcoholism Gilpin notes in her text), there is pure anguish, deep sadness. The flag that covers half the picture resonates with the loss of the son and the failed promises of the United States that have characterized Navajo life for over a century. Gilpin's text does not leave the Nakais there, but records their recovery, then the death of Francis Nakai from pneumonia, and, finally, Gilpin and Forster's last tear-filled visit to Mrs. Francis, which ends as she gives Gilpin "a beautiful hand-woven belt she had recently made" and "Betsy had them all smiling and happy" (248), an economy of exchange that must be read in counterpoint to the image.

In virtually ending her book with these images of the Nakais, Gilpin allows me one last glance at her relationship with Cather, the topic that occasioned these pages. For the only book we know the well-read Forster had with her while she lived in Red Rock was *Death Comes for the Archbishop,* and we know that because she mentions lending it to Francis Nakai (*Denizens,* 79). Gilpin mentions Cather once, not in *The Enduring Navaho,* but in *The Pueblos;* in the text accompanying a photograph of Acoma, she alludes to *Death Comes for the Archbishop* as a "graphic" and "beautiful" text (120). The novel also appears in the bibliography of *The Rio Grande.* Cather's book is, of course, generically a historical romance, the genre I have argued is Gilpin's as well.

So, imagine that Gilpin's Cather project was Forster's. Put beside the archbishop and his male companion, setting off into the Southwest, the intrepid figures of Gilpin and Forster. Recall the story that Gilpin told over and again of how they came to be there. They were on a camping and photographing trip and, given bad directions by an Anglo, found themselves out of gas in the desert. Gilpin trudged off—it was a ten-mile walk to the nearest trading post—leaving Forster to guard the car. From what? Gilpin asks in the dedicatory letter to *The Enduring Navaho,* admitting the folly of the fears that beset her, the stuff of false romance. On her return she found Forster surrounded by Navajo playing cards with her, "like a swarm of bees about a honeysuckle" (*Enduring Navaho,* v). The desert that they had thought bare teemed with life; the woman-in-distress was this honeysuckle, and there was nothing to fear. The stuff of true romance. Indeed, as Gilpin tells the story as Forster told it to her, before she appeared over the horizon to "rescue" her friend left in the wilderness, the Navajo knew she was coming: "Here comes your friend. She's in Frasier's car." "But," Gilpin continues, "there wasn't a car in sight; it was still over the hill."[58] The Navajo saw without seeing, and not just Frasier's car.

This "mystery" of life in the desert is the particular wonder of so many of Gilpin's photographs, amazing images like the one of "The little shepherd" (*Enduring Navaho,* 92–93), a small boy in a vast expanse, his sheep feeding in a landscape that to Anglo eyes appears incapable of supporting life, a landscape without visible home or habitation (figure 14). It is there in that utterly mysterious image of two men, one on horse, one on foot, meeting in the desert, as Gilpin tells it, a wonder to her and Forster too when they saw these two figures appear as out of nowhere: "We spoke to no one, they paid no attention to us whatsoever, yet I doubt not that later in the day they knew who we were and a surprising lot about us" (*Enduring Navaho,* 91). That unstated knowledge is what illuminates these images, what makes something as ordinary as a meeting resonate with the sublime landscape that seems so unavailable to meaning and yet provides the meaning for such knowledge.

What knowledge is this? It need not be exclusively lesbian, but it is certainly about personal relationships. Hence the final pair of photographs in *The Enduring Navaho* (251): a young couple, close-up, then, below, the same scene, long distance, the man and woman almost invisible in a landscape seemingly without life, nothing but sand and sky. Would we even read their faint shapes as human without the close-up to guide us? What is there to be seen in this landscape, among these people? Pondering these questions, I would also recall Willa Cather and Edith Lewis making their first trip to Mesa Verde, where they too got lost.[59] The parallel is not exact. No Navajo came and swarmed; Cather and Lewis simply sat on a rock, watched the sun set, and Tom Outland's story, Cather's style, clicked into place.

To St. Peter this plain account was almost beautiful, because of the stupidities it avoided and the things it did not say. . . . Yet through this austerity one felt the kindling imagination, the ardour and excitement of the boy, like the vibration in a voice when the speaker

14. Laura Gilpin, *Navaho Shepherd Boy (The Little Shepherd)*. Gelatin silver print, 1950. (© 1979, Amon Carter Museum, Fort Worth, Texas. Gift of Laura Gilpin.)

strives to conceal his emotion by using only conventional phrases. (*Professor's House,* 238)

It is because of such understatement that so little can mean so much in Cather. In *Death Comes for the Archbishop,* the Cather text that bound Gilpin to Forster, Forster to the Navajo, the central relationship of Bishop Latour and Father Vaillant, however much it is a brotherhood of the cloth, is also a strange brotherhood, two friends who chose each other above every other relationship, even possibly their relationship to God, as Latour recognizes in his desire to have Vaillant with him, or when he imagines heaven as the place where they will be together forever. "*Since your brother was called to his reward,*" he writes to Vaillant's sister, "*I feel nearer to him than before.*"[60] Cather's sublimated, displaced relationships are perhaps nowhere more painful or sublime than in this release into a more than mortal union, a holding fast to the first moment when they came together—"he was standing in a tip-tilted green field among his native mountains, and he was trying to give consolation to a young man who was being torn in two before his eyes by the desire to go and the necessity to stay" (299) — a memory that is Latour's last conscious moment. Father Joseph awakens in Jean Latour "extraordinary personal devotion," and what makes it extraordinary is that it is a feeling "aroused and retained so long, in red men and yellow men and white" (289). In *Death Comes for the Archbishop* the relationship of Father Jean and Father Joseph is thereby generalized, and made of a piece with Latour's declaration after he sees his Navajo friend Eusabio for the last time: "I have lived to see two great wrongs righted; I have seen the end of black slavery, and I have seen the Navajos restored to their own country" (292).

While the relationship of the two fathers is one maintained at a distance throughout the novel (making all the more poignant Latour's yearning for and ultimate union with Vaillant), Latour's more usual and frequent partner is the Native American Jacinto. They are "two companions" who commune together and yet who maintain their own thoughts (92). Latour has "human companionship with his Indian boy" (93), and the novel immediately retracts and rewrites this nomination, "boy" signifying an elasticity and youthfulness that has nothing to do with naivete, meaning "nothing boyish in the American sense, nor even in the European sense" (93). The novel's negations here point to the special ur-meaning of "boy" in Cather and, in the articulation of its untranslatability, reinforce the sense that the companionship of Latour and Jacinto is not one in which the Westerner seeks to impose himself on the alterity valued in the native. It is only at the level of unspoken, unspeakable emotion that union is possible, a union deferred to a futurity, or realized only through the Navajo, in the way they are said to take possession by dispossession. "It was the Indian's way to pass through a country without disturbing anything; to pass and leave no trace, like fish through the water, or birds through the air. It was the Indian manner to vanish into the landscape, not to stand out against it" (233). This Navajo way of being names the artistic principle joining Cather and Gilpin.

In *Death Comes for the Archbishop* there is no doubting that Cather was aware that Western possessiveness involves mastery and ownership, that the vanishing of the Navajo entailed their being made to disappear. It is always possible to treat the exaltation of sublime reunion as an ideological ruse, to mistrust the naivete of Latour's joy in living to see the end of slavery and the restoration of Navajo land as concealing the part he played (if not personally then as a European) in those deprivations, to mistrust the belatedness of this celebration as the mirror of the brotherly meeting he dreams of as he leaves the world. But it is also possible—and it has been the aim of this book to imagine this possibility—that the affective charge of that otherworldly meeting lies in its power to figure an alterity otherwise unimaginable *except as the alterity that coexists with ordinary relationships.* And thus to imagine and to realize in and through others an alterity otherwise unimaginable.

Notes

Preface

1 Willa Cather, "The Novel Démeublé," in *Not Under Forty* (Lincoln: University of Nebraska Press, 1988 [1922]), p. 50.
2 Willa Cather, *The Song of the Lark* (Boston: Houghton Mifflin, 1988 [1937]), p. 72.
3 See Janet Halley, *Don't* (Durham: Duke University Press, 1999); Michael Warner, *The Trouble With Normal* (New York: Free Press, 1999).
4 Sedgwick's essay appeared initially in *SAQ* 88, no. 1 (1989): 53–72; the theoretical introduction was incorporated into the opening chapter of her *Epistemology of the Closet* (Berkeley: University of California Press, 1990), while a version of the Cather essay appears in *Tendencies* (Durham: Duke University Press, 1997).
5 Butler's essay is included in her *Bodies That Matter* (London: Routledge, 1993).
6 Julie Abraham, "Willa Cather's New World Histories," in *Are Girls Necessary?* (New York: Routledge, 1996); Christopher Nealon, "Affect-Genealogy: Feeling and Affiliation in Willa Cather," *American Literature* 69, no. 1 (March 1997): 5–37. A version of this essay appears as a chapter in Nealon's *Foundlings* forthcoming from Duke University Press.

Other Names

1 Sharon O'Brien, " 'The Thing Not Named': Willa Cather as a Lesbian Writer," *Signs* 9, no. 4 (summer 1984): 576–99.
2 Citations of "My First Novels (There Were Two)" from appendix B to *Alexander's Bridge,* ed. Marilee Lindemann (Oxford: Oxford University Press, 1997), pp. 97–98, from which all citations from the novel also will be drawn. The *Colophon* essay also is included in *Willa Cather on Writing* (Lincoln: University of Nebraska, 1988 reprint of 1949 collection).
3 Sharon O'Brien, *Willa Cather: The Emerging Voice* (Oxford: Oxford University Press, 1987), pp. 392–93.
4 Hermione Lee, *Willa Cather: Double Lives* (New York: Vintage, 1989), p. 11.

5   For a telling analysis of such critical procedures, see Eve Kosofsky Sedgwick, *Epistemology of the Closet* (Berkeley: University of California Press, 1990), "Introduction: Axiomatic," especially pp. 52–53.

6   On this, see the case that Joanna Russ makes, detailing her difficulty in placing an essay on Cather's lesbianism in 1986 ("To Write 'Like a Woman': Transformations of Identity in the Work of Willa Cather," reprinted and revised in Russ, *To Write Like a Woman* [Bloomington: Indiana University Press, 1995]. The clearest sign of the times is a piece by Joan Acocella, "Cather and the Academy," *The New Yorker* (27 November 1995), pp. 56–71, which excoriates most feminist and gay affirmative criticism of Cather, but endorses Russ, precisely because she can take, from its account of closeted writing practice, the opportunity to practice what Eve Kosofsky Sedgwick has summarized as the strategy of (un)knowingness that reduces to "Don't ask. Or, less laconically: You shouldn't know" (*Epistemology of the Closet,* p. 52). Acocella affirms that Cather was a lesbian, but that she never had lesbian sex, and that her sexuality therefore has nothing to do with her success as a writer. Acocella's essay, while claiming to be doing nothing more than rescuing Cather from the ideological extremes and flattening aims of her critics, is an exercise in a familiar "populist" antiintellectualism. This is even more explicit in the slightly expanded version of her essay that appeared as *Willa Cather and the Politics of Criticism* (Lincoln: University of Nebraska Press, 2000), which ends with a brief chapter in which Red Cloud inhabitants are allowed to voice versions of their difficult lives which are assumed to be identical to the message of Cather's novels. For all her claims to be rescuing Cather and attending to her literary value, Acocella reduces Cather's texts to banalities, themes of the kind she no doubt was taught that Cather represented when she read her in high school ("Nature was the inspirer of Cather's irony," she intones, "and of her tragic vision. Nature showed her that the world might be beautiful, and loud with life, yet wholly indifferent to the happiness of its creatures" [p. 89], Willa Cather and the enduring theme of "Man vs. Nature"). It is part of the mean-spiritedness of Acocella's book that she fails to realize the passionate investment in Cather—and not least in her as a writer—of the critics she so nastily and ignorantly dismisses.

7   The half-heartedness of the use of "queer" in Marilee Lindemann, *Willa Cather: Queering America* (New York: Columbia University Press, 1999), can be seen in the opening sentences of the book: "Willa Cather was not a Queer Nationalist, and neither am I. She might have been a Queer theorist, but I don't claim that lofty title for myself. Indeed, I didn't think I was even a Queer critic—merely a practicing

lesbian whose work as a feminist critic occasionally attended to sex as well as gender—until I began searching for a way to frame a study of Willa Cather's entanglements in the social and literary histories of the United States in the first quarter of the twentieth century" (pp. 1–2).

8   See "Jane Austen and the Masturbating Girl," in Eve Kosofsky Sedgwick, *Tendencies* (Durham: Duke University Press, 1997), p. 126.

9   The 1922 preface appears as appendix A in the Oxford edition of *Alexander's Bridge;* my citations from the beginning and end of the piece appear on pp. 94 and 96 respectively.

10 In "The Cowboy, the Dandy, and Willa Cather" (in *The Cowboy and the Dandy* [New York: Oxford University Press, 1999], pp. 85–94), Perry Meisel makes this claim in the course of an argument about Cather's ability to cross the divide that bears comparison with my own, although Meisel phrases these meetings of east and west, inside and outside, male and female (in *Alexander's Bridge* particularly) as Bloomian metalepses; unlike O'Brien, who finds Cather's opposites reconciled in the feminine, Meisel finds them reconciled in *The Professor's House,* but gives no sexual terms that might complicate this masculinist meeting. For another reading of "Cather's Dandy" and its French connections, see Jessica R. Feldman, *Gender on the Divide* (Ithaca: Cornell University Press, 1993), chapter 5.

11 The best exposition of the function of Bergsonian intuition of which I am aware is chapter 1 of Gilles Deleuze, *Bergsonism,* trans. Hugh Tomlinson and Barbara Habberjam (New York: Zone Books, 1991). For an analysis of intuition as key to postmodern politics, see Brian Massumi, "The Autonomy of Affect," *Cultural Critique* 31 (1995): 83–109. My thanks to Kathy Trevenen for suggesting Massumi's essay to me, since it led me to further understand the significance of Bergson for Cather. Cather's relationship to Bergson is attested by Elizabeth Shepley Sergeant, as Loretta Wasserman notes in "The Music of Time: Henri Bergson and Willa Cather," *American Literature* 57, no. 2 (1985): 226–39, an essay redacted as "William James, Henri Bergson, and Remembered Time in *My Ántonia,*" in Susan J. Rosowski, ed., *Approaches to Teaching Cather's "My Ántonia"* (New York: MLA, 1989), pp. 83–88. The fullest treatment of the cultural significance of Bergson for early twentieth-century America is Tom Quirk, *Bergson and American Culture* (Chapel Hill: University of North Carolina Press, 1990), which devotes most of chapter 3 (especially pp. 113–38) to comparing *Alexander's Bridge* to *O Pioneers!* in terms of the Bergsonism of the latter novel, organic vitalism replacing mechanism; chapter 4 surveys Cather's later writing for the Bergsonism of her central artistic tenets involving memory, its retentiveness of primordial pastness in

the present (pp. 158–59 offer one useful summary of these connections).

12   The essay, "Katherine Mansfield," appears in Willa Cather, *Not Under Forty* (Lincoln: University of Nebraska Press, 1988), from which I cite.

13   Elizabeth Shepley Sergeant, *Willa Cather: A Memoir* (1953; I cite the Ohio University Press 1992 reprint); Sergeant is paraphrasing Cather demeaning her verse as "callow," *The Troll Garden* as "unfledged," and telling her "to wait till she got on paper a story she was brooding over that might prove her first novel: it was about a bridge-builder, with a double nature" (p. 72).

14   Cited from L. Brent Bohlke, ed., *Willa Cather in Person: Interviews, Speeches, and Letters* (Lincoln: University of Nebraska Press, 1986), p. 6.

15   O'Brien moralizes Sarah Orne Jewett's comment in a 27 November 1908 letter to Cather on a male character in one of her stories: "The lover is as well done as he could be when a woman writes in the man's character,—it must always, I believe, be something of a masquerade." In fact, while Jewett offers several points of advice about this and raises the possibility that Cather might have made the relationship one between two women, she ends by commending this male masquerade in just the kind of terms that Cather would use to describe her preferred road: "But oh, how close—how tender—how true the feeling is! the sea air blows through the very letters on the page." Citations from Annie Fields, ed., *Letters of Sarah Orne Jewett* (Boston: Houghton Mifflin, 1911), pp. 246–47.

16   Cited in O'Brien, *Willa Cather*, p. 83.

17   Gertrude Stein, "What Are Masterpieces," in *Writing and Lectures*, ed. Patricia Meyerowitz (Harmondsworth: Penguin, 1967), p. 155 for the citation.

18   Cather's lifelong companion, Edith Lewis, notes how numinous Alexander's boy reverie is by connecting it in her 1953 memoir, *Willa Cather Living* (Athens: Ohio University Press, 1989), p. 79, to the early story, "The Enchanted Bluff," as well as to moments in *My Ántonia* and *Death Comes for the Archbishop*. The connection to *The Professor's House* is made first in the "authorized" biography begun by E. K. Brown and completed by Leon Edel, *Willa Cather* (New York: Knopf, 1953), p. 118 in the 1980 Avon reprinting. It's the main point in Bernice Slote's introduction to her edition of *Alexander's Bridge* (Lincoln: University of Nebraska Press, 1977), pp. xx–xxvi, treated in terms of Cather's attraction to the theme of the "divided self." In her "Introduction" to the Oxford *Alexander's Bridge*, Lindemann notes similarities between Alexander and later "male characters," including Jim Burden, Claude Wheeler, and Godfrey St. Peter, "disappointed by adulthood, marriage, and professional success" (p. x). To this list might be added

Clement Sebastian in *Lucy Gayheart* (New York: Vintage, 1976 [1935]), who believes he might "pick . . . up" his youth "again, somewhere" (77), and does—in Lucy, and before her, in a boy named Marius. In an oft-cited essay by Blanche H. Gelfant, "The Forgotten Reaping-Hook: Sex in *My Ántonia*," *American Literature* 43 (1971): 60–82, moments like these are treated as "regressive," and Gelfant, like critics of the 1930s, takes Cather to task for her inability to represent a mature heterosexuality.

19 The question of Cather's male-male representations is handled with great acuity in Julie Abraham, *Are Girls Necessary?* (New York: Routledge, 1996).

20 To repeat: I don't see this conclusion as supporting Lindemann in her claim that the novel "promotes a conservative ideology of love and sexuality by punishing he who transgresses the norms of procreative, marital heterosexuality with death" (*Alexander's Bridge,* introduction, p. xxviii); when, toward the end of her introduction, Lindemann does suggest that the novel is more ambivalent than that, she locates its ambivalences around questions of national identity.

21 All citations from Willa Cather, *O Pioneers!* (New York: Penguin, 1989).

22 Judith Butler, *Bodies That Matter* (London: Routledge, 1993), pp. 143–66.

23 Butler's argument here could be compared to Judith Fetterley, "*My Ántonia,* Jim Burden, and the Dilemma of the Lesbian Writer," in Karla Jay and Joanne Glasgow, eds., *Lesbian Texts and Contexts* (New York: New York University Press, 1990): "the inability to speak directly is the heart of the problem" (p. 154).

24 All citations of *My Ántonia* are to the 1988 reprint of the 1926 version of the text except when I quote from the original 1918 text; all editions were published in Boston by Houghton Mifflin.

25 In fact, Cather's difficulty and dissatisfaction with the "Introduction" are recorded; see, e.g., E. K. Brown, *Willa Cather* (New York: Knopf, 1953), p. 153.

26 For the history of how immigrant cultures have been racialized, see Matthew Frye Jacobson, *Whiteness of a Different Color* (Cambridge: Harvard University Press, 1998).

27 Mike Fischer, "Pastoralism and its Discontents: Willa Cather and the Burden of Imperialism," *Mosaic* 23, no. 1 (1990): 31–44.

28 For Bourne's cosmopolitan views, see his 1916 essay, "Trans-National America," reprinted in *War and the Intellectuals,* ed. Carl Resek (New York: Harper and Row, 1964), and the discussion in David A. Hollinger, *Postethnic America* (New York: Basic Books, 1995). Bourne's 1918 review of *My Ántonia,* which praises the book but does not stress its

"trans-national" aspects, is reprinted in *Critical Essays on Willa Cather,* ed. John J. Murphy (Boston: G. K. Hall, 1984), pp. 145–46.

29   Guy Reynolds, *Willa Cather in Context* (New York: St. Martin's Press, 1996), p. 80.

30   Willa Cather, *The Song of the Lark* (Boston: Houghton Mifflin, 1988 reprint of 1937 edition), p. 214.

31   Katrina Irving, "Displacing Homosexuality: The Use of Ethnicity in Willa Cather's *My Ántonia,*" *Modern Fiction Studies* 36, no. 1 (spring 1990): 91–102.

32   L. Brent Bohlke, ed., *Willa Cather in Person,* p. 44, from a 6 November 1921 interview in the *Lincoln Sunday Star.*

33   All citations from the 1975 Vintage reprinting of *Sapphira and the Slave Girl* (New York: Random House, 1940). Cather's name signs a brief endnote to the novel (p. 295), a signature in proximity to a character in the novel whose only name is "I," and who appears first on p. 279 and fades, just a bit before the end of the novel, into the voice of Till.

34   Toni Morrison, *Playing in the Dark* (New York: Vintage, 1992); the discussion of Cather occupies pp. 18–28, from which all citations are drawn.

35   Elizabeth Ammons, "*My Ántonia* and African American Art," in Sharon O'Brien, ed. *New Essays on "My Ántonia"* (Cambridge: Cambridge University Press, 1999), p. 62. Ammons makes a similar case in *Conflicting Stories* (New York: Oxford University Press, 1991), and ends a chapter on Cather with a devastating reading of Thea Kronborg's reference to a "nigger" laundry woman, pp. 138–39. In her essay on *My Ántonia,* Ammons looks mainly at the figure of the black pianist Blind D'Arnault, a racial grotesque, but also, as she goes on to show, a figure in whom Cather strongly invests.

36   Naomi Morgenstern, " 'Love is home-sickness': Nostalgia and Lesbian Desire in *Sapphira and the Slave Girl,*" *Novel* 29 (1995–96): 184–205. "What Morrison and other critics seem to at once approach and avoid is a lesbian reading. Sapphira wants to rape Nancy" (p. 191). Morgenstern is not the only critic to make this argument; Julie Abraham ends her chapter on Cather in *Are Girls Necessary?* by allying the depiction of Sapphira's bloated body and will to power as representations of the monstrosity of "a woman's sexual designs on another woman" (p. 58); Lindemann carries the case further by reading the novel as policing — and revealing as "hellish" — the desires it depicts (p. 138).

37   The presentation of Cather as nativist modernist is the burden of Walter Benn Michaels, *Our America* (Durham: Duke University Press, 1995).

38   See Hortense Spillers, "Mama's Baby, Papa's Maybe: An American Grammar Book," reprinted from *Diacritics* 17, no. 2 (1987) in Ange-

lyn Mitchell, ed., *Within the Circle* (Durham: Duke University Press, 1994). For a similar analysis of Cather's novel, see Angela M. Salas, "Willa Cather's *Sapphira and the Slave Girl:* Extending the Boundaries of the Body," *College English* 24 (1997): 97–108. "Cather does not construct Till as a reactionary example of the putative 'deficiencies' of African-American mothers; she portrays her, instead, as a mother from whom the power to protect her child has been stolen" (p. 101).

39 Toni Morrison, "Unspeakable Things Unspoken: The Afro-American Presence in American Literature," *Michigan Quarterly Review* 28, no. 1 (winter 1989): 1–34. This essay is a version of The Tanner Lecture in Human Values that also lies behind *Playing in the Dark.*

40 Cited in Anne Goodwyn Jones, "Displacing Dixie: The Southern Subtext in *My Ántonia,*" in O'Brien, ed., *New Essays,* p. 87.

Cather Diva

1 See, e.g., E. K. Brown, *Willa Cather: A Critical Biography* (New York: Knopf Books, 1953), pp. 140–44 or James Woodress, *Willa Cather: A Literary Life* (Lincoln: University of Nebraska Press, 1987), pp. 252–58.

2 All citations from Willa Sibert Cather, "Three American Singers," *McClure's Magazine* 42, no. 2 (December 1913): 33–48.

3 For a more heightened account, see Elizabeth Moorhead, *These Too Were Here: Louise Homer and Willa Cather* (Pittsburgh: University of Pittsburgh Press, 1950), recalling how Cather did not share Moorhead's enthusiasm for Homer: "Her lips were closed, her face was inscrutable. She was reserving her enthusiasm for Olive Fremstad whom she considered a supreme artist" (p. 41).

4 This is the thesis about Fremstad that Carl Van Vechten offers in his glowing chapter about her in *Interpreters and Interpretation* (New York: Knopf, 1917).

5 See, e.g., Mildred R. Bennett, *The World of Willa Cather* (Lincoln: University of Nebraska Press, 1951), p. 37 (Ray Kennedy modeled on Cather's brother Douglass's railroad housemate); p. 110 (Dr. Archie modeled on Dr. G. E. McKeeby, himself a model for the aspiring Will Cather, M. D.); p. 153 (A. Wunsch's model in Professor Shindelmeisser, Cather's piano teacher and musical mentor). Cf. Woodress, *Willa Cather,* p. 267.

6 All citations from Edith Lewis, *Willa Cather Living* (Athens: Ohio University Press, 1989, reprint of 1953 edition).

7 See, for example, Sharon O'Brien, *Willa Cather: The Emerging Voice* (New York: Oxford University Press, 1987), which deploys these metaphors throughout, and the concluding pages of which attend

to *The Song of the Lark* in these terms. (The move from contralto to soprano would map onto the move to woman-centered writing accomplished in *O Pioneers!*) This is also the thesis of Susan J. Leonardi and Rebecca A. Pope, *The Diva's Mouth* (New Brunswick: Rutgers University Press, 1996), who argue that in representations of the diva, "the diva's voice motivates another woman to discover and use her own . . . voice" (p. 73), "voice" thereby serving "as both a mode of and metaphor for female empowerment" (p. 74).

8 Most official accounts give 1871 as the year of Fremstad's birth. However, the obituary notice that appeared in *Opera News* 16 (15 October 1951) gives 1872, as does the 22 April 1951 obituary notice in the *New York Herald Tribune;* the *New York Times* obituary of 23 April 1951 reports that "accounts of her career do not report her exact age"; her year of birth appears as 1868 in Robert Tuggle, *The Golden Age of Opera* (New York: Holt Rinehart and Winston, 1983), as 1870 in Oscar Thompson, *The American Singer* (New York: Dial Press, 1937). She was at least 41 when Cather met her, perhaps 45. While it is to be expected that the diva's age is not exactly a matter of record, it is the case that almost all aspects of Fremstad's career, especially before she came to the Metropolitan Opera, but even then in terms of performances outside that house, are poorly documented with the most widely conflicting accounts offered as fact (for example, in *McClure's,* Cather claims Fremstad sang in Munich for ten years; most sources say three years, some six, and there does not appear to be any convenient way of checking these assertions).

9 All citations of *The Song of the Lark* will be from the 1937 reprinting of the novel unless otherwise indicated. All references are to Willa Cather, *The Song of the Lark* (Boston: Houghton Mifflin, 1915, 1937).

10 Hermione Lee, *Willa Cather: Double Lives* (New York: Vintage, 1989), p. 121.

11 The literature on this topic is large; I would point to Judith Butler, *Gender Trouble* (New York: Routledge, 1990) and Diana Fuss, *Identification Papers* (New York: Routledge, 1995) for important discussions.

12 Lewis's account seems to match that in a letter of Cather's to Elizabeth Sergeant describing Fremstad's enthusiasm for the novel paraphrased in Woodress, *Willa Cather,* p. 271. See also Sergeant's own account, presumably based on the same letter, in Elizabeth Shepley Sergeant, *Willa Cather: A Memoir* (Athens: Ohio University Press, 1987 [1953]), p. 143.

13 The information can be found in William H. Seltsam, *Metropolitan Opera Annals* (New York: H. W. Wilson, 1947), invaluable for its listing of casts and dates of performances; for my tally I depend as well on a summary sheet on file in the Metropolitan Opera Archives. These

only count performances at the Metropolitan Opera House, however, and do not include regular performances in Brooklyn or Philadelphia or on tour. My thanks to John Pennino for allowing me access to the Metropolitan Opera Archives.

14 For the last point, see Phyllis Robinson, *The Life of Willa Cather* (New York: Holt, Rinehart and Winston, 1983), p. 194. Henry Krehbiel's *Tribune* account of the final performance is reprinted in Seltsam, *Annals*, p. 269; Richard Aldrich's account of her "rousing farewell" appeared in the *New York Times* on 24 April 1914. Fremstad's opera performances after her retirement from the Met included some appearances in Chicago as Kundry (see the 13 January 1916 *Musical Courier* for a review); as Tosca with the Boston Opera Company on 24 November 1915. (See Quaintance Eaton, *The Boston Opera Company* [New York: Appleton-Century, 1965]; she had previously sung two Isoldes in Boston in the winter of 1913; for further, if somewhat conflicting, information, see Thompson, *American Singer*, pp. 232–33.) On 16 December 1914 she gave the first of three recitals in New York (the second was on 15 February 1916; the last, on 19 January 1920, was her final public appearance).

15 James Woodress, *Willa Cather*, p. 273.

16 All references to Mary Watkins Cushing, *The Rainbow Bridge* (New York: G. P. Putnam's Sons, 1954).

17 Walter Schmucker, "A Tribute to Olive Fremstad," *Opera News* 16 (31 December 1951), p. 23.

18 I don't mean to suggest, of course, that Fremstad's appearance as Giulietta was the only time in her career that she substituted for an indisposed singer, although all the other instances I have found do not involve her stepping into a role midway through a performance; the *Hoffman* moment is the one that registered for Cather. When Fremstad appeared for Marie Duchene (who, in fact, was not sick, simply trapped in an elevator), she took up a part she had sung a few times earlier in the season and had abandoned as not particularly suited to her talents or ambition. See Cushing, *Rainbow Bridge*, pp. 217–19, for a version of the episode of her last-minute substitution as Giulietta worth comparing to the scene when Thea is called to sing Sieglinde in *Song of the Lark*, pp. 376–84.

19 For one example, see W. J. Henderson, *The Art of Singing* (New York: Dial Press, 1938): "as time passed it became clear that Mme. Fremstad had to pay the inevitable price of pushing up her voice. She suffered loss of resonance, of quality and indeed of all tone in some of the high flights of the score" (p. 498). He is discussing her singing of Isolde; Henderson was daily music reviewer for the New York *Sun* during the years Fremstad sang at the Met.

20 Cited in Tuggle, *The Golden Age of Opera*, p. 91. A couple of years later, on 9 March 1908, reviewing Fremstad in the part, St. John-Brenon was a good deal more generous in the *Morning Telegraph:* "Olive Fremstad was the Brünnhilde. In poetry of gesture, in romantic heroism of bearing, this fine actress was the intense self she is always. She threw herself into the part, she felt it and she lived it. She spared herself in no way." This opinion is, in fact, closer to that voiced in most reviews of Fremstad's first Brünnhilde. Richard Aldrich in the *New York Times* (14 December 1905), for example, understood that Fremstad would want to sing the part, and that while her "voice is not intended by nature to sing this music," he finds her performances in many ways "superb" despite some forcing and unsteadiness in the highest reaches of the part (which are killing). Aldrich expresses confidence that future performances will be better, depending on a fact mentioned in review after review of Fremstad, that her performances grew over time: viewers went to see Fremstad because they could expect something better each time.

21 I therefore do not endorse the usual view, offered by Robin Heyeck and James Woodress, "Willa Cather's Cuts and Revisions in *The Song of the Lark*," *Modern Fiction Studies* 25, no. 4 (winter 1979–80): 651–58, that the 1937 changes represent Cather fixing artistic lapses and removing unnecessary detail in order to produce a more time-transcending and conventional piece of writing with a more acceptably feminine protagonist. Rather, the analysis I offer here — in which disidentification, sacrifice, and aggressivity, accompany acts of identification — depends upon Judith Butler's chapter on Cather in *Bodies That Matter* (New York: Routledge, 1993), and the case I am making here could be compared to arguments in chapter 1 detailing the murderousness of Sapphira's desire for Nancy.

22 All citations from Marcia Davenport, *Of Lena Geyer* (New York: Charles Scribner's Sons, 1936). In making this comparison I follow several critics who have explored the relationship between Fremstad and various fictionalizations of her career; these include Terry Castle, "In Praise of Brigitte Fassbaender (A Musical Emanation)" in her *The Apparitional Lesbian* (New York: Columbia University Press, 1993); Elizabeth Wood, "Sapphonics," in Philip Brett, Elizabeth Wood, and Gary C. Thomas, eds., *Queering the Pitch* (New York: Routledge, 1994), and Leonardi and Pope, *The Diva's Mouth*. As I mentioned earlier, Cather critics have handled the relationship to Fremstad in a fairly perfunctory way. These three studies do include Cather, and their approaches to her and to questions of gender and sexuality intersect with my own.

23 For these details, see Henry-Louis de la Grange, *Gustav Mahler* (Ox-

ford: Oxford University Press, 1995). Alma Mahler reports: "Mahler said after a performance of *Tristan* with Fremstad and Burrian: 'The stars were kind. I have never known a performance of *Tristan* to equal this'" (*Gustav Mahler: Memories and Letters,* trans. Basil Creighton; ed. Donald Mitchell, third ed. [Seattle: University of Washington Press, 1975], p. 131). Versions of Mahler's admiration can also be found in *Song of the Lark,* pp. 347, 366.

24 It is only Alma Mahler who records this performance. See *Mahler: Memories and Letters,* p. 133: "It was a feast for the ear, not the eyes. Don Giovanni, Scotti; Donna Anna, Fremstad; Elvira, Gadski; Zerline [*sic*], Farrar; Ottavio, Bonci; Leporello, Chaliapin." Although Fremstad's Munich repertoire had included at least one Mozart part, Dorabella in *Così fan tutte,* she sang no Mozart parts at the Met. The cast Davenport provides comes close to the one Mahler reports, Eames and Sembrich substituted for Gadski and Farrar (perhaps because Gadski was Fremstad's rival, while Farrar was the Lilli Lehmann student who retained her teacher's love).

No Philadelphia performance of Fremstad as Donna Anna is recorded in the updated *Annals of the Metropolitan Opera,* ed. Gerald Fitzgerald (Boston: G. K. Hall, 1989), which, unlike the earlier Seltsam compilation, does list performances by the company that took place outside the Metropolitan Opera House. In this listing, the total number of performances Fremstad gave comes to 351, of which 106 did not take place at the Metropolitan Opera House.

25 Davenport was born in 1903; her mother sang at the Met from 1909 to 1911, and Davenport attended Met performances at that time: "the sopranos I heard oftenest and remembered best were Emmy Destinn, Geraldine Ferrar, and Olive Fremstad," she comments in her autobiography, *Too Strong for Fantasy* (New York: Charles Scribner's Sons, 1967), p. 53, noting also that Fremstad's Isolde, which she heard with Toscanini conducting, set a high standard even for Kirsten Flagstad (p. 31). The narrator's reminiscences in *Of Lena Geyer* of childhood visits to the Met, pp. 305 ff., tally with the memories Davenport includes in her autobiography, which reveals the sources for some of the aspects of Geyer, e.g., that her funeral is based on Marcella Sembrich's, that her repertoire echoes Lilli Lehmann's, that the erotics of her voice matches Davenport's experience hearing Lotte Lehmann (an "ecstasy," she says, "comparable only to falling in love," pp. 162–63). She provides no further details about Fremstad's role in creating Geyer: "anybody who knows the history of opera can name the prototypes" (p. 225), she avers.

26 James McCourt, *Mawrdew Czgowchwz* (New York: Farrar, Straus and Giroux, 1975). McCourt dubs his diva an "oltrano"—her unclassifi-

able voice encompasses all ranges and styles, and like Fremstad, she turns from contralto parts to soprano roles.

27 A parallel to this: without the work that Elizabeth Wood has done in "Sapphonics" around the lesbian composer Ethel Smyth, one might not know that Fremstad sang a lead part in the world premiere of Smyth's *Der Wald* in 1902 and repeated the role the next year, the last of her two seasons at London's Covent Garden; her other parts there were the expected Ortrud (her debut role), Brangaene, Sieglinde, Fricka (in *Rheingold*), and Venus. For brief mention of Fremstad's career at Covent Garden, see Harold Rosenthal, *Two Centuries of Opera at Covent Garden* (London: Putnam, 1958).

28 "Venus or Valkyr" was reprinted in James Huneker, *Bedouins* (New York: Charles Scribner's Sons, 1920); the Fremstad-Huneker correspondence is in the Huneker collection in the Dartmouth College Baker Library; I am grateful to Philip N. Cronenwett for allowing me access. For the authoritative study of Huneker, which includes discussion of his relationship to Fremstad, see Arnold T. Schwab, *James Gibbons Huneker: Critic of the Seven Arts* (Stanford: Stanford University Press, 1963). In a letter of 1 October 1896, Fremstad responds to Huneker's "Venus or Valkyr," in which the protagonist flirts with both a Wagnerian soprano and a Rumanian beauty, worried that she will be recognized, and "very jealous": "Jim, you had a dark beauty in Bayreuth who discarded you—and while there was no one else around, you came to me, is that right? You see how hateful I can be!"

29 The piece appeared in *Century* 77 (1908): 143–45 and is reprinted in Arnold T. Schwab, ed., *Americans in the Arts: Critiques by James Gibbons Huneker* (New York: A. M. S. Press, 1985), pp. 106–08, a collection that also includes a few other brief reviews of Fremstad, among them a 1905 notice that lists some of her Munich roles: Carmen, Brangaene, Venus, Sieglinde. In a letter from Munich on 19 September 1901, Huneker adds Dorabella, Ortrud, and Waltraute to the list; see Josephine Huneker, ed., *Letters of James Gibbons Huneker* (New York: Charles Scribner's Sons, 1922), p. 7. For Huneker's position as a critic with advanced views (as opposed to the more staid Henderson and Krehbiel), and for Fremstad as an innovative Wagnerian, see Joseph Horowitz, *Wagner Nights* (Berkeley: University of California Press, 1994), a richly informative account of Wagner in the United States in the late nineteenth century. Horowitz focuses on the figure of Anton Seidl, under whom Fremstad gave her first public performance (the reviewer in the *Musical Courier* of 11 November 1891, who may have been Huneker, praises her "remarkable voice" for its "power, quality, and range. Her lower tones are rich, full and of great volume, her upper notes brilliant and unforced," before offering caveats

about her limited artistry: "She sang 'Ah, don fatal,' from Verdi's 'Don Carlos,' with plenty of fire, but lacking sadly in control and judgment. This was more manifest in her encore piece, a trashy ballad, which she delivered in a most artificial and amateurish fashion"). Horowitz ends his book with several pages on Fremstad as the last great Wagnerian singer, an opinion echoed in Rupert Christiansen's account of Fremstad's career in *Prima Donna* (Harmondsworth: Penguin, 1984), who claims that "Fremstad had no successor, and the quality of Wagnerian sopranos at the Met did not recover for nearly twenty years" (p. 188). He is thinking of Kirsten Flagstad, who debuted at an age close to that at which Fremstad was forced to retire; Horowitz does not think that Flagstad came close to the achievement of Fremstad.

For another firsthand review of Fremstad's Isolde in Mahler's debut performance, see Samuel Chotzinoff, *Day's at the Morn* (New York: Harper and Row, 1964), pp. 122–24, which emphasizes the brilliance of characterization and vocalization culminating in the overwhelming joy in annihilation of Fremstad's *Liebestod:* "By her rapturous, other-worldly smile as she gazed at her dead lover, she illuminated the hidden idea of the story—that it was not King Mark who had stood between her and Tristan, but life itself" (p. 124).

30 Davenport's novel in fact capitalizes on a rumor that Fremstad was writing her memoirs, lamented as untrue, for instance, by Lawrence Gilman in the *Herald Tribune* on 22 April 1934.

31 Leonardi and Pope, *Diva's Mouth,* p. 108 and p. 258 n. 26; Eve Kosofsky Sedgwick's "Across Gender, Across Sexuality: Willa Cather and Others," *SAQ* 88 (1989): 53–72, is cited in support of a comparison that seems to want to make Davenport's representation properly lesbian and Cather's questionably so, hardly Sedgwick's point.

32 Cushing's account as well as Davenport's novel give many details of Fremstad's rigorous routine; worth consulting, too, is Mary Watkins Cushing, "Isolde Between the Lines," *Opera News* 19 (14 March 1955): 8–10, 26–27, which reproduces Fremstad's extensive marginalia in her score of *Tristan,* indicating that every move and gesture was planned beforehand. Leonardi and Pope valuably emphasize how much Davenport pictures singing as labor.

33 Elizabeth Wood, "Sapphonics," p. 40.

34 Terry Castle, *The Apparitional Lesbian,* p. 215.

35 For the episode, see Cushing, p. 124, and its recounting in Wayne Koestenbaum, *The Queen's Throat* (New York: Poseidon, 1993), p. 99.

36 Cf. Leonardi and Pope, *The Diva's Mouth,* pp. 130–31, which, while attentive to these issues of the complexity of naming the relationship between Fremstad and Watkins, also opts for a desexualized reading.

37 See Eve Kosofsky Sedgwick, *Epistemology of the Closet* (Berkeley: University of California Press, 1990), chapter 1.

38 Suggestive in this respect is the opening chapter of David Schwarz, *Listening Subjects* (Durham: Duke University Press, 1997), on music as a "sonorous envelope," and the transgressive boundary-crossing energies that it awakens in the listener. Schwarz provides a Lacanian pedigree for these speculations; to the texts he cites might be added Michel Poizat, *The Angel's Cry*, trans. Arthur Denner (Ithaca: Cornell University Press, 1992), which, although quite determinately within a heterosexual framework, does have some interesting discussion of the voice as a primordial object of desire, especially the diva's divine voice. The locus classicus for discussion of voice in Lacan is "The Subversion of the Subject and the Dialectic of Desire in the Freudian Unconscious," in Jacques Lacan, *Ecrits: A Selection,* trans. Alan Sheridan (New York: Norton, 1977), especially pp. 314 ff. on erogenous zones; "psychoanalysis is not the rite of the Oedipus complex," Lacan further remarks (p. 316).

    For an analysis of voice as object that resonates with arguments I make below, see Slavoj Žižek, " 'I hear you with my eyes': or, The Invisible Master," in Renata Saleci and Slavoj Žižek, ed., *Gaze and Voice as Love Objects* (Durham: Duke University Press, 1996), pp. 90–126, particularly the discussion of voice and muteness (p. 93), voice and the "drive of the life substance" (p. 94) and its consequent resistance to meaning (pp. 103–04). Žižek draws attention to Edvard Munch's painting *The Scream,* by definition silent, as a kind of parallel, while Neil Hertz, in his thoughtful response to this essay, drew my attention to Munch's *Summer Night,* in which a singer, with mouth closed, is represented, her throat displaced as the elongated reflection of the moon in water, as akin to the representation of the erotics of the mute voice unheard by the ear in Cather. For a Kantian transcendentalizing account of the noumenal limits of voice, see Gary Tomlinson, *Metaphysical Song* (Princeton: Princeton University Press, 1999).

39 See, e. g., Carolyn Abbate, "Opera: or, the Envoicing of Women," in Ruth A. Solie, ed., *Musicology and Difference: Gender and Sexuality in Music Scholarship* (Berkeley: University of California Press, 1993), pp. 225–58. Abbate is obviously writing in answer to Cathérine Clément's *Opera, or the Undoing of Women,* and her main interest is the way in which the music is carried by the performer beyond the control of some original (usually male) composer and beyond the plotting (in which the heroine is most often sacrificed). Crucial here, and for my argument as well, is that this "beyond" has no other locus than in the actuality of materially embodied performance. This body could be that of the actual diva onstage, or that of a recording.

40 Cushing remained a lifelong friend of Fremstad, however, while other women served as the diva's companions in the long years between her 1920 retirement and her death in 1951. Information about these years is not readily available; a *New York Herald Tribune* article of 24 February 1933 announcing "Mme. Fremstad to Reappear at the Metropolitan" (she attended a gala for the farewell of Guilio Gatti-Casazza, the director who had fired her years before) mentions and names a live-in female companion, Dorothy B. Leake. In his "Tribute to Olive Fremstad," Schmucker reports that "her old age was spent in the company of her devoted friends, the Misses Wellington and Wallace" (p. 23). In an on-line biographical essay by George Parous (http://www.cantabile-subito.de/Sopranos/Fremstad_Olive /fremstad_olive.htm), Fremstad is located "in the sapphic circles of . . . the Misses De Forest and Callendar, for many years New York society's answer to Gertrude Stein and Alice B. Toklas."

41 Undated letter in Dartmouth Library. In a letter of 16 May 1920, probably close in time to the undated letter, Fremstad refers to herself as "der 'einsame Fichtenbaume' " and closes her letter to Huneker by citing the line "Der Fichtenbaum steht einsam—aber fest!" It is, of course, possible that Huneker compared Fremstad to a singing tree knowing her fondness for the self-designation.

42 Leonardi and Pope also deny that Geyer's death from cervical cancer is meant as a sexual punishment; however Davenport explicitly casts it as the "price" (p. 467) Geyer must pay for her first sexual experience—intercourse that resulted in the birth of an illegitimate, stillborn child. I take this as a further sign that Davenport wishes her diva had been normatively heterosexual, or that her reader not think the novelist endorses transgressive sex. I suspect too that this plot has something to do with Davenport's relationship to her mother.

43 Originally published in 1920. I cite James Huneker, *Painted Veils* (New York: Horace Liveright, 1929).

44 For example, of her Met debut: "Lilli Lehmann, retired; Ternina retired—who was there except Olive Fremstad to take their place! Fremstad would prove a serious rival to Easter" (p. 263).

45 Schwab, *James Gibbons Huneker,* pp. 267–68, briefly details the parallels to Fremstad but insists that the lesbianism is Huneker's invention in a book that seems programmatically to be trying to represent every form of sex it thinks outrageous.

46 Here I demur from Christopher Nealon's reading of this moment in "Affect-Genealogy: Feeling and Affiliation in Willa Cather," *American Literature* 69, no. 1 (March 1997): 5–37. Nealon takes the shared gender identity of Thea and Fred as boys to indicate that she is averse to sexual relations with him (pp. 15–16); while I agree that Thea's desires

here are not conventionally heterosexual, it seems to me that Cather indicates this by making the two have the same gender.

47 See John H. Flannigan, "Thea Kronborg's Vocal Transvestism: Willa Cather and the 'Voz Contralto'," *Modern Fiction Studies* 40, no. 4 (winter 1994): 737–63.

Another kind of literalization of Fremstad in the novel is through the figure of Oliver Landry, Thea's accompanist ever since their time together in Germany. While Oliver might seem to name Olive in the masculine, he is a somewhat effeminate bachelor (he collects fans) with a diminutive voice, and a family history of abuse by his father and pampering by a maiden aunt, who leaves him her Greenwich Village apartment. Landry moreover is nursed when he has erysipelas by Thea; the latter is a piece of Cather's history with Fremstad. Landry also looks ahead to her Claude Wheeler of *One of Ours*. In other words, the figure of the effeminate man figures both Cather and Fremstad, much as Fred's name seems to be a version of Fremstad's, while Cather projects her desire through Fred's resemblances to Huneker as well.

48 8 August 1896 letter to James Huneker in the Dartmouth College Library. Insofar as he follows Kronborg's German career, and loves but cannot marry the diva because he is already married, Fred strongly echoes Huneker. Fremstad's solution—wishing she were male—could be read as an avoidance of sex through same-gender companionship but seems more likely to propose homosex as an alternative, as well as a nonthreat, to the marital tie. Fremstad did marry twice, in both cases for short periods of time; her longest documented relationship was with Mary Watkins.

49 For the significance of this couple for Cather, see O'Brien, *Willa Cather*, pp. 108, 264, 412.

50 The disquieting racialism of dominance here—or in Cather's ecstasies over Fremstad's Scandinavian skin—is at least complicated by the connection between whiteness and femaleness that positions Cather's "dusky" and "male" desire.

51 For a benign version of this, consider the diva's self-appraisal in *Mawrdew Czgowchwz:* "She was, she thought, perhaps if anything *too* whole, *too* entirely present to herself, like a rogue friend from youth turned all too suddenly a lover" (p. 96).

52 Friedrich Kittler, "World-Breath: On Wagner's Media Technology," in *Opera Through Other Eyes,* ed. David J. Levin (Stanford: Stanford University Press, 1994), p. 231. Kittler describes an amplification system of the soprano voice and orchestra that might be compared with Carolyn Abbate's claims about the more than authorial voice of music

embodied in soprano performance; see, for example, her stunning final chapter, "Brünnhilde Walks by Night," in *Unsung Voices* (Princeton: Princeton University Press, 1991), which concludes with a discussion of what she calls "voice-Brünnhilde" and how it dominates the score of Wagner's *Ring* (pp. 244–48).

53 Cather quotes her in "Three American Singers": "The Swedish voice is always long" (p. 45).

54 See J. Dennis and Louis Migliorini, "Olive Fremstad," *The Record Collector* 7 (March 1952): 53–65. Dennis offers a career summary followed by a listing of the recordings (p. 59), which are then discussed individually by Migliorini in the remaining pages. This is the most complete discussion of the recordings. I should here mention my gratitude to Jan McGee and her colleagues in the recorded sound division of the Library of Congress who were of inestimable help in researching and hearing these recordings. Our knowledge—and evaluation— of these recordings may be altered when they are released on a forthcoming CD engineered by Ward Marston.

55 *Prima Donna*, p. 186.

56 Migliorini, on the other hand, thinks it and Brünnhilde's war cry the weakest of the operatic selections.

57 J. B. Steane, *The Grand Tradition* (Portland, OR: Amadeus Press, 1993); all citations from pp. 95–96.

58 I refer, of course, to Cather's essay "The Novel Démeublé," reprinted in Willa Cather, *Not Under Forty* (Lincoln: University of Nebraska Press, 1936), and cite from p. 50: "Whatever is felt upon the page without being specifically named there—that, one might say, is created. It is the inexplicable presence of the thing not named, of the overtone divined by the ear but not heard by it, the verbal mood, the emotional aura of the fact or the thing or the deed. . . ."

59 Rimbaud writes "Je est un autre" in a letter to Georges Izambard (13 May 1871) and reaffirms the sentiment in a letter two days later to Paul Demeny; Arthur Rimbaud, *Oeuvres Complètes: Correspondance,* ed. Louis Forestier (Paris: Robert Laffont, 1972), pp. 230, 233.

War Requiems

1 I cite Barker's novels from the Plume paperback editions (New York: Penguin): *Regeneration* (1993); *The Eye in the Door* (1995); *The Ghost Road* (1996); Cather's *One of Ours* from the Vintage Classics edition (New York: Vintage, 1991).

2 See Richard Slobodin, *W. H. R. Rivers* (New York: Columbia Univer-

sity Press, 1978), pp. 1–85, for a biography. For a recent assessment of Rivers as an anthropologist, see Adam Kuper, *The Invention of Primitive Society* (London: Routledge, 1988), chapters 8 and 9.

3 All citations from A. T. Fitzroy, *Despised and Rejected* (London: GMP, 1988). For information about the author I depend upon Jonathan Cutbill's introduction in this reprinting. Susan R. Grayzel, *Women's Identities at War* (Chapel Hill: University of North Carolina Press, 1999), notes another unconventional love story in Allatini's 1915 novel *Payment,* but fails to provide further details, as well as a 1919 novel about a young man killed in World War I, *Requiem* (p. 253 n. 54). Paul Hammond's discussion of *Despised and Rejected* in *Love Between Men in English Literature* (London: Macmillan, 1996), pp. 212–21, is little more than useful plot summary; it is suggestively positioned following a discussion of Owen (pp. 203–12) that documents the centrality of representations of homosexuality in Owen's poetry.

4 All citations from Christopher Nealon, "Affect-Genealogy: Feeling and Affiliation in Willa Cather," *American Literature* 69, no. 1 (March 1997): 5–37. For a quite different take on these questions, see Timothy R. Cramer, "Claude's Case: A Study of the Homosexual Temperament in Willa Cather's *One of Ours,*" *South Dakota Review* 31, no. 3 (fall 1993): 147–60, which reads Claude by way of "Paul's Case" (an entirely convincing conjunction) as another instance of Cather's internalized homophobia. Valuable in such a view is its insistence on homophobic violence.

To anticipate the concluding discussion of this essay, it might be worth comparing Nealon's affect-genealogy to the application of Leo Bersani's insistence on a sameness as essential to homosexuality in Jim Ellis's "Strange Meeting: Wilfred Owen, Benjamin Britten, Derek Jarman, and the *War Requiem,*" in Richard Dellamora and Daniel Fischlin, eds., *The Work of Opera* (New York: Columbia University Press, 1997): 277–96. Ellis notes that Jarman's film provides virtually identical and undifferentiated pasts for its English and German figures, and that the community formed between these men conveys the pacifist and homoerotic element in the film as an answer to the sacrificial demands of a society whose bellicosity cannot be disentangled from its homophobia. The "strange meeting" of the film refuses the boundaries of nationality and other normative terms for identity.

5 Nealon considers the early reviews of the novel by H. L. Mencken, Sinclair Lewis, and Ernest Hemingway, all of which can be found in James Schroeter, ed., *Willa Cather and Her Critics* (Ithaca: Cornell University Press, 1967). What he underscores in these accounts also underlies Stanley Cooperman, "The War Lover: Claude" (in *World War I and*

the American Novel [Baltimore: Johns Hopkins University Press, 1967]; reprinted in John J. Murphy, ed., Critical Essays on Willa Cather [Boston: G. K. Hall, 1984]), which analyzes Claude's war aggressivity as a function of his failure to be heterosexual.

6   In pointing to this thematic, I mean to invoke Eve Kosofsky Sedgwick, Epistemology of the Closet (Berkeley: University of California Press, 1990), which guides me throughout my analysis.

7   On the inseparability of sadism and masochism, indeed the priority of masochism, see Leo Bersani, Homos (Cambridge: Harvard University Press, 1995), pp. 95–97.

8   For a reading of One of Ours that sees it motivated by a critique of the war effort and its implication in the transformation of the United States into a global, militaristic power, see Joseph R. Urgo, Willa Cather and the Myth of American Migration (Urbana: University of Illinois Press, 1995), pp. 143–67.

9   See W. E. B. DuBois, "An Essay Toward a History of the Black Man in the Great War" and "The Souls of White Folk" in the Library of America Edition of DuBois, Writings (New York: Literary Classics of the United States, 1986), pp. 879–938.

10   This view can be found in Sharon O'Brien, Willa Cather: The Emerging Voice (New York: Oxford University Press, 1987) and in her "Combat Envy and Survivor Guilt: Willa Cather's 'Manly Battle Yarn'," in Helen M. Cooper, Adrienne Auslander Munich and Susan Merrill Squier, eds., Arms and the Woman (Chapel Hill: University of North Carolina Press, 1989), pp. 184–204. See, e. g., Willa Cather, pp. 249–50, for Cather's transformation of her relationship to Dorothy Canfield Fisher into the relationship between Claude and David Gerhardt; see "Combat Envy," especially pp. 190, 198, for Cather's identifications with Claude and/as her nephew, G. P. Cather.

11   On this point, see Mark J. Madigan, "Willa Cather and Dorothy Canfield Fisher: Rift, Reconciliation, and One of Ours," Cather Studies 1 (1990): 126.

12   As Maureen Ryan comments in "No Woman's Land: Gender in Willa Cather's One of Ours," Studies in American Fiction 18 (spring 1990): 65–75, "Enid's is the untold story of One of Ours. A singularly unattractive character, she quietly violates the norms of her time and place" (p. 70).

13   Better Angel was published under the pseudonym "Richard Meeker" and was recently reissued under the author's proper name (Boston: Alyson, 1995), with an introduction by Hubert Kennedy and an epilogue by Brown. Nealon closes his essay with considerations of gendered difference of the kind I pursue here, which prompts my treat-

ment of the relationship between Claude and Gladys in the light of what Nealon refers to as "clumsy, difficult cross-identifications" (p. 33).

14 This piece of information is provided in Hermione Lee, *Willa Cather: Double Lives* (New York: Vintage, 1991 [1989]), p. 165. For Cather's account of her relationship to Hochstein, see the 1922 interview reprinted in L. Brent Bohlke, ed., *Willa Cather in Person* (Lincoln: University of Nebraska, 1986), pp. 51–57.

15 Frederick T. Griffiths, "The Woman Warrior: Willa Cather and *One of Ours*," *Women's Studies* 11 (1984): 261–85; see especially p. 267. This is close to the point about the scene offered in Julie Abraham, *Are Girls Necessary?* (New York: Routledge, 1996), pp. 44–46, which emphasizes the fatality of homosexuality to the homosocial; this view is endorsed in Marilee Lindemann's reading of the scene, *Willa Cather: Queering America* (New York: Columbia University Press, 1999), pp. 74–76, which, however, complicates its reading of the "homophobia" of the scene by recognizing the "panic" produced by the potential collapse of "the lines between queer and un-queer, enemy and ally, pervert and chum, foreign and native" (p. 76).

16 James Woodress, *Willa Cather: A Literary Life* (Lincoln: University of Nebraska Press, 1987), pp. 332–33.

17 On this point, see Michel Foucault, *The History of Sexuality,* trans. Robert Hurley (New York: Pantheon, 1978), pp. 118–19, and the concluding discussion of bio-power that follows from this linkage of race and sex, a topic discussed further in Foucault, "Faire vivre et laisser mourir: la naissance du racisme," *Les Temps Modernes* 46 n.535 (February 1991): 37–61, a transcript of the final lecture he delivered at the Collège de France in 1976 (the complete set of lectures is now available as *Il faut défendre la société* [Paris: Seuil/Gallimard, 1997]). Michael McKeon, in "Historicizing Patriarchy: The Emergence of Gender Difference in England, 1660–1760," *Eighteenth-Century Studies* 28, no. 3 (1995): 295–322, digresses from his historical point to ponder the asymmetries in the contemporary critical lexicon of race, class, and gender, and suggests (p. 205) that race and sex are perhaps more profitably thought together, since each rests on a suspect biologization of essence.

18 For further information see Pat Barker, author's note, *Eye in the Door,* pp. 278–80; Samuel Hynes, *A War Imagined* (New York: Atheneum, 1991), pp. 226–32, which seems to have influenced Barker's view of a war front at home directed against pacifists and homosexuals as traitors; for some more recent considerations of the case, see William Fiennes, review of Philip Hoare, *Wilde's Last Stand: Decadence, Conspiracy and the First World War, London Review of Books* (18 September

1997), pp. 26–27. Hoare's book was released in the United States as *Oscar Wilde's Last Stand: Decadence, Conspiracy, and the Most Outrageous Trial of the Century* (New York: Arcade, 1998) and offers the fullest narrative of these events. See also Lucy Bland, "Trial by Sexology?: Maud Allan, *Salome* and the 'Cult of the Clitoris' Case," in Lucy Bland and Laura Doan, eds., *Sexology in Culture* (Chicago: University of Chicago Press, 1998), pp. 183–98, which includes further bibliographical guidance.

19 The reading of shell shock as the male counterpart of female hysteria that Barker offers appears indebted to Elaine Showalter, *The Female Malady* (New York: Pantheon, 1985), chapter 7, redacted as "Rivers and Sassoon: The Inscription of Male Gender Anxieties," in Margaret Higgonet et al, eds., *Behind the Lines* (New Haven: Yale University Press, 1987), pp. 61–69. "If it was the essence of manliness not to complain, then shell shock was the body language of masculine complaint, a disguised male protest, not only against the war, but against the concept of manliness itself" (p. 64). Showalter follows a connection made on the opening page of Eric Leed's chapter on neuroses and war in his *No Man's Land: Combat and Identity in World War I* (Cambridge: Cambridge University Press, 1979), p. 163.

In *A War Imagined*, Hynes insists that the kind of rethinking of gender that Barker represents through Rivers is the point to emphasize about him and next to which "sexuality is too simple a concept for the releasing of emotions that Rivers encouraged" (p. 186). This downplaying of sexuality—by which Hynes means homosexuality—is consistent with views that I explore later in this essay—and not the point that Barker seeks to make.

20 For the relationship between the homosocial and the policing of homosexuality see Eve Kosofsky Sedgwick, *Between Men* (New York: Columbia University Press, 1985).

21 This "strict Freudian view" cannot, to my knowledge, actually be found in Freud, although it may be extrapolated from his "Psychoanalysis and War Neuroses," a preface he wrote to a 1919 volume of the same name. (It is reprinted in *Character and Culture*, ed. Philip Rieff [New York: Collier Books, 1963], from which I cite.) In it, and telling for the discussion that follows, Freud sees war neuroses as arising from the conflict between the aggressivity of the war ego which functions as a "newly formed parasitic double" (p. 217) threatening the life of the old peaceful ego. Thus, fear of aggression is turned into "an internal enemy" (p. 219), and narcissistic libido is traumatized. It is easy enough to see how this dynamic can be mapped onto psychoanalytic views that collapse homosexuality into narcissism and sadomasochistic paranoia.

In "Traumatic Cures: Shell Shock, Janet, and the Question of Memory," *Critical Inquiry* 20 (summer 1994): 623–62, Ruth Leys connects Ernst Simmel's claim that shell shock represents a splitting of the personality to Freud's work on hysteria, concluding that shell shock represents the traumatic loss of the mother (see pp. 632–34).

22 For a recent historicizing study of the phenomenon of multiple personality, see Ian Hacking, *Rewriting the Soul* (Princeton: Princeton University Press, 1995). In *The Harmony of Illusions* (Princeton: Princeton University Press, 1995), Allan Young assesses Rivers's contributions to the theory of trauma.

23 All citations from W. H. R. Rivers, *Conflict and Dream* (New York: Harcourt Brace, 1923).

24 See W. H. R. Rivers, *Instinct and the Unconscious* (Cambridge: Cambridge University Press, 1924), p. 26; further citations refer to this edition.

25 For Rivers as "father-confessor," see Siegfried Sassoon, *Sherston's Progress* (Garden City, NY: Doubleday, Doran and Co., 1936), p. 45; for his presence as Sherston's (Sassoon's name for his alter ego) ghostly conscience, see pp. 136, 162, as well as Sassoon's poem, "Revisitation (W.H.R.R.)" in *Collected Poems, 1908–1956* (London: Faber and Faber, 1961), p. 221.

26 Citations from Willa Cather, *Not Under Forty* (Lincoln: University of Nebraska Press, 1988).

27 All citations from Paul Fussell, *The Great War and Modern Memory* (London: Oxford University Press, 1975). For a parallel, consider Jon Stallworthy, *Wilfred Owen* (London: Oxford University Press/Chatto and Windus, 1974), the standard biography written by the editor of the standard new edition of Owen's *Complete Poems and Fragments* (London: Chatto and Windus/Oxford University Press, 1983). At numerous points in considering Owen's early verse, Stallworthy comments on homoerotic elements which he characterizes variously as unclean (p. 70) or immature (pp. 72–73), cloying (p. 141), of possible psychological, but not poetic, interest (p. 195). From the start, however, Stallworthy also wants to insist that an episode that led to Owen's departure from his position of employment in the vicarage at Dunsden must have been about "Christ rather than Eros" (p. 85)—it is, however, more likely that it had to do with his being discovered entertaining a young man in his room—in order to prepare for the conclusion of the book, in which Owen's "disciplined sensuality" and "passionate intelligence" (p. 280) characterize his mature poems.

28 Siegfried Sassoon, *Memoirs of a Fox-Hunting Man* (London: Faber and Faber, 1928), opens with the promising sentence, "My childhood was

a queer and not altogether happy one" (p. 9); the dream figure of the "ideal companion" appears shortly thereafter (p. 11) and is variously embodied in the household groom, Tom Dixon; a hunting companion and eventual master of hounds with whom Sherston lives, Denis Milden; his companion in the hunt, Stephen Colwood; and his battle friend, Dick Tiltwood; it is the death in war of all of these figures except Milden, and the end of an era of innocence metaphorized in fox hunting, that moves Sassoon's autobiographical story of his outdoorsman half, George Sherston.

29 See James S. Campbell, " 'For you may touch them not': Misogyny, Homosexuality, and the Ethics of Passivity in First World War Poetry," *ELH* 64, no. 3 (fall 1997): 823–42, p. 827, for the characterization of Adrian Caesar, *Taking It Like a Man* (Manchester: Manchester University Press, 1993), from which I cite below. Campbell's thesis echoes Caesar; like him, he insists on an ethical stance that involves condemning homosexuality as responsible for misogyny; Campbell fetches his ethical position from Levinas, and although he notes that Irigaray has faulted his masculinism, somehow that does not impugn his ethics, I assume because Levinas, unlike Owen or Sassoon, is presumed heterosexual. These arguments are anticipated by a brief discussion in Sandra M. Gilbert and Susan Gubar, *No Man's Land: Sexchanges* (New Haven: Yale University Press, 1989), noting "an inextricable tangle of (male) misogyny and (male) homosexuality" (p. 302).

30 Cited from Siegfried Sassoon, *The War Poems,* ed. Rupert Hart-Davis (London: Faber and Faber, 1983), p. 29.

31 For a study of some of the ways in which these double trajectories are in play in the military, Steven Zeeland provides much illumination in his books: *The Masculine Marine* (New York: Haworth, 1996); *Sailors and Sexual Identity* (New York: Haworth, 1995), as does Richard Rambuss in "Machinehead," *Camera Obscura* 42 (September 1999): 97–124, an essay on the Stanley Kubrick film *Full Metal Jacket.*

32 See, e.g., his pamphlet *Wilfred Owen,* #246 in the *Writers and Their Work* series (London: British Council, 1974), which refers to the "homosexual and sado-masochistic elements in his [Owen's] nature" (p. 15), and dismisses "Greater Love" as a "deplorable poem" (p. 21). For a feminist appraisal that finds value in Owen's representations of gender, see the "Critical Commentary" in Jennifer Breen, ed., *Wilfred Owen: Selected Poetry and Prose* (London: Routledge, 1988), pp. 171–93.

33 *Character and Culture,* p. 132.

34 See, inter alia, Guy Reynolds, *Willa Cather in Context* (New York: St. Martin's Press, 1996), pp. 113–18; Reynolds is more convincing in his discussion of the contexts for Cather's conflicted views about the war and American society than he is in detailing questions of gender.

35 Philip Hoare, *Serious Pleasure* (New York: Penguin, 1990), p. 11. The anecdote recounted below is also cited from Hoare.

36 Patricia Lee Younger, "Willa Cather's Aristocrats," *Southern Humanities Review* 14, no. 1 (1980): 43–56, chalks up the attraction to Tennant's flamboyant wealth, while Hoare imagines that the asexual although lesbian Cather (a characterization he takes from Hermione Lee) did not see Tennant's "obvious homosexuality," and read his effeminacy as Englishness; he concludes that "neither her own orientation, nor Stephen's, intruded on their friendship" (p. 212), which he attributes to Tennant's acuity as a critic. No doubt Cather was attracted to how expensively Tennant lived, how unguarded he was (she kept a gift of his softcore pornographic drawings in a drawer, sharing them with Edith Lewis), how much he adored Cather's writing, but that cannot be the entire story.

37 Stephen Tennant, ed., *Willa Cather on Writing* (Lincoln: University of Nebraska Press, 1988), cited below.

38 For this well-established connection, see, inter alia, Mervyn Cooke, *Britten: War Requiem* (Cambridge: Cambridge University Press, 1996), especially pp. 49–52.

39 For musicological analysis, see Cooke as well as Peter Evans, *The Music of Benjamin Britten* (Minneapolis: University of Minnesota Press, 1979), chapter 18; James D. Herbert, "Bad Faith at Coventry: Spence's Cathedral and Britten's *War Requiem*," *CI* 25 (spring 1999): 535–65.

40 For the text of the poem that Britten worked from, see Wilfred Owen, *Poems,* with a memoir and notes by Edmund Blunden (1931; I cite from the 1949 reprint in the New Classics series [no publisher given]). It is the final poem in the volume, pp. 116–17, and also includes a series of variants in the notes which Britten used for the text he set in the *War Requiem*. It is worth noting that one source for the strange meeting in the poem is Dante's encounter with his former teacher Brunetto Latini in the circle of sodomites in *Inferno* 15.

41 I have, however, repunctuated in keeping with the text of letter #512 in the *Collected Letters,* ed. Harold Owen and John Bell (London: Oxford University Press, 1967), p. 461.

42 I allude here to the sentence upon which Jacques Derrida meditates in *Politics of Friendship,* trans. George Collins (London: Verso, 1997), and seek to make it available for this study of affect-genealogy in contrast to Derrida's worries that the friendship tradition in its exclusions of women is a necessarily suspect male-male configuration (the suspicion is, once again, of homosexuality, not of male homosocial, that is, heterosexual social organizations).

43 Siegfried Sassoon, introduction to his edition of Wilfred Owen,

Poems (New York: B. W. Huebsch, Inc., n.d. [American reprint of the 1920 English edition]), p. v.

Strange Brothers

1   For a history of visitors to Luhan's house, see Lois Palken Rudnick, *Utopian Vistas* (Albuquerque: University of New Mexico Press, 1996); Cather stayed while she was writing *Death Comes for the Archbishop;* Luhan employed Gilpin some twenty years later.

Judith Fryer Davidov's *Women's Camera Work* (Durham: Duke University Press, 1998) appeared shortly after the initial publication of the essay on Cather and Gilpin in *American Literature* that is the basis for the final section of this chapter. Her book usefully locates Gilpin in the context of other American women photographers, and forcefully revises standard histories of photography of the Western landscape or of pictorialism, the traditions in which Gilpin worked. Davidov makes occasional comparisons between Gilpin and Cather, noting the failed project that I pursue, and she too assumes that Cather's antipathy to films of her work would have extended to a photographic edition of *The Professor's House* (see pp. 413 n. 11; 472 n. 118). She too measures the distance between Gilpin's early romanticized photos of Native Americans with her later images of the Navajo, and offers in passing the point that structures my discussion below, that it was the relationship of Betsy Forster (Gilpin's lifelong partner) to the Navajo that made for Gilpin's: "Gilpin learned to love the people Forster loved" (p. 141).

2   Blair Niles, *Strange Brother* (London: Gay Men's Press, 1991), p. ii. Subsequent citations from the novel are from this edition. Burton's point echoes Roger Austen's treatment of the novel in *Playing the Game: The Homosexual Novel in America* (Indianapolis: Bobbs-Merrill, 1977), pp. 57–92, which also notes Niles's travel writing, as well as her novels about unjust treatment of criminals. Joseph Allen Boone picks up these points in opening his discussion of *Strange Brother* in *Libidinal Currents: Sexuality and the Shaping of Modernism* (Chicago: University of Chicago Press, 1998), describing Niles as "a white female novelist, journalist, and travel writer whose interest in and empathy for 'foreign' cultures marks all her writing" (p. 266).

3   Blair Niles, *Passengers to Mexico* (New York: Farrar and Rinehart, 1943).

4   C. William Beebe, *Two Bird-Lovers in Mexico* (Boston: Houghton, Mifflin, 1905). Citations from chapter xv, "How We Did It," by Mrs. C. William Beebe; p. 366 on the proper "spirit"; p. 372 on the need to

employ a cook ("have it distinctly understood that she is camping for *pleasure*"); pp. 374–75 on the pleasures of nature.

5 Blair Niles, *Journeys in Time* (New York: Coward-McCann, 1946), p. 3.

6 Blair Niles, *The James* (New York: Farrar and Rinehart, 1939), p. 12.

7 C. William Beebe and Mary Blair Beebe, *Our Search for a Wilderness* (New York: Henry Holt and Co., 1910), pp. 80–81.

8 Robert Henry Welker, *Natural Man: The Life of William Beebe* (Bloomington: Indiana University Press, 1975), p. 26, from a chapter on Beebe's marriage.

9 Blair Niles, *Casual Wanderings in Ecuador* (New York: The Century Company, 1923), p. 3.

10 Boone, *Libidinal Currents*, p. 475 n.137.

11 All citations from Blair Niles, *Black Haiti* (New York: Grosset and Dunlap, 1926). J. Michael Dash, *Haiti and the U.S.: National Stereotypes and the Literary Imagination,* 2d ed. (London: Macmillan, 1997 [1988]), notes the complicity with colonization in Niles's "well-meaning" account of Haiti (p. 25), whose primitivist focus ignores real-world problems of economic development (p. 31); Dash also connects her views on Haiti to what he describes as fashionable 1920s antipuritanical views of Harlem (p. 34).

12 David Harrell, "Willa Cather's Mesa Verde Myth," *Cather Studies* 1 (1990): 130–43; citing p. 130. Harrell extends his arguments in *From Mesa Verde to "The Professor's House"* (Albuquerque: University of New Mexico Press, 1992). Richard Wetherill's first sighting has been disputed by his brother Al; see Maurine S. Fletcher, ed., *The Wetherills of the Mesa Verde* (Lincoln: University of Nebraska Press, 1977), especially part 2. (The book is a version of Al Wetherill's autobiographical papers.)

13 The essay is reprinted in Susan J. Rosowski and Bernice Slote, "Willa Cather's 1916 Mesa Verde Essay: The Genesis of *The Professor's House,*" *Prairie Schooner* 58, no. 4 (1984): 81–92; "On *The Professor's House*" is included in *Willa Cather on Writing* (Lincoln: University of Nebraska Press, 1988), pp. 30–33.

14 Willa Cather, "On *The Professor's House,*" p. 32.

15 He seems always to be Richard in the biographical account offered by Frank McNitt, *Richard Wetherill: Anasazi* (Albuquerque: University of New Mexico Press, 1957, 1966); in the reminiscences of his wife compiled by Kathryn Gabriel, *Marietta Wetherill* (Boulder: Johnson Books, 1992); in his brother Al's autobiographical writings. For Gilpin's naming, see Laura Gilpin, *The Pueblos: A Camera Chronicle* (New York: Hastings House, 1941), p. 34. The essays by Butler are included in her *Bodies That Matter* (New York: Routledge, 1993).

16 Edith Lewis, *Willa Cather Living* (Athens: Ohio University Press, 1989 [1953]), pp. 94–95.

17 Sharon O'Brien, *Willa Cather: The Emerging Voice* (New York: Oxford University Press, 1987), for instance, while certainly aware of the importance of Lewis's role in Cather's life, nonetheless complains that "one doesn't learn much about this relationship from Lewis' cautious memoir" (p. 354). In her foreword to *Willa Cather Living*, Marilyn Arnold is rather circumspect about the personal relationship of the two women, but acute in noting how the book shows "the merging of one mind and life into that of another" (p. xxiii).

18 It is occupied, as suggested above in "War Requiems," by Stephen Tennant.

19 See Leon Edel, "A Cave of One's Own," in *Stuff of Sleep and Dreams* (New York: Harper and Row, 1982), p. 238. Edel's broader pyschological reading of the novel I find quite unconvincing in its recourse to themes of regression and maternal domination.

20 Doris Grumbach, "A Study of the Small Room in *The Professor's House*," *Women's Studies* 11 (1984): 327–45; citing p. 339. Grumbach's recognition of the homoerotics of the relationship is welcome, of course, and not something most critics notice, nor would I deny Cather's identification with St. Peter, the most telling sign of which, in this context, is the fact that the study that Isabelle McClung earlier provided for Cather in her Pittsburgh house was a room, like the professor's, shared with a seamstress.

21 All citations from *The Professor's House* (New York: Vintage, 1990 [1925]).

22 It also explains Kathleen's otherwise unmotivated assurance to Scott that he is "the real one" (p. 93) after they witness a scene in which Rosie seems to betray some feeling for Outland; the assurance concludes an elliptical conversation which may suggest that Scott knew that there was Tom before he came along, and before Kathleen lost him to her sister.

23 On that episode, see Eve Kosofsky Sedgwick, "Across Gender, Across Sexuality: Willa Cather and Others," *SAQ* 88, no. 1 (1989), pp. 62–63. Similar energies are deployed in *The Professor's House* against St. Peter's rival colleague Horace Langtry, derisively named "Lily" (41) and "Madame" (43). Langtry seems akin to the professor of "The Professor's Commencement," and his doubled relationship to St. Peter is a sign of an attempted splitting of the professor, just as Louie and Tom serve as alter egos. On the possibilities of mobilizing anti-Semitism for antigay purposes, see Daniel Boyarin, "Freud's Baby, Fliess's Maybe: Homophobia, Anti-Semitism, and the Invention of

Oedipus," *GLQ* 2 (1995): 115–47. For a reading of Louie in terms consonant with the ones I provide, see Julie Abraham, *Are Girls Necessary?* (New York: Routledge, 1996), p. 51. Abraham's chapter on Cather, which appeared after I wrote "Strange Brothers" in 1995, attempts important connections between her representations of homosexuality and heterosexuality, of male–male and lesbian identifications facilitated by the figure of the "boy," and attends, in its pages on *The Professor's House,* to the relationship between Tom and Roddy as well as between Tom and St. Peter.

24 Hermione Lee, *Willa Cather: Double Lives* (New York: Vintage, 1989), p. 241.

25 One of the most extraordinary descriptions of the hand can be found in "Neighbour Rosicky" (Willa Cather, *Stories, Poems, and Other Writings* [New York: Library of America, 1992], p. 616); I owe to Judith Butler, and her "The Lesbian Phallus and the Morphological Imaginary" (in *Bodies That Matter*), the warrant for thinking about hands in this sexual fashion. I have also been implying that in this confluence of hand and back garden, Cather may share with her mentor Henry James a rich anal erotics. On this in James, see Eve Kosofsky Sedgwick, "Is the Rectum Straight? Identity and Identification in *The Wings of The Dove,"* in *Tendencies* (Durham: Duke University Press, 1993). On Cather's anal erotics, see the forthcoming essay by Michèle Aina Barale in her *Below the Belt* to be published by Duke University Press.

26 "The Enchanted Bluff," in Willa Cather, *Twenty-Four Stories,* ed. Sharon O'Brien (New York: Penguin/Meridian, 1987), p. 255.

27 This suggests that Native American civilization may have served something of the same function for Cather as it provided a site for homosexual projection in Hart Crane; on this, see Jared Gardner, "'Our Native Clay': Racial and Sexual Identity and the Making of Americans in *The Bridge,"* *American Quarterly* 44, no. 1 (1992): 24–50.

28 George Chauncey, *Gay New York: Gender, Urban Culture, and the Making of the Gay Male World, 1890–1940* (New York: Basic Books, 1994), pp. 6–7, 273–80, 375 n. 8. It is, of course, ironic that Hermione Lee subtitles her book "Double Lives" without registering the salience of that term in this context.

29 Lillian Faderman, *Odd Girls and Twilight Lovers* (New York: Penguin, 1991). While Faderman alludes to the title of a 1950s lesbian novel, the term "twilight" has both gay male and lesbian currency in the 1920s and 30s.

30 Blair Niles, *Condemned to Devil's Island* (New York: Harcourt, Brace and Company, 1928), p. xii.

31 Blair Niles, *Free* (New York: Harcourt, Brace and Company, 1930),

p. 154. After *Strange Brother*, Niles continued to write similar novels championing the causes of those she considered unjustly treated by society. *Light Again* (1933), for example, is set in an insane asylum. Her final novels bring together her interests in race and the history of slavery and conquest; *Maria Paluma* (1934) is a historical novel set in Guatemala; *Day of Immense Sun* (1936) in Peru, while *East By Day* (1941) is about slaves returning to Africa. Niles also continued to write travel books about South America. Her last book was a biography of George Washington, *Martha's Husband* (1951).

32   See *The Professor's House*, pp. 59–60, for the pageant of the sons-in-law, Louie in "a green dressing gown and turban," Scott attired like Richard Plantagenet (giving a crusading excuse for Scott's anti-Semitism, as well as pointing to the kind of possible homo resonance Sedgwick notes in the Berengaria ["Across Gender, Across Sexuality," p. 71]; p. 233 for the allusion to *Othello* 1.1.135, which suggests the further parallel between Tom's storytelling and the Moor's.

33   See Lee, *Willa Cather: Double Lives*, p. 251, who also reads Roddy sympathetically; as she notes he is "an unusual figure in Cather's work, a radical working man," although I think much of what his "working-man" status conveys is often the work of immigrant culture in other Cather novels and stories—those Bohemians who may encode another form of *la vie de bohème* as well (Cather herself was a Greenwich Village denizen, of course). As Lee puts it, Roddy's "personal tenderness has led him, in Forster's phrase, to betray his country rather than his friend; Tom's idealism makes him betray his friend in the interests of his country." I am not convinced by arguments like those of Walter Benn Michaels originally published in "The Souls of White Folks" (in *Literature and the Body*, ed. Elaine Scarry [Baltimore: Johns Hopkins University Press, 1988] and in "Race Into Culture: A Critical Genealogy of Cultural Identity," *Critical Inquiry* 18, no. 4 (1992): 655–85, or in "The Vanishing American," *American Literary History* 2:2 (1990): 220–41, Michaels's application of the race-into-culture argument to *The Professor's House*, and now recast in Walter Benn Michaels, *Our America* (Durham: Duke University Press, 1995). What I think requires more thought here is the degree to which the evocation of national culture is to be taken straight or simply as Cather's political position. It is certainly the case that Cather opposed melting-pot models for the assimilation of immigrants, but she did so from an aversion to "turning them into stupid replicas of smug American citizens" (*Willa Cather in Person* [Lincoln: University of Nebraska Press, 1966], p. 71, from a 1924 *New York Times* interview), which suggests that American citizenship may have not been as central to Cather as Michaels seems to believe. In "Affect-

Genealogy": Feeling and Affiliation in Willa Cather, *American Literature* 69.1 (1997): 5–37, Christopher Nealon shows how Cather "assembled a lesbian strategy for imagining an America in which feeling, not family, would be the basis of affiliation" (p. 11). Such an argument wrests "culture" from "ideology" and makes valuable and valued space for sexuality and affect.

34 Possibly Cather made the Proustian connection, of anti-Dreyfus sentiment and homophobia. On this point, see Abraham, *Are Girls Necessary?* pp. 50–51, 187 n. 14.

35 See Martha Sandweiss, *Laura Gilpin: An Enduring Grace* (Fort Worth: Amon Carter Museum, 1986), a book-length biography, and "Laura Gilpin and the Tradition of American Landscape Photography," in *The Desert Is No Lady*, ed. Vera Norwood and Janice Monk (New Haven: Yale University Press, 1987), pp. 62–73. Further citations from these sources appear in the text, abbreviated as *LG* and *Desert*, respectively.

36 Laura Gilpin, *The Mesa Verde National Park: Reproductions From a Series of Photographs by Laura Gilpin* (Colorado Springs: Gilpin Publishing, 1927).

37 The letter of 21 March 1929 from Boughton about the project and its failure is exceedingly ambiguous. Reporting that Cather was away in California tending her ailing mother and not expected home soon, Boughton comments on Gilpin's "hard luck in missing her"; this remark leaves open the question of whether this was the first such misfortune. Boughton also says that it is "too bad" that Gilpin had failed to land "the illustrations job," suggesting, perhaps, that it had not been initiated by Gilpin or that Cather had at least known about the plan. I cite the letter from the Laura Gilpin Papers, Amon Carter Museum Archives, Fort Worth, Texas, and thank Paula Stewart, the archivist, for supplying me with a copy of it, and Martha Sandweiss, for directing me to Ms. Stewart.

38 A small exception to this is the 1937–1941 edition of Cather's *Novels and Stories* brought out by Houghton Mifflin. This thirteen-volume set includes illustrations: one of the Benda cuts adorns *My Ántonia*; other volumes feature reproductions of manuscript pages or hand-corrected typescripts of the novels and stories; four photos of Cather are also included. Thus, with the exception of the Benda print, the author and her working habits are illustrated, not the texts. In the context of this discussion, it is probably worth saying something about the photographs of the author included, at least to remark that the professional images are stylistically akin to Gilpin's, ranging from the rather stagy pictorialism of the 1924 Muray portrait that serves as a frontispiece to *A Lost Lady*, to the far more "straight" and modernist 1926 image by Steichen tucked in the middle of a volume including

Obscure Destinies and the essays gathered as *Not Under Forty,* here re-titled *Literary Encounters* (volume 12, published in 1938). It is also worth noting that the one image in which Cather interacts with the camera was taken in the garden of Isabelle McClung's home in Ville d'Avray. It is the image in which Cather is nuzzling a pet dog that appears on the cover of this book; I assume Cather's smile is for McClung. The 1922 photo is the frontispiece to *One of Ours* (volume 5, published in 1937).

39 All citations from Laura Gilpin, *The Pueblos: A Camera Chronicle* (New York: Hastings House, 1941) are noted parenthetically in the text as *Pueblos.*

40 Gilpin herself comments on the mixed style of her work, from her early "soft focus" period to a later style that she regards as a sign of her development as a photographer; see her preface to *The Pueblos.* It is this double style that Vera Norwood plots along an axis of romance versus realism in her essay "The Photographer and the Naturalist: Laura Gilpin and Mary Austin in the Southwest," *Journal of American Culture* 5 (summer 1982): 1–28, an opposition I comment upon and cite below.

41 The interviews in question are Paul Hill and Tom Cooper, "Camera Interview: Laura Gilpin," *Camera* 11 (November 1976): 11, 27, 35–37, and David Vestal, "Laura Gilpin: Photographer of the Southwest," *Popular Photography* 80 (February 1977): 100–05, 130–34. For another late interview, see also, Margaretta K. Mitchell, *Recollections: Ten Women of Photography* (New York: Viking, 1979), 120–39.

42 John Collier Jr., "Laura Gilpin: Western Photographer," *New Mexico Quarterly* 20 (winter 1950–1951): 488, 489.

43 Evan Connell, "Mesa Verde," and John Chavez, "Gilpin's Rio Grande as Seen by Another," in *Perpetual Mirage: Photographic Narratives of the Desert West* (New York: Whitney Museum of Art, 1996), p. 77 [Connell]; p. 151 [Chavez]. The exhibit, curated by May Castleberry, was on display from 27 June to 22 September 1996.

44 See Davidov, *Women's Camera Work* (Durham: Duke University Press, 1998), pp. 356–66; all citations from Laura Gilpin, *The Rio Grande: River of Destiny* (New York: Duell, Sloan and Pearce, 1949).

45 For another critique of Gilpin, one that does not accord value to *The Enduring Navaho,* considering it also to be manipulative, see James C. Faris, *Navajo and Photography* (Albuquerque: University of New Mexico Press, 1996), chapter 6. "However well-intentioned, Gilpin was just one more non-Navajo representing Navajo" (p. 240), Faris writes; but this is also the case with Faris, and whether he can claim any more privilege to represent Navajo is questionable.

46 "Deeply personal" is the phrase used by Robert Adams to summa-

rize Sandweiss's argument about the value and motivating force behind Gilpin's portraits in *The Enduring Navaho;* see Adams, *Why People Photograph* (New York: Aperture, 1994), p. 95. The essay on Gilpin in this volume is a review of Sandweiss's book on Gilpin as well as of the show of Gilpin's which it accompanied.

47 For one guide to this distinction, see Alan Trachtenberg, *Reading American Photographs* (New York: Hill and Wang, 1989), chapter 4, especially pp. 174–76.

48 Laura Gilpin, "Historic Architecture Photography: The Southwest," in *The Complete Photographer: An Encyclopedia of Photography,* ed. Willard D. Morgan (New York: National Educational Alliance, 1949), pp. 1986–95. This volume reprints a publication of Gilpin's that first appeared in *Complete Photographer,* 20 July 1942.

49 Several of these images illustrate William N. Goetzmann's "The Arcadian Landscapes of Edward S. Curtis," in *Perpetual Mirage,* pp. 86–87. It was the Curtis image of Canyon de Chelly in her childhood home that, Gilpin affirms, set her on the path toward her photographic career. It is in that context worth noting that her final, unfinished project was to have been a book of Canyon de Chelly photographs.

50 The 1891 photographs by Nordenskiöld to which I refer are beautifully reproduced in *Perpetual Mirage,* pp. 68–69, 76.

51 Reproductions of these images can be found in Alfred Stieglitz, *Camera Work: A Pictorial Guide,* ed. Marianne Fulton Margolis (New York: Dover, 1978), pp. 73–74. Boughton's images could be compared to those of Sicilian boys made by von Gloeden or to F. Holland Day's nude adolescent males, which are often described as if they were nothing but academic studies in an antique style, although their undeniable homoerotic impulses are usually unmentioned by conventional art historians. For an exception, see John Pultz, *The Body and the Lens* (New York: Abrams, 1995). For the homosexual history of this academic tradition, from eighteenth-century French painting and Winckelmann on, I have been enlightened by Michael Moon, *A Small Boy and Others* (Durham: Duke University Press, 1998).

52 This happens in Karen Hust's " 'The Landscape (Chosen by Desire)': Laura Gilpin Renegotiates Mother Nature," *Genders* 6 (November 1989): 20–48, when Hust notes that "an analysis of Gilpin as a lesbian photographer remains potential in my argument" (p. 47 n. 30), the potential seemingly to be found in reading female-female relations as mother-daughter ones (this is how Hust reads Gilpin's relationship to landscape and her negotiation of an otherwise male photographic terrain). This need not necessarily be the case, as is suggested in Carol Mavor's *Pleasures Taken* (Durham: Duke University Press, 1995), which considers the sexuality involved in mother-

daughter images and argues for identification-as-a-mother as a possible route for same-sex identifications; and in Mavor's *Becoming: The Photographs of Clementina, Viscountess Hawarden* (Durham: Duke University Press, 1999), which furthers these arguments by considering the adolescent daughter's desire, and by insisting on a dynamic between the mother/photographer and daughter/subject which is decidedly queer, and insistently erotic.

My point, therefore, should not be read as an attack on mothers or maternity but rather is aimed against the kinds of reductions that often are made in the name of the mother, although happily not in Mavor's work. I would like to believe my critique is informed by Adrienne Rich's *Of Woman Born* (New York: Norton, 1976), a crucial early feminist intervention against the institutionalization of motherhood as the only way in which a woman fulfills herself.

53 The procedures described here are scrutinized by Eve Kosofsky Sedgwick in *Epistemology of the Closet* (Berkeley: University of California Press, 1990).

54 Laura Gilpin, *The Enduring Navaho* (Austin: University of Texas Press, 1968), p. v.

55 *Laura Gilpin: An Enduring Grace,* directed by Anita Thacher, 1986. Many thanks to Millie Seubert of The Museum of the American Indian for providing me with a copy of this tape.

56 Elizabeth W. Forster and Laura Gilpin, *Denizens of the Desert,* ed. Martha A. Sandweiss (Albuquerque: University of New Mexico Press, 1988), p. 33. Further citations are given parenthetically.

57 Willa Cather, *My Ántonia* (1918; reprint, Boston: Houghton Mifflin, 1988), p. 8. Worth comparing too is the movement from this sense of obliteration to the connection affirmed a bit later: "that is happiness; to be dissolved into something complete and great" (p. 14), the passage that provided the words on Cather's tombstone.

58 Mitchell, *Recollections,* p. 122.

59 For this episode, see Edith Lewis, *Willa Cather Living* (1953; reprint, Athens: Ohio University Press, 1989), pp. 95, 99.

60 Willa Cather, *Death Comes for the Archbishop* (New York: Vintage, 1971 reprinting of the 1927 edition), p. 265, from which all further citations are drawn. A kind of key to this analysis can be found in Cather's portrait of Cecile's reading of the lives of martyrs in *Shadows on the Rock* (New York: Knopf, 1931), pp. 39–40, in which Cecile finds something like "the glow of worldly pleasure" in these tales of self-abnegation.

Bibliography

Abbate, Carolyn. "Opera: or, the Envoicing of Women." *Musicology and Difference: Gender and Sexuality in Music Scholarship.* Ed. Ruth A. Solie. Berkeley: University of California Press, 1993.

———. *Unsung Voices.* Princeton: Princeton University Press, 1991.

Abraham, Julie. *Are Girls Necessary?* New York: Routledge, 1996.

Acocella, Joan. "Cather and the Academy," *The New Yorker* (27 November 1995): 56–71.

———. *Willa Cather and the Politics of Criticism.* Lincoln: University of Nebraska Press, 2000.

Adams, Robert. *Why People Photograph.* New York: Aperture, 1994.

Austen, Roger. *Playing the Game: The Homosexual Novel in America.* Indianapolis: Bobbs-Merrill, 1977.

Barker, Pat. *Regeneration.* New York: Penguin, 1993.

———. *The Eye in the Door.* New York: Penguin, 1995.

———. *The Ghost Road.* New York: Penguin, 1996.

Beebe, C. William. *Two Bird-Lovers in Mexico.* Boston: Houghton Mifflin, 1905.

Beebe, C. William and Mary Blair Beebe. *Our Search for a Wilderness.* New York: Henry Holt and Co., 1910.

Bennett, Mildred R. *The World of Willa Cather.* Lincoln: University of Nebraska Press, 1951.

Bersani, Leo. *Homos.* Cambridge: Harvard University Press, 1995.

Bland, Lucy. "Trial by Sexology? Maud Allan, *Salome* and the 'Cult of the Clitoris' Case," *Sexology in Culture.* Ed. Lucy Bland and Laura Doan. Chicago: University of Chicago Press, 1998.

Boone, Joseph Allen. *Libidinal Currents: Sexuality and the Shaping of Modernism.* Chicago: University of Chicago Press, 1998.

Bourne, Randolph. *War and the Intellectuals.* Ed. Carl Resek. New York: Harper and Row, 1964.

Boyarin, Daniel. "Freud's Baby, Fliess's Maybe: Homophobia, Anti-Semitism, and the Invention of Oedipus," *GLQ* 2 (1995): 115–47.

Breen, Jennifer, ed. *Wilfred Owen: Selected Poetry and Prose.* London: Routledge, 1988.

Brown, E. K. *Willa Cather.* New York: Knopf, 1953.

Brown, Richard Forman. *Better Angel.* Boston: Alyson, 1995.

Butler, Judith. *Gender Trouble.* New York: Routledge, 1990.

———. *Bodies That Matter.* London: Routledge, 1993.

Caesar, Adrian. *Taking It Like a Man.* Manchester: Manchester University Press, 1993.

Campbell, James S. " 'For you may touch them not': Misogyny, Homo-sexuality, and the Ethics of Passivity in First World War Poetry," *ELH* 64, no. 3 (fall 1997): 823–42.

Castle, Terry. *The Apparitional Lesbian.* New York: Columbia University Press, 1993.

Castleberry, May, ed. *Perpetual Mirage: Photographic Narratives of the Desert West.* New York: Whitney Museum of Art, 1996.

Cather, Willa. *Alexander's Bridge.* Ed. Bernice Slote. Lincoln: University of Nebraska Press, 1977 [1912].

———. *Alexander's Bridge.* Ed. Marilee Lindemann. Oxford: Oxford University Press, 1997 [1912].

———. *O Pioneers!* New York: Penguin, 1989 [1913].

———. "Three American Singers," *McClure's Magazine* 42, no. 2 (December 1913): 33–48.

———. *The Song of the Lark.* Boston: Houghton Mifflin, 1988 [1915].

———. *My Ántonia.* Boston: Houghton Mifflin, 1988 [1918].

———. *Not Under Forty.* Lincoln: University of Nebraska Press, 1988 [1922].

———. *One of Ours.* New York: Vintage, 1991 [1923].

———. *The Professor's House.* New York: Vintage, 1990 [1925].

———. *Death Comes for the Archbishop.* New York: Vintage, 1971 [1927].

———. *Shadows on the Rock.* New York: Vintage, 1990 [1925].

———. *Lucy Gayheart.* New York: Vintage, 1976 [1935].

———. *Novels and Stories.* 13 vols. Boston: Houghton Mifflin, 1937–41.

———. *Sapphira and the Slave Girl.* New York: Vintage, 1975 [1940].

———. *Willa Cather on Writing.* Ed. Stephen Tennant. Lincoln: University of Nebraska Press, 1988 [1949].

———. *Willa Cather in Person.* Ed. L. Brent Bohlke. Lincoln: University of Nebraska Press, 1986.

———. *Twenty-Four Stories.* Ed. Sharon O'Brien. New York: Penguin/ Meridian, 1987.

———. *Stories, Poems, and Other Writings.* New York: Library of America, 1992.

Chauncey, George. *Gay New York.* New York: Basic Books, 1994.

Chotzinoff, Samuel. *Day's at the Morn.* New York: Harper and Row, 1964.

Christiansen, Rupert. *Prima Donna.* Harmondworth: Penguin, 1984.

Clément, Cathérine. *Opera, or the Undoing of Woman.* Trans. Betsy Wing. Minneapolis: University of Minnesota Press, 1988.

Collier, John, Jr. "Laura Gilpin: Western Photographer," *New Mexico Quarterly* 20 (winter 1950–51): 485–93.

Cooke, Mervyn. *Britten: War Requiem.* Cambridge: Cambridge University Press, 1996.

Cooperman, Stanley. *World War I and the American Novel.* Baltimore: Johns Hopkins University Press, 1967.

Cramer, Timothy R. "Claude's Case: A Study of the Homosexual Temperament in Willa Cather's *One of Ours,*" *South Dakota Review* 31, no. 3 (fall 1993): 147–60.

Cushing, Mary Watkins. *The Rainbow Bridge.* New York: G. P. Putnam's Sons, 1954.

———. "Isolde Between the Lines," *Opera News* 19 (14 March 1955), 8–10, 26–27.

Dash, J. Michael. *Haiti and the U.S.: National Stereotypes and the Literary Imagination.* 2d ed. London: Macmillan, 1997 [1988].

Davenport, Marcia. *Of Lena Geyer.* New York: Charles Scribner's Sons, 1936.

———. *Too Strong for Fantasy.* New York: Charles Scribner's Sons, 1967.

Davidov, Judith Fryer. *Women's Camera Work.* Durham: Duke University Press, 1998.

De la Grange, Henry-Louis. *Gustav Mahler.* Oxford: Oxford University Press, 1995.

Deleuze, Gilles. *Bergsonism.* Trans. Hugh Tomlinson and Barbara Habberjam. New York: Zone, 1991.

Dennis, J. and Louis Migliorini. "Olive Fremstad," *The Record Collector* 7 (March 1952): 53–65.

Derrida, Jacques. *Politics of Friendship.* Trans. George Collins. London: Verso, 1997.

Du Bois, W. E. B. *Writings.* New York: Literary Classics of the United States, 1986.

Eaton, Quaintance. *The Boston Opera Company.* New York: Appleton-Century, 1965.

Edel, Leon. *Stuff of Sleep and Dreams.* New York: Harper and Row, 1982.

Ellis, James. "Strange Meeting: Wilfred Owen, Benjamin Britten, Derek Jarman." *The Work of Opera.* Ed. Richard Dellamora and Daniel Fischlin. New York: Columbia University Press, 1997.

Evans, Peter. *The Music of Benjamin Britten.* Minneapolis: University of Minnesota Press, 1979.

Faderman, Lillian. *Odd Girls and Twilight Lovers.* New York: Penguin, 1991.

Faris, James C. *Navajo and Photography.* Albuquerque: University of New Mexico Press, 1996.

Feldman, Jessica R. *Gender on the Divide.* Ithaca: Cornell University Press, 1993.

Fetterley, Judith. "*My Ántonia,* Jim Burden, and the Dilemma of the Lesbian Writer." *Lesbian Texts and Contexts.* Ed. Karla Jay and Joanne Glasgow. New York: New York University Press, 1990.

Forster, Elizabeth W. and Laura Gilpin. *Denizens of the Desert.* Ed. Martha A. Sandweiss. Albuquerque: University of New Mexico Press, 1988.

Fields, Annie, ed. *Letters of Sarah Orne Jewett.* Boston: Houghton Mifflin, 1911.

Fischer, Mike. "Pastoralism and Its Discontents: Willa Cather and the Burden of Imperialism," *Mosaic* 23, no. 1 (1990): 31–44.

Fitzgerald, Gerald, ed. *Annals of the Metropolitan Opera.* Boston: G. K. Hall, 1989.

Fitzroy, A. T. *Despised and Rejected.* London: Gay Men's Press, 1988.

Flannigan, John H. "Thea Kronborg's Vocal Transvestism: Willa Cather and the 'Voz Contralto'," *Modern Fiction Studies* 40, no. 4 (winter 1994): 737–63.

Fletcher, Maurine S., ed. *The Wetherills of the Mesa Verde.* Lincoln: University of Nebraska Press, 1977.

Foucault, Michel. *The History of Sexuality.* Trans. Robert Hurley. New York: Pantheon, 1978.

——. "Faire vivre et laisser mourir: la naissance du racisme," *Les Temps Modernes* 46 n. 535 (February 1991): 37–61.

——. *Il faut défendre la société.* Paris: Seuil/Gallimard, 1997.

Freud, Sigmund. "Psychoanalysis and War Neuroses," *Character and Culture.* Ed. Philip Rieff. New York: Collier Books, 1963.

Fuss, Diana. *Identification Papers.* New York: Routledge, 1995.

Fussell, Paul. *The Great War and Modern Memory.* London: Oxford University Press, 1975.

Gabriel, Kathryn. *Marietta Wetherill.* Boulder: Johnson Books, 1992.

Gardner, Jared. " 'Our Native Clay': Racial and Sexual Identity and the Making of Americans in *The Bridge*," *American Quarterly* 44, no. 1 (1992): 24–50.

Gelfant, Blanche. "The Forgotten Reaping-Hook: Sex in *My Ántonia*," *American Literature* 43 (1971): 60–82.

Gilbert, Sandra M. and Susan Gubar. *No Man's Land: Sexchanges.* New Haven: Yale University Press, 1989.

Gilpin, Laura. *The Mesa Verde National Park: Reproductions from a Series of Photographs by Laura Gilpin.* Colorado Springs: Gilpin Publishing, 1927.

——. *The Pueblos: A Camera Chronicle.* New York: Hastings House, 1941.

——. *The Rio Grande: River of Destiny.* New York: Duell, Sloan and Pearce, 1949.

——. "Historic Architecture Photography: The Southwest," *The Complete Photographer: An Encyclopedia of Photography.* Ed. Willard D. Morgan. New York: National Educational Alliance, 1949.

———. *The Enduring Navaho.* Austin: University of Texas Press, 1968.

Grayzel, Susan R. *Women's Identities at War.* Chapel Hill: University of North Carolina Press, 1999.

Griffiths, Frederick T. "The Woman Warrior: Willa Cather and *One of Ours,*" *Women's Studies* 11 (1984): 261–85.

Grumbach, Doris. "A Study of the Small Room in *The Professor's House,*" *Women's Studies* 11 (1984): 327–45.

Hacking, Ian. *Rewriting the Soul.* Princeton: Princeton University Press, 1995.

Halley, Janet. *Don't.* Durham: Duke University Press, 1999.

Hammond, Paul. *Love Between Men in English Literature.* London: Macmillan, 1996.

Harrell, David. "Willa Cather's Mesa Verde Myth," *Cather Studies* 1 (1990): 130–43.

———. *From Mesa Verde to "The Professor's House."* Albuquerque: University of New Mexico Press, 1992.

Henderson, W. J. *The Art of Singing.* New York: Dial, 1938.

Herbert, James D. "Bad Faith at Coventry: Spence's Cathedral and Britten's *War Requiem,*" *CI* 25 (spring 1999): 535–65.

Heyeck, Robin and James Woodress. "Willa Cather's Cuts and Revisions in *The Song of the Lark,*" *Modern Fiction Studies* 25, no. 4 (winter 1979–80): 651–58.

Hibbard, Dominic. *Wilfred Owen.* London: British Council, 1974.

Hill, Paul and Tom Cooper. "Camera Interview: Laura Gilpin," *Camera* 11 (November 1976): 11, 27, 35–37.

Hoare, Philip. *Serious Pleasure.* New York: Penguin, 1990.

———. *Oscar Wilde's Last Stand: Decadence, Conspiracy and the Most Outrageous Trial of the Century.* New York: Arcade Publishing, 1998.

Hollinger, David A. *Postethnic America.* New York: Basic Books, 1995.

Horowitz, Joseph. *Wagner Nights.* Berkeley: University of California Press, 1994.

Huneker, James. *Painted Veils.* New York: Horace Liveright, 1929.

———. *Bedouins.* New York: Charles Scribner's Sons, 1920.

Huneker, Josephine, ed. *Letters of James Gibbons Huneker.* New York: Charles Scribner's Sons, 1922.

Hust, Karen. "'The Landscape (Chosen by Desire)': Laura Gilpin Renegotiates Mother Nature," *Genders* 6 (November 1989): 20–48.

Hynes, Samuel. *A War Imagined.* New York: Atheneum, 1991.

Irving, Katrina. "Displacing Homosexuality: The Use of Ethnicity in Willa Cather's *My Ántonia,*" *Modern Fiction Studies* 36, no. 1 (spring 1990): 91–102.

Jacobson, Matthew Frye. *Whiteness of a Different Color.* Cambridge: Harvard University Press, 1998.

Kittler, Friedrich. "World-Breath: On Wagner's Media Technology," *Opera Through Other Eyes*. Ed. David J. Levin. Stanford: Stanford University Press, 1994.

Koestenbaum, Wayne. *The Queen's Throat*. New York: Poseidon, 1993.

Kuper, Adam. *The Invention of Primitive Society*. London: Routledge, 1988.

Lacan, Jacques. *Ecrits: A Selection*. Trans. Alan Sheridan. New York: Norton, 1977.

Lee, Hermione. *Willa Cather: Double Lives*. New York: Vintage, 1989.

Leeds, Eric. *No Man's Land: Combat and Identity in World War I*. Cambridge: Cambridge University Press, 1979.

Leonardi, Susan J. and Rebecca A. Pope. *The Diva's Mouth*. New Brunswick: Rutgers University Press, 1996.

Lewis, Edith. *Willa Cather Living*. Athens: Ohio University Press, 1989 [1953].

Leys, Ruth. "Traumatic Cures: Shell Shock, Janet, and the Question of Memory," *Critical Inquiry* 20 (summer 1994): 623–62.

Lindemann, Marilee. *Willa Cather: Queering America*. New York: Columbia University Press, 1999.

Madigan, Mark J. "Willa Cather and Dorothy Canfield Fisher: Rift, Reconciliation, and *One of Ours*," *Cather Studies* 1 (1990): 115–29.

Mahler, Gustav. *Gustav Mahler: Memories and Letters*. Trans. Basil Creighton. Ed. Donald Mitchell. Seattle: University of Washington Press, 1975.

Massumi, Brian. "The Autonomy of Affect," *Cultural Critique* 31 (1995): 83–109.

Mavor, Carol. *Pleasures Taken*. Durham: Duke University Press, 1995.

———. *Becoming: The Photographs of Clementina, Viscountess Hawarden*. Durham: Duke University Press, 1999.

McCourt, James. *Mawrdew Czgowchwz*. New York: Farrar, Straus and Giroux, 1975.

McKeon, Michael. "Historicizing Patriarchy: The Emergence of Gender Difference in England, 1660–1760," *Eighteenth-Century Studies* 28, no. 3 (1995): 295–322.

McNitt, Frank. *Richard Wetherill: Anasazi*. Albuquerque: University of New Mexico Press, 1966 [1957].

Meisel, Perry. *The Cowboy and the Dandy*. New York: Oxford University Press, 1999.

Michaels, Walter Benn. "The Souls of White Folks," *Literature and the Body*. Ed. Elaine Scarry. Baltimore: Johns Hopkins University Press, 1988.

———. "The Vanishing American," *American Literary History* 2, no. 3 (1990): 220–41.

————. "Race into Culture: A Critical Genealogy of Cultural Identity," *Critical Inquiry* 18, no. 4 (1992): 655–85.

————. *Our America*. Durham: Duke University Press, 1995.

Mitchell, Margaretta K. *Recollections: Ten Women of Photography*. New York: Viking, 1979.

Moon, Michael. *A Small Boy and Others*. Durham: Duke University Press, 1998.

Moorhead, Elizabeth. *These Too Were Here: Louise Homer and Willa Cather*. Pittsburgh: University of Pittsburgh Press, 1950.

Morgenstern, Naomi. " 'Love is home-sickness': Nostalgia and Lesbian Desire in *Sapphira and the Slave Girl*," *Novel* 29 (1995–96): 184–205.

Morrison, Toni. "Unspeakable Things Unspoken: The Afro-American Presence in American Literature," *Michigan Quarterly Review* 28, no. 1 (winter 1989): 1–34.

————. *Playing in the Dark*. New York: Vintage, 1992.

Murphy, John J., ed. *Critical Essays on Willa Cather*. Boston: G. K. Hall, 1984.

Nealon, Christopher. "Affect-Genealogy: Feeling and Affiliation in Willa Cather," *American Literature* 69, no. 1 (March 1997): 5–37.

Niles, Blair. *Casual Wanderings in Ecuador*. New York: Century, 1923.

————. *Black Haiti*. New York: Grosset and Dunlap, 1926.

————. *Condemned to Devil's Island*. New York: Harcourt, Brace and Company, 1928.

————. *Free*. New York: Harcourt Brace, 1930.

————. *The James*. New York: Farrar and Rinehart, 1939.

————. *Passengers to Mexico*. New York: Farrar and Rinehart, 1943.

————. *Journeys in Time*. New York: Coward-McCann, 1946.

————. *Strange Brother*. London: GMP, 1991.

Norwood, Vera. "The Photographer and the Naturalist: Laura Gilpin and Mary Austin in the Southwest," *Journal of American Culture* 5 (summer 1982): 1–28.

O'Brien, Sharon. " 'The Thing Not Named': Willa Cather as a Lesbian Writer," *Signs* 9, no. 4 (summer 1984): 576–99.

————. *Willa Cather: The Emerging Voice*. Oxford: Oxford University Press, 1987.

————. "Combat Envy and Survivor Guilt: Willa Cather's 'Manly Battle Yarn'," *Arms and the Woman*. Ed. Helen M. Cooper, Adrienne Auslander Munich and Susan Merrill Squier. Chapel Hill: University of North Carolina Press, 1989.

————, ed. *New Essays on "My Ántonia."* Cambridge: Cambridge University Press, 1999.

Owen, Wilfred. *Poems*. Ed. Siegfried Sassoon. New York: B. W. Huebsch, n.d. [1920].

————. *Poems*. Ed. Edmund Blunden. New Classics, 1949 [1931].

————. *Collected Letters*. Ed. Harold Owen and John Bell. London: Oxford University Press, 1967.

————. *Complete Poems and Fragments*. Ed. Jon Stallworthy. London: Chatto and Windus/ Oxford University Press, 1983.

Poizat, Michel. *The Angel's Cry*. Trans. Arthur Denner. Ithaca: Cornell University Press, 1992.

Pultz, John. *The Body and the Lens*. New York: Abrams, 1995.

Quirk, Tom. *Bergson and American Culture*. Chapel Hill: University of North Carolina Press, 1990.

Rambuss, Richard. "Machinehead," *Camera Obscura* 42 (September 1999): 97–124.

Reynolds, Guy. *Willa Cather in Context*. New York: St. Martin's Press, 1996.

Rich, Adrienne. *Of Woman Born*. New York: Norton, 1976.

Rimbaud, Arthur. *Oeuvres Complètes: Correspondances*. Ed. Louis Forestier. Paris: Robert Laffon, 1972.

Rivers, W. H. R. *Conflict and Dream*. New York: Harcourt Brace, 1923.

————. *Instinct and the Unconscious*. Cambridge: Cambridge University Press, 1924.

Robinson, Phyllis. *The Life of Willa Cather*. New York: Holt, Rinehart and Winston, 1983.

Rosenthal, Harold. *Two Centuries of Opera at Covent Garden*. London: Putnam, 1958.

Rosowski, Susan J. and Bernice Slote. "Willa Cather's 1916 Mesa Verde Essay: The Genesis of *The Professor's House*," *Prairie Schooner* 58, no. 4 (1984): 81–92.

Rudnick, Lois Palken. *Utopian Vistas*. Albuquerque: University of New Mexico Press, 1996.

Russ, Joanna. *To Write Like a Woman*. Bloomington: Indiana University Press, 1995.

Ryan, Maureen. "No Woman's Land: Gender in Willa Cather's *One of Ours*," *Studies in American Fiction* 18 (spring 1990): 65–75.

Salas, Angela M. "Willa Cather's *Sapphira and the Slave Girl*: Extending the Boundaries of the Body," *College English* 24 (1997): 97–108.

Sandweiss, Martha. *Laura Gilpin: An Enduring Grace*. Fort Worth, TX: Amon Carter Museum, 1986.

————. "Laura Gilpin and the Tradition of American Landscape Photography," *The Desert is No Lady*. Ed. Vera Norwood and Janice Monk. New Haven: Yale University Press, 1987.

Sargeant, Elizabeth Shepley. *Willa Cather: A Memoir*. Athens: Ohio University Press, 1992 [1953].

Sassoon, Siegfried. *Memoirs of a Fox-Hunting Man.* London: Faber and
Faber, 1928.
———. *Sherston's Progress.* Garden City, NY: Doubleday, Doran and
Company, 1936.
———. *Collected Poems, 1908–1956.* London: Faber and Faber, 1961.
———. *The War Poems.* Ed. Rupert Hart-Davis. London: Faber and
Faber, 1983.
Schmucker, Walter. "A Tribute to Olive Fremstad," *Opera News* 16
(31 December 1951): 23.
Schroeter, James, ed. *Willa Cather and Her Critics.* Ithaca: Cornell Univer-
sity Press, 1967.
Schwab, Arnold T. *James Gibbons Huneker: Critic of the Seven Arts.* Stan-
ford: Stanford University Press, 1963.
———, ed. *Americans in the Arts: Critiques by James Gibbons Huneker.*
New York: A. M. S., 1985.
Schwarz, David. *Listening Subjects.* Durham: Duke University Press, 1997.
Sedgwick, Eve Kosofsky. *Between Men.* New York: Columbia University
Press, 1985.
———. "Across Gender, Across Sexuality: Willa Cather and Others,"
SAQ 88, no. 1 (1989): 53–72.
———. *Epistemology of the Closet.* Berkeley: University of California
Press, 1990.
———. *Tendencies.* Durham: Duke University Press, 1997.
Seltsam, William H. *Metropolitan Opera Annals.* New York: H. W. Wil-
son, 1947.
Showalter, Elaine. *The Female Malady.* New York: Pantheon, 1985.
———. "Rivers and Sassoon: The Inscription of Male Gender Anxi-
eties," *Behind the Lines.* Ed. Margaret Higgonet et al. New Haven: Yale
University Press, 1987.
Slobodin, Richard. *W. H. R. Rivers.* New York: Columbia University
Press, 1978.
Spillers, Hortense. "Mama's Baby, Papa's Maybe: An American Gram-
mar Book," *Within the Circle.* Ed. Angelyn Mitchell. Durham: Duke
University Press, 1994.
Stallworthy, Jon. *Wilfred Owen.* London: Oxford University Press/
Chatto and Windus, 1974.
Steane, J. B. *The Grand Tradition.* Portland, OR: Amadeus, 1993.
Stein, Gertrude. *Writing and Lectures.* Ed. Patricia Meyerowitz. Har-
mondsworth: Penguin, 1967.
Stieglitz, Alfred. *Camera Work: A Pictorial Guide.* Ed. Marianne Fulton
Margolis. New York: Dover, 1978.
Thatcher, Anita, dir. *Laura Gilpin: An Enduring Grace.* 1986.
Thompson, Oscar. *The American Singer.* New York: Dial, 1937.

Tomlinson, Gary. *Metaphysical Song*. Princeton: Princeton University Press, 1999.

Trachtenberg, Alan. *Reading American Photographs*. New York: Hill and Wang, 1989.

Tuggle, Robert. *The Golden Age of Opera*. New York: Holt, Rinehart and Winston, 1983.

Urgo, Joseph R. *Willa Cather and the Myth of American Migration*. Urbana: University of Illinois Press, 1995.

Van Vechten, Carl. *Interpreters and Interpretation*. New York: Knopf, 1917.

Vestal, David. "Laura Gilpin: Photographer of the Southwest," *Popular Photography* 80 (February 1977): 100–05, 130–34.

Warner, Michael. *The Trouble with Normal*. New York: Free Press, 1999.

Wasserman, Loretta. "The Music of Time: Henri Bergson and Willa Cather," *American Literature* 57, no. 2 (1985): 226–39.

———. "William James, Henri Bergson, and Remembered Time in *My Ántonia*," *Approaches to Teaching Cather's "My Ántonia."* Ed. Susan J. Rosowski. New York: MLA, 1989.

Welker, Robert Henry. *Natural Man: The Life of William Beebe*. Bloomington: Indiana University Press, 1975.

Wood, Elizabeth. "Sapphonics," *Queering the Pitch*. Ed. Philip Brett, Elizabeth Wood and Gary C. Thomas. New York: Routledge, 1994.

Woodress, James. *Willa Cather: A Literary Life*. Lincoln: University of Nebraska Press, 1987.

Young, Allan. *The Harmony of Illusions*. Princeton: Princeton University Press, 1995.

Younger, Patricia Lee. "Willa Cather's Aristocrats," *Southern Humanities Review* 14, no. 1 (1980): 43–56.

Zeeland, Steven. *Sailors and Sexual Identity*. New York: Haworth, 1995.

———. *The Masculine Marine*. New York: Haworth, 1996.

Žižek, Slavoj. " 'I hear you with my eyes'; or, The Invisible Master," *Gaze and Voice as Love Objects*. Ed. Renata Saleci and Slavoj Žižek. Durham: Duke University Press, 1996.

Index

Jonathan Goldberg is Sir William Osler Professor of English at

The Johns Hopkins University. He has written and edited numerous

books including *Desiring Women Writing: English Renaissance Examples;*

Reclaiming Sodom; Queering the Renaissance (Duke, 1994); and

Sodometries: Renaissance Texts, Modern Sexualities.

Library of Congress Cataloging-in-Publication Data

Goldberg, Jonathan.
Willa Cather and others / Jonathan Goldberg.
p.   cm. — (Series Q)
Includes bibliographical references (p.   ) and index.
ISBN 0-8223-2677-9 (cloth : alk. paper) —
ISBN 0-8223-2672-8 (pbk. : alk. paper)
1. Cather, Willa, 1873–1947—Criticism and interpretations.
2. Women and literature—United States—History—20th century.
3. Cather, Willa, 1873–1947—Contemporaries.   I. Title.   II. Series.
PS3505.A87 Z647   2001
813'.52—dc21   00-063658